0-07-005203-4	Berson/Anderson	*Sybase and Client / Server Computing*
0-07-024036-1	Graham	*The Networker's Practical Reference*
0-07-015839-8	Davis/McGuffin	*Wireless Local Area Networks: Technology, Issues, and Strategies*
0-07-005119-4	Baker	*Network Security: How to Plan For It and Achieve It*
0-07-024842-7	Grinberg	*Computer / Telecom Integration: The SCAI Solution*
0-07-911889-5	Nemzow	*Enterprise Network Performance Optimization*
0-07-035968-7	Kumar	*Broadband Communications: A Professional's Guide to ATM, Frame Relay, SMDS, SONET, and B-ISDN*
0-07-049663-3	Peterson	*TCP / IP Networking: A Guide to the IBM Environment*
0-07-057628-9	Simon	*Workgroup Computing: Workflow, Groupware, and Messaging*
0-07-911857-7	Ananthaswamy	*Data Communications Using Object-Oriented Design and C++*

D1085023

To order or receive additional information on these or any other McGraw-Hill titles, in the United States please call 1-800-822-8158. In other countries, contact your local McGraw-Hill representative.   **BC15XXA**

TCP/IP NETWORKING

TCP/IP NETWORKING

A Guide to the IBM Environment

David M. Peterson
Transition Data Group

McGraw-Hill, Inc.

New York   San Francisco   Washington, D.C.   Auckland   Bogotá
Caracas   Lisbon   London   Madrid   Mexico City   Milan
Montreal   New Delhi   San Juan   Singapore
Sydney   Tokyo   Toronto

Library of Congress Cataloging-in-Publication Data

Peterson, David M.
    TCP/IP networking : a guide to the IBM environment / David M. Peterson.
        p.   cm.
    Includes index.
    ISBN 0-07-049663-3
    1. TCP/IP (Computer network protocol)   2. IBM computers.   I. Title.
TK5105.55.P47   1995
004.6'5—dc20

94-46511
CIP

1 2 3 4 5 6 7 8 9 0   DOC/DOC   9 0 0 9 8 7 6 5

ISBN 0-07-049663-3

*The sponsoring editor for this book was Jerry Papke, the editing super-
visor was Jim Halston, and the production supervisor was Suzanne
W. B. Rapcavage.*

Printed and bound by R. R. Donnelley & Sons Company.

McGraw-Hill books are available at special quantity discounts to use
as premiums and sales promotions, or for use in corporate training programs. For more information, please write to the Director of Special
Sales, McGraw-Hill, Inc., 11 West 19th Street, New York, NY 10011.
Or contact your local bookstore.

*To Madeleine once again, and
to my fellow long-distance runners.*

Contents

Preface

The Amazing Story of TCP/IP

When I talk to people whose job does not involve programming or otherwise tending the computer, and explain what I do, the subject of IBM and its future always seems to come up. Perhaps based on a recent *BusinessWeek* or *Wall Street Journal* article, they give me their opinion. In light of IBM's layoffs and the stock slide of a few years back, people invariably advise "don't count IBM out."

Interesting. Having spent so much of my career working with IBM products and technologies, I have always had a sense of loyalty, and have never counted them out.

But at the same time, if one steps back away from the MVS assembler, latest OS/2 C compiler, and SNA data formats to get a better view, it is clear that their domain is under attack. On several fronts the company is doing battle. At the same time, it is also obvious that they are making more concessions. Rather than dominating the process of technology creation and production, we see more of the IBM solutions as "open" and nonproprietary. This tack involves using products that are based on other standards, drawn from: independent groups, de facto consensus, companies that IBM buys into, and even non-IBM proprietary products.

Some of this shift has been inevitable as the industry has accelerated and expanded, like a river in flood. The old IBM was structured around the mainframe, a bit too large and slow to respond quickly where necessary. But much has also resulted from a lack of vision and anticipation, as well as by (some would say) gross incompetence on the part of some of the top IBM executives.

Some of the more notable examples of where these competitive dynamics are revealed include:

- Microprocessors - After tapping Intel to provide the microprocessor for its first PC, IBM then looked on as the next big computer revolution took place. While IBM is a large producer of PCs, it is not in control of the core technology. The recent PowerPC family of chips, created in alliance with Motorola, is meant to combat this threat posed by the newly empowered Intel.
- Desktop client platform - Although technically superior, OS/2 has been trailing Windows by huge margins for years. And now with Win95, NT, and the future Cairo, IBM faces the almost impossible task of reclaiming what they, just as in the case of Intel, gave away.
- Server platforms - With the vastly improved performance and falling prices of the microprocessors, it seems the servers are getting small, more functional, and less expensive. The proprietary IBM servers, such as MVS and the AS/400 line, must compete with workstations of all sizes and shapes. IBM has responded by introducing the new System/390 Parallel Server family of machines based on CMOS technology. Initially they may only appeal to a small percentage of the high-end MVS shops. However, IBM is expected to gradually enhance these boxes, making them more general-purpose and also less expensive. This trend portends a new direction for the MVS mainframe and capabilities of the software. Also, some would point with hope to the RS/6000 and the new SP2 processors. But the strategic operating system here is AIX (i.e., UNIX, of AT&T fame).
- System software at the server - This can fall into several different categories, primarily: database management and transaction processing monitors. Take databases, for example. IBM created the theory underlying the hugely popular relational DB model. But other companies were quicker to introduce mainstream products, most of the time on non-IBM boxes (i.e., UNIX). As corporations continue to downsize, IBM has moved the functionality of its premier system, DB2, to other platforms such as OS/2 and the RS/6000.

- Distributed computing - Where APPC had once been the sole strategic program-to-program development option, IBM now supports a variety of options (i.e., middlewares). Perhaps most important among these is DCE, which was created and is maintained by OSF.
- Distributed Transaction Processing - IBM recently acquired the Transarc Corporation, and its Encina family of products.
- Object oriented development - IBM has its Distributed System Object Model (DSOM), but this will be compliant with CORBA, from the independent OMG. IBM also offers Smalltalk products, a technology developed by Xerox.
- Object-oriented databases - IBM has invested heavily in Object Design, Inc. and their product ObjectStore.
- Network management - While mainframe NetView was an IBM invention, NetView/6000 (at least in its earlier releases) was almost completely based on OpenView as licensed from Hewlett-Packard.
- Network communication architectures - Traditional SNA has long been the only option for mainframe users. APPN, or the so-called "new" SNA, reduces the hierarchy and mirrors the requirements of the distributed workstations and PCs which can operate more autonomously. However, IBM seems to have been a little slow off the gun with APPN, and now has conceded to offer several networking options to its customers. It has favored the more fully functional OSI model where possible, but to no avail. TCP/IP has rapidly invaded the IBM world, from top to bottom.

This last item, of all the others in the partial list, is the subject of this book. It is the story of exactly how IBM has implemented the TCP/IP architecture across its product line. Does this TCP/IP support undermine SNA ? It seems to me that it does, at least to some extent and/or until IBM can differentiate itself with next generation high-speed technologies. But I guess it depends on your point of view. The use of traditional SNA appears to be stable or perhaps falling (with the mainframe), while APPN (actually more similar to TCP/IP) has not yet found a widespread usage outside of the midrange line (i.e., AS/400).

Perhaps someone will point to TCP/IP and say that IBM is merely responding to the legitimate needs of its commercial customers. This may be true as far as it goes, but after such a long delay with APPN and APPC does IBM really have a choice ? That is, these technologies have been around for roughly a decade (although APPN wasn't "formally" announced until 1991). Saying that IBM is just following the market ignores the advantage that IBM had, and what might have been possible from their vantage point in the late 1970s and early 1980s. I would classify such statements along with those advocating NAFTA because it will be good for the average U.S. worker, or that cutting taxes and raising spending won't hurt us because deficits don't matter. In both of these cases, as well as with IBM's embrace of TCP/IP, only time will tell.

Goals of the Book

The goal of the book is reflected in the title. It has been written to provide a guide to where and how IBM has implemented the protocols found within the TCP/IP networking architecture. This has meant providing a complete picture. Not only must the platforms be described, but also the connectivity options, routers, controllers, applications, programming options, monitoring, and management. Also, the TCP/IP framework itself is presented.

One can easily see what a large body of material this has turned out to be. This is compounded by the fact that both the architecture itself as well as IBM's product lines continue to be enhanced. I have tried to deal with these and other issues by arranging the material in a logical order and by providing as much depth as possible.

Stylistic Matters

With a degree in electrical engineering, and years of development experience, I revel in the bits and bytes. Give me the low-level details. But, not everyone needs this type of information or would benefit from such an approach.

Therefore, as with my first book, I have established three major goals regarding the style and content. These include:

- Broad coverage of the subject matter.
- Consistent level of detail throughout.
- Clear, objective, and useful descriptions.

This is a very broad text then, by definition. I have tried to cover each of the major areas with a consistent level of detail.

Organization

The book has 14 chapters and is divided into three parts, an arrangement that seemed to make sense given the diversity of material.

The first part covers the TCP/IP architecture. These four chapters represent a much condensed and compressed version, but still serve to pave the way for the rest of the book. There are several good texts available on TCP/IP for the interested reader, some of which are listed in the bibliography. And of course the RFC documents are the authoritative source (see Appendix A).

Part two discusses the basics of the IBM environment. This includes the six major platform implementations, host connectivity options, router support, and finally the recent AnyNet family as cast from the Networking Blueprint.

Finally, the third part, consisting of five chapters, extends the discussion started in part 2 to more advanced topics. This includes application support, programming options, support, performance, and network/systems management.

It has been my goal to have each part, as well as each chapter, build on the previous so as to gradually expand the reader's knowledge and appreciation of this large subject area.

Audience

There are undoubtedly a variety of computer professionals who would benefit from this text. Given its broad approach, and consequent restricted depth, it will be especially useful to those with some networking background (e.g., SNA) but new to TCP/IP.

I hope that the audience will include junior network systems programmers or operators who desire a complete introduction to this important subject. Others in the mainframe area will include non-network systems programmers, network analysts, client/server professionals, and managers.

Finally, I hope that it creates a potential for a cross-pollination effect among those using IBM products. For example, it might provide insights to the PC and workstation specialists as to what's available at the mainframe (and how to connect). Mainframers might expand their perspective to ease a transition to the LAN world, possibly in the planning stages.

Completeness and Accuracy

As mentioned above, the material included is designed to be as complete as possible within the confines of a book of this size, without diminishing its detail and usefulness. The text strives to provide the complete picture, cutting across several subject areas.

In the process of performing the research and writing, I have worked to maintain a high degree of accuracy. In the end, however, I must accept responsibility for the content of this book and any mistakes or inaccuracies.

If when reading the book, you have any comments, suggestions, or corrections, please contact the author directly through the Internet (peterson@cerf.net). As an alternative, you can send this information to:

McGraw-Hill
P.O. Box 338
Grand Central Station
New York, NY 10163-0338

And of course, as TCP/IP and its support by IBM continue to evolve, there will be new products and updated features. I look forward to the possibility of a second edition, at which time new information can be included and any errors corrected.

David Peterson

Acknowledgments

After spending so much time in a product development environment, it has been refreshing to take a break over the past year or so in order to pursue other interests. During this "break," however, it seems that I've been busier than ever, balancing assignments in writing, teaching, and consulting. This experience has, however, given me a new perspective on the rapidly changing industry. I would like to thank a few of the individuals who have helped during this time, directly or indirectly contributing to this book.

First, thanks to Jay Ranade for suggesting this subject area as the topic for my second book. Looking back on some of the other ideas we both came up with, this now seems to have been a good choice.

Also, thanks to Keith Landowitz at Merrill Lynch who reviewed the manuscript. His depth of knowledge has helped to refine the organization of the material and also to correct several errors.

Many thanks go out to the staff at the University of California extension department in Irvine, and especially to Mario Vidalon. During my association with UCI, he has allowed me to make a contribute to the development of his program by proposing and creating several new courses.

Thanks also to a few of the quality people I worked with at Candle, then in West Los Angeles. It was there that I got my start in several ways, working as a member of the network R&D group. This included writing for the *Candle Computer Report*, where my first articles on SNA appeared in 1988. Best regards to Mr. Chernick, especially with his SystemView development relationship with IBM which started shortly after I left in 1991 (i.e., Automation Center/400 product).

Finally, thanks go out to my editor at McGraw-Hill, Jerry Papke, for his encouragement and patience as the deadline for this book seemed to continually slip (but not quite so much as the first one !).

1

TCP/IP Architecture

Structural Overview

The Transmission Control Protocol/Internet Protocol (TCP/IP) networking architecture grew out of the early ARPANET project, as sponsored by the Department of Defense in the late 1960s. Since that time, it has evolved to accommodate the requirements of its rapidly expanding user base.

The TCP/IP data formats and protocols are loosely arranged within a layered model, with some flexibility in terms of the implementation options. The protocols are designed to support a wide variety of host computing platforms and networking configurations. This independence from the operating system and underlying physical transport have contributed to its appeal and widespread usage.

In addition to the basic framework for data transport and routing, there is a suite of standard applications that are usually supplied with a particular implementation. These services, along with the various application programming interfaces, allow TCP/IP to be quickly established as a useful tool in the operation of an enterprise-wide data communication network.

1.1 Internetworking Model

The communications network has become a common and necessary element in the operation and use of today's computing systems. There is not only a wide variety of computer hardware and software platforms, but also of networking protocols available. Along with this diversity, the need to share data and services among connected computer users has accelerated as individuals, corporations, universities, and countries depend on each other in the competitive business world. This is especially true as distributed processing, and the special case of the hugely popular client/server computing, becomes more widespread.

Physical connections between computing machines can be, at times, a simple one-to-one link. However, it is increasingly more common that a group of local machines (i.e., a network) is joined with another group. In this case, entire networks can be integrated allowing users of one network to access resources in another network.

Large Virtual Network

Such a collection of interconnected networks forms an internetwork, or internet. The individual networks can maintain their local autonomy, while still participating in the larger internet.

The internet provides users with a transparent access across network boundaries. In this sense, the internet is a type of virtual network, with consistent standards for data transmission, routing, and processing.

The internetworking concept is central to the TCP/IP architecture. In this case, instances of the Internet Protocol (IP) are distributed across mainframes, minicomputers, workstations, PCs, and routers in order to form a single virtual IP network.

Any collection of networks using TCP/IP can be considered to be an internet. However, the Internet (capital "I") is a special case, with its wide recognition and exponentially expanding user base. In fact, the development and evolution of the Internet is intertwined with and dependent upon the TCP/IP architecture, as discussed below.

Datagram Flow

The term "datagram" has been widely used in the communication field. Within the TCP/IP networking architecture, a datagram is the fundamental packet of information flowing through the IP network, as processed by the Internet layer.

Each datagram is routed independently, based on a unique destination and source address. The format of the IP address, as well as other contents within the IP header, are illustrated below. The content and format of the data portion carried by the packet depend on the Transport layer protocol and application in use.

1.2 Protocol Evolution

The evolution and development of TCP/IP has proceeded differently than the other major communication architectures found in widespread usage today.

For example, Systems Network Architecture (SNA) provides a foundation for guiding the creation of IBM's networking products. While the manufacturer has at times demonstrated a sensitivity to emerging technologies and user requests for open systems standards, SNA is still a proprietary, commercial framework developed to support the IBM product plan and its interests.

The model for Open Systems Interconnection (OSI), as sponsored by the International Standards Organization (ISO), is an ambitious attempt at creating broad interconnection and interoperability standards for networked computer users. It has been designed in a formal fashion, according to arduous committee consensus. Each aspect of the OSI model is completed before the actual OSI-compliant products are built.

The evolution of TCP/IP, on the other hand, has been accomplished using a more open approach, largely based on actual user requirements and their pragmatic interests. A wider participation in its content and characteristics is possible, because any of the users within the TCP/IP community can construct and submit a proposal for enhancements and new features. These documents, known as Request For Comments (RFCs), are maintained on-line and distributed freely by a central managing authority.

TCP/IP is unique not only in its development, but also in its contribution to the data communications field in general. In fact, the early designers of the original project leading to TCP/IP actually pioneered several technologies, such as:

- Packet switching
- Protocol layering

In some ways, the early TCP/IP networks included revolutionary concepts and design aspects which forged the path for interoperability within data communication networks. Recently, however, the flow of ideas is also moving noticeably in the other direction. That is, many of the concepts and characteristics put forth in the OSI and SNA standards have been indirectly absorbed by TCP/IP.

Early Government and Scientific Users

The Advanced Research Projects Agency (ARPA), later changed by prefixing the word Defense (i.e., DARPA), sponsors research in emerging technology fields. In the late 1960s, data communications was recognized to be an important area for research, and was therefore allocated funding.

The result of this investment was the ARPA Network, or ARPANET, which became operational in 1969. ARPANET utilized packet switching technology, and was initially designed for use by the government and scientific communities.

While the idea behind the ARPANET was sound, the network had several limitations which revealed themselves in the form of frequent system crashes and outages. It became obvious that a change would need to be made.

Transition to TCP/IP Protocols

In 1974, a proposal was made by Vinton Cerf and Robert Kahn, published as a paper in the *IEEE Transactions on Communications*, for a new communication architecture. The resulting recommendation was to keep the ARPANET infrastructure largely intact, while upgrading the network protocols. The replacement architecture, TCP/IP, was debated and modified until taking its current form around 1978.

The architecture is named after its two major operational protocols: TCP and IP. However, this framework actually includes a wide range of protocols and applications designed to support interoperability and end-user computing.

The network users made a gradual transition to TCP/IP from the older ARPANET protocols, which was completed in 1983. In the same year, the government, again through DARPA funding, contracted to have TCP/IP woven directly into the Berkeley Software Distribution (BSD) version of UNIX; the socket API was thus created. This was designed primarily as a method for interconnecting UNIX machines. At the same time, the Department of Defense approved the TCP/IP standard, another important step toward establishing its widespread acceptance.

In 1984, the ARPANET was split into two parts:

- ARPANET - for continued research and scientific usage.
- MILNET - for unclassified military usage.

The ARPANET continued to grow and evolve until finally being dissolved in 1990. In its transition to and support of TCP/IP, the ARPANET formed the first backbone of the U.S. Internet.

U.S. Internet

The Internetwork, or Internet, is a large collection of interconnected networks each operated and administered in an autonomous fashion. In recent years, the Internet has experienced exponential growth in terms of connected devices and registered users.

While TCP/IP is primarily associated with the Internet, it is of course used in other cases. For example, many businesses are adopting the architecture as an enterprise-wide standard.

The Internet, while composed of a large number of interconnected networks, does have a center. The earlier ARPANET served as the first backbone for the Internet. With its dissolution in 1990, the National Science Foundation Network (NSFNET) replaced ARPANET as the Internet's primary backbone.

The networks comprising NSFNET are grouped into three levels according to functional characteristics and usage. These levels include:

- Backbone
- Mid-level networks
- Campus networks

The core backbone, which has continued to evolve as requirements dictate, supports the mid-level and local campus networks.

In addition, there are several other networks worldwide which participate in the Internet. In most cases, these operate independently, connecting to the Internet in order to provide services such as mail exchange. Figure 1.1 provides a list of these networks. In addition, there are several corresponding networks in Europe, and elsewhere in the world.

Administration and RFC Process

The Internet Architecture Board (IAB) is empowered to oversee the architecture's continued development. The IAB consists of two major bodies:

- Internet Engineering Task Force (IETF)
- Internet Research Task Force (IRTF)

The Internet Engineering Task Force provides immediate (i.e., tactical) support, while the Internet Research Task Force focuses on

Network	Description
NFSNET	National Science Foundation Network - replaced the earlier ARPANET as the primary backbone for the Internet.
MILNET	Military Network - separated from ARPANET in 1984 and used for unclassified military data.
CREN	Corporation for Research and Educational Networking - created in 1989 based on merger of CSNET and BITNET.
DRI	Defense Research Internet - a testbed for wide area and high-speed networking protocols for IP traffic.
NSI	NASA Science Internet - combination of several NASA networks, such as Space Physics Analysis Network (SPAN).
ESNET	Energy Sciences Network - network maintained by the U.S. Department of Defense, with Internet access.

Figure 1.1 Major networks which interoperate with the Internet.

long-term (i.e., strategic) issues.

The Network Information Center (NIC) provides registration and information distribution services. Part of the task of guiding the architecture's evolution is managing the dynamic collection of RFC documents. Once submitted for consideration, each RFC is reviewed and then assigned a unique number by the RFC editor, currently:

Dr. Jon Postel
Information Sciences Institute
University of Southern California

postel@isi.edu
(310) 822-1511

RFCs describing protocols can be assigned one of several different states; a list of these is provided in Figure 1.2.

State	Description
Experimental	A protocol is first thoroughly tested on a limited number of participating systems.
Proposed	At this point, the protocol begins the process toward standardization, with revision very lately.
Draft	The IAB more seriously considers the protocol, with more input and updates solicited.
Standard	The protocol has become an official standard, and may safely be implemented.
Informational	Information and protocols used outside of the Internet are published for convenient review.
Historic	Protocols that have been superseded or abandoned are not likely to become standards.

Figure 1.2 States used to characterize an RFC document.

In addition, the RFC can also have a status, identifying the requirement for the protocol, including:

- Required
- Recommended
- Elective
- Limited use
- Not recommended

In administering a TCP/IP-based network, the end user must also interact with the Internet authorities. One example of this is the registration of IP addresses.

Each host that is connected to the Internet must be assigned a unique 32-bit IP address. The address is actually divided into a two parts. The most significant of the two, the network address, is assigned to guarantee uniqueness. The lower part, the host address, is locally administered.

The Internet Assigned Numbers Authority (IANA) controls all protocol numbers within the TCP/IP protocol suite. The Internet Registry, part of IANA, manages the IP addresses.

Current and Future Uses

The Internet is designed to facilitate information access and sharing between a widely dispersed group of users. While the backbone is not adequate to handle high volume commercial traffic, the TCP/IP protocols are suitable for this purpose within other networks, including the corporate networks.

TCP/IP is the basis for several application-oriented technologies. For example, the X Window System from MIT allows for distributed presentation based on TCP/IP. Various Graphical User Interface (GUI) styles can be used, such as Motif. Also, the Distributed Computing Environment (DCE) can utilize TCP/IP.

Another influence on TCP/IP, at least in the IBM world, is the recently announced Networking Blueprint. This initiative is designed to accommodate multiple network architectures, such as TCP/IP, by effectively decoupling them from the applications. If the effort is successful, the underlying transports may slowly become a commodity.

1.3 Division of Function

The TCP/IP architecture, as stated above, is named after its two most prominent protocols. TCP is the reliable Transport layer protocol which makes use of the underlying IP routing function. TCP is therefore conceptually positioned above IP.

Taking it a step further, all of the TCP/IP networking protocols can be loosely arranged into a layered model consisting of four main levels. Figure 1.3 contains an illustration of the TCP/IP model compared to OSI and SNA.

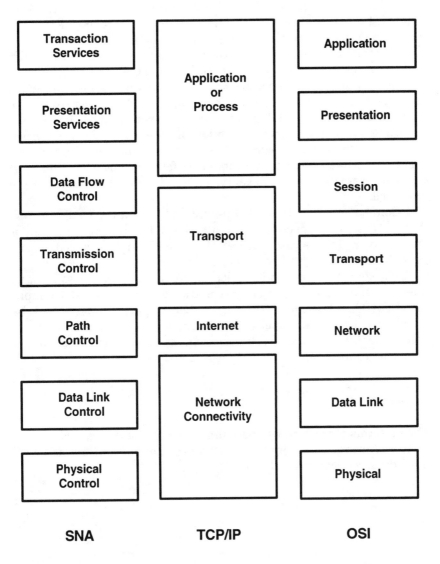

Figure 1.3 Comparison of the layered structure of SNA, TCP/IP, and OSI.

Connection-Oriented versus Connectionless

An important concept when approaching TCP/IP, as well as networking architectures in general, is the "connection" (or session). Some protocols require that a connection first be established before allowing the exchange of data between sender and receiver. Other protocols do not require a connection, with each packet viewed separately as a a self-contained data unit. These communication models therefore fall into two main categories: connection-oriented and connectionless.

Connection-oriented implies that a logical connection or link must first be established between the two sides (e.g., applications) before any data is exchanged. The setup usually involves following a standard procedure. The data packets can then be sent and received within the connection, and are logically related to each other. This can be the case when a remote request or unit of work is initiated. After the information has been exchanged, the connection can be terminated. This type of operation, while involving additional performance overhead, usually has several advantages. For example, reliability and flow control can be improved.

Connectionless service is different in that data packets are exchanged without the need to first create a formal link between the sender and receiver. In this case, the initial overhead can be reduced, with a penalty incurred with respect to reliable delivery.

The concept of connection-oriented versus connectionless is found in several networking architectures, and at several levels. For example, the IEEE 802.2 Logical Link Control sublayer, part of lower Data Link layer, provides the developer with both types of service. And within the TCP/IP architecture, an application can choose to use, or not use, a transport connection.

Layered Model

The protocols of most network architectures are commonly arranged in a layered model. Each layer has a protocol boundary with the layers immediately above and below.

In theory, this layering approach has several major advantages, such as:

- Reduced complexity, because each layer needs to only be aware of its adjacent layer immediately above and below.
- Maintenance, enhancement, and complete replacement of each layer is becomes easier, another result of isolation.
- Peer layers in different nodes communicate through operations on shared data formats.

In practice however, especially with TCP/IP, the layer boundaries are not strictly defined and observed. However the model is still appropriate and useful to describe the architecture.

Referring to Figure 1.3, the Transport and Internet layers have been described by the architecture. In addition, many of the applications which utilize these protocols are also included as part of the standard. Therefore, TCP/IP is a large collection of separately defined protocols.

The bottom Network Connectivity layer is not specifically included in the architecture. However, the Internet layer is designed to integrate with several different physical transports (e.g., X.25), as described in the RFC documents.

Upper Layer Protocols

The transport layer includes two protocols:

- Transmission Control Protocol (TCP)
- User Datagram Protocol (UDP)

An application utilizes one of these protocols, through the provided programming interfaces, in order to send and receive network data. In practice, the protocols can be implemented as a separate process or "protocol machine" which connects to the lower IP to support the local applications.

TCP provides a connection-oriented service to its applications, including data sequencing and flow control. UDP is a connectionless protocol, with fewer features and less sophistication; most notably UDP does not guarantee delivery.

Flexible IP Routing

Beneath the Transport layer lies the Internet layer, which actually consists of several different protocols. The Internet Protocol (IP), one of the protocols in this layer, is connectionless. The concern of reliable delivery is left to the higher level TCP, or application in the case of UDP.

IP supports several major functions, including:

- Accept data from the upper layer protocols to create datagrams.
- Maintain an IP routing table.
- Send outgoing datagrams based on its routing table entries.
- Receive incoming datagrams, either rerouting out into the network or directing them to a local application.
- Assist in supporting the IP to hardware layer mappings.
- Report on routing errors in the network.

To summarize, IP encapsulates TCP/UDP data into IP datagrams which are sent through the network. The IP instance at the receiving host removes the IP header to recreate the original data for delivery to the destination application.

The processing of each datagram is consistent at each step through the network, whether host or router. The routing and control functions are more balanced. In this way, TCP/IP networks can be compared to IBM's Advanced Peer-to-Peer Networking (APPN) architecture, an enhancement to the traditional SNA.

1.4 Network Characteristics

Unlike the traditional, hierarchical SNA network, TCP/IP operates in an autonomous, peer-to-peer fashion. An application on one host can dynamically initiate a connection to an application on a peer host without requiring a central, controlling server. This allows enterprise-wide system resources to be easily shared.

A TCP/IP network is composed of two major functional elements:

- Hosts
- Routers

The host is a computer system containing a full-stack implementation of TCP/IP in order to support the applications. Hosts can range in size from mainframes down to personal computers.

The routers connect one network to another, allowing traffic to flow between the internetworked hosts. Routing is based on the IP address; the network portion corresponds to each network and must be unique across the internet. It is interesting to note that the TCP/IP literature really uses the term "gateway" instead of router. However, this can cause some confusion with the IBM terminology, as discussed below.

One large virtual network is formed through the combination of the Internet layers distributed among the connected hosts and routers.

Connecting Hosts

The primary goal of TCP/IP, as with other architectures, is to provide the ability for applications and end users to connect and exchange information. As mentioned above, the host computer can take many forms in the TCP/IP network. In the IBM world, TCP/IP hosts include all of the major platforms, from MVS and VM to OS/2 and DOS. Each is referred to as a host.

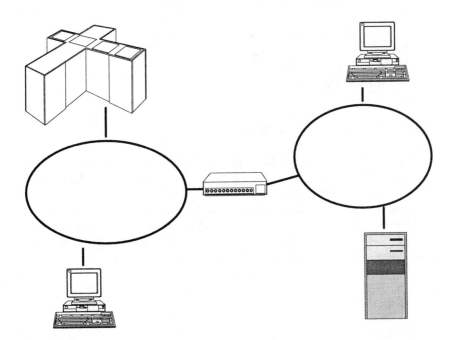

Figure 1.4 An example of how networks can be interconnected using TCP/IP.

Figure 1.4 presents a simple example of an interconnection of two networks. The hosts support the application systems and their access to the network through the Transport layer implementation. The router in this example joins the two networks.

Typical Link-Level Protocols

The physical medium is, of course, very important in the operation of the network. However, these protocols are not specifically defined and managed by the IAB. Rather, the Internet layer is designed to utilize a wide range of standard protocols, support for which can vary from implementation to implementation. Examples include:

- Token ring
- Ethernet
- X.25
- Frame Relay
- High-level Data Link Control (HDLC)

The use of one protocol instead of another depends on several factors. The decision can effect several areas of network operation, including performance. For example, the IP fragmentation protocol is based on the maximum frame size that a specific network can handle, which varies based on the link-level protocol utilized.

Refer to the appendix for a survey of the most common network communication standards.

Bridges, Routers, and Gateways

In many cases, two host machines not on the same physical network must communicate. This involves traversing two or more networks in order to exchange the datagram packets.

The TCP/IP standard, as mentioned above, differentiates between hosts and routers (gateways). IBM establishes a further distinction among this router functionality, with slightly different terminology depending upon the addressing and functions provided.

The three primary functions include:

- Bridge
- Router
- Gateway

A bridge supports the connection between two networks at the lower physical and data link layers. It establishes a method to connect LAN segments in a manner that is independent of and transparent to the data being carried (e.g., TCP/IP, SNA, etc.). In effect, the bridging function is invisible to IP routing.

A router, or what is called a gateway in the formal TCP/IP documentation, provides the interconnection at the higher-level networking layer. In the case of TCP/IP, routers handle packets based on the IP address, rather than the physical frame header address. The recent routers can also bridge different link-level protocols.

If the sender and receiver are both on the same local network, the router function is not required and the packet can be sent directly to the destination. In the case of remote hosts, data flows through a router in an indirect manner until reaching the destination network for final delivery. In addition to the dedicated routing devices, each host can also act as a router when multiple networking interfaces have been configured.

In IBM terminology, a gateway provides support for a protocol even higher than the bridges and routers. For example, a translation or mapping from one application protocol to another is common (e.g., mail or document exchange).

1.5 Data Formats and Addressing

As with SNA and OSI, the TCP/IP architecture uses well-defined data formats in order to transfer control information and end-user data between applications. The peer layers in connected nodes communicate control and routing information, as described below.

Segments, Datagrams, and Frames

The developer has several TCP/IP communication options available when creating an application. The largest number of applications utilize TCP in order to provide a more reliable, connection-oriented service.

Figure 1.5 provides an illustration of the data formats used during an exchange over a typical connection.

The application sends a stream of bytes to TCP which at some point will create a segment. The TCP segment contains a TCP header, followed by the data. The segment is passed to IP which then constructs a datagram as shown. The datagram begins with an IP header immediately followed by the segment. Next, the Service Access Point (SAP) for the IEEE 802.2 Logical Link Control (LLC) is used. An LLC Protocol Data Unit (PDU) is created, containing the datagram as well as the source and destination SAP addresses. Finally, the token ring Media Access Control (MAC) frame is sent over the LAN, containing the LLC PDU. The physical MAC frame is made up of several fields, including the source and destination link station address, each 48 bits long.

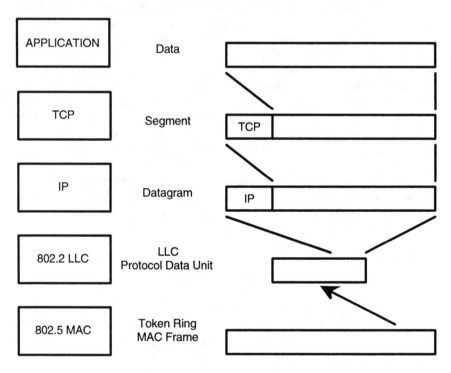

Figure 1.5 Data formats and addresses used during transmission of TCP/IP network data.

During this operation, several types of addresses are used. Beginning from the top layer, these major addresses include:

■ Port number identifying the application, in the TCP header.
■ Transport layer protocol in use (i.e., TCP), in the IP header.
■ IP addresses identifying the connected hosts, in the IP header.

- Data link address for the Service Access Point (i.e.,
  IEEE 802.2 LLC SAP), in the LLC Protocol Data Unit.
- Physical address identifying the token ring link
  station, in the MAC frame header.

Each of the addressing specifications is examined and processed at different points in the layered model, as shown in Figure 1.5.

1.6 Use of Transport Layer Protocols

An application will usually use either TCP or UDP to handle the transportation of data through IP (although a "raw" IP interface is consistently supported as well). In both cases, a port is utilized by the transport protocol to support its applications through a multiplexing scheme.

That is, the IP address is used to route the datagrams through the internet. Once the packet arrives at its destination host it is then processed by either TCP or UDP. Each of these protocols then examines the 16-bit destination port number to determine which of the local applications will receive the data. Looked at slightly differently, the port number, protocol (e.g., TCP), and IP address (used by the local host) can be combined to form a unique path from the application out into the network.

Application Access

The TCP and UDP RFC documents describe the service interface available to the higher-level applications. The definition of TCP is more well-defined than UDP, identifying six primitives; refer to Chapter 3 for a more complete description.

A specific TCP/IP platform implementation can provide its own unique, high-level interface to either of the protocols. However, to improve consistency, interoperability, and portability, several API standards have been commonly accepted and implemented. Figure 1.6 provides a list of the major APIs usually available to applications using TCP/IP as a transport. Note that some are directly integrated with and therefore a part of TCP/IP, while others are built on top of TCP/IP. Additional interfaces can also exist for a few of the TCP/UDP applications (e.g., FTP, SNMP).

Development Interface	Description
Socket	The de facto standard for TCP/IP development; can support other transport protocols as well.
Transport Layer interface	The TLI standard was created for the AT&T UNIX System V, and competes with the socket interface.
NETBIOS	NETBIOS was created for the IBM PC Network, and now can be used to access TCP and UDP services.
Remote Procedure Call	An important client/server technology used to invoke procedures on remote machines.
X Window System	Created at MIT and allows for distributed graphical presentation using X terminals or emulators.
Basic TCP/UDP	Possible to directly access TCP or UDP for a given product implementation.

Figure 1.6 Programming interfaces used to access TCP/IP services, or built on top of (and associated with) TCP/IP.

Perhaps the most widely utilized is the socket interface, first developed for the Berkeley Software Distribution (BSD) version of UNIX in the early 1980s. Each application "plugs into" a local socket, which is really a handle used by the application for network access. Two socket applications can connect and exchange data; refer to Chapter 3, and the last part of the book, for more information on the socket programming interface.

1.7 Implementation Characteristics

Several influences have affected the creation and evolution of TCP/IP. A typical implementation has several characteristics, as discussed below.

UNIX Roots

TCP/IP has been closely associated with the UNIX operating system, after it was included with the BSD version. The two major aspects of UNIX which have affected TCP/IP, particularly the socket interface, include:

- Process
- File

A process is a collection of system resources, including at least (and many times at most) one task thread. As with the analogous MVS address space, a protected virtual storage map is used.

On any active system, there are dozens or even hundreds of processes concurrently active. Many times, information must be exchanged among the processes. UNIX therefore provides for interprocess communication (IPC).

Applications using TCP/IP engage in a type of IPC, among distributed machines. Also, many of the networking protocols themselves are described as implementations within separate processes.

The process also becomes important when understanding several of the application-level protocols (e.g., file transfer). Many times a main server process is assumed to be able to create child processes, in a master-slave relationship, to carry out specific work requests.

Another aspect of UNIX influencing the access to TCP/IP is the file. Once opened, a file is referenced by a "handle," or integer number. All I/O operations (e.g., read) can then be performed using the handle as an operand on the API call. This is analogous to the socket address, which is first created and then used on subsequent socket API calls.

Client/Server Model

Client/server computing has rapidly gained interest in recent years among both vendors and end users. The client/server model is a special case of cooperative processing, whose acceptance is being driven by the increasing power of desktop workstations and PCs, and by the sophisticated Graphical User Interface (GUI) technology now available.

The objective with client/server computing is to identify a specific set of resources that are managed and controlled by one or more servers. The clients, implemented across the enterprise typically as separate PCs, can then establish network connections allowing access to the server's resource or service.

The TCP/IP architecture is ideally suited to this type of processing. In fact, most of the standard applications operate using this type of model; servers wait for incoming client requests.

Basic Services

A TCP/IP host implementation will contain three basic application services, as listed in Figure 1.7. Of these, the mail service is perhaps the most familiar and widely used.

TCP/IP Application	Description
Mail	Simple Mail Transfer Protocol (SMTP) provides for direct, or store-and-forward, mail exchange.
Remote logon	TELNET provides a simple, but flexible, technique for logging on to a remote host application.
File exchange	File Transfer Protocol (FTP) is used to exchange data files among connected TCP/IP hosts.

Figure 1.7 Three major applications provided with TCP/IP implementation.

1.8 Network Administration

While the RFC documents describe the architecture, actual product implementations vary. In each case, however, the network planner and system administrator must perform several tasks in order to install, configure, and maintain the TCP/IP network.

NIC Registration Services

TCP/IP is an architecture which can be implemented with or without a connection to the U.S. Internet. However, even though normal commercial traffic has been traditionally disallowed on the Internet backbone, many corporations choose to access the Internet for services that can be provided (e.g., universal mail exchange).

One aspect in the planning for TCP/IP product installation includes deciding whether or not to register certain networking values with the NIC to ensure uniqueness. The major parameters that can be registered include:

- IP address
- Domain name
- Autonomous System (AS) number
- Port number(s)

A range of IP addresses can be assigned, based on the size of the user's network. A domain is characterized by a single point of administrative control, and is assigned a unique name in the hierarchical domain tree. The combination of domain name and local user ID is a convenient way to access a particular host user without the need to know the corresponding IP address. Refer to Chapter 2 for more information IP addressing, and to Chapter 4 for the Domain Name System (DNS).

An AS number can be used in identifying a group of networks. This value can be used for several purposes, most notably in some of the newer IP routing protocols.

As mentioned above, and again in Chapter 3, the port is used together with the Transport layer protocol (e.g., TCP) to identify a specific local application. The port number is 16 bits long, ranging from 0 to 64K. The first 1K, or 0 through 1023, are referred to as "well-known" ports, effectively reserved for use by the standard applications. Of course, a vendor or user can petition to reserve a port for universal use.

Planning and Product Configuration

The planning of a TCP/IP network is a large and, at times, complex subject area. It involves establishing standards for all parts of network operation, including:

- Physical connectivity (i.e., LANs)
- Host software implementations
- Bridges and routers

- Address and name assignments
- IP subnetworks
- Multiple protocol and integration issues

The remainder of this book is designed to assist the administrator in understanding TCP/IP in the IBM environment, and to clarify many of the options available.

Support

As with any network protocol, TCP/IP requires support. The tasks required include:

- Growth enablement
- Trouble-shooting
- Performance
- Network management

Unlike SNA, TCP/IP is a relatively new phenomenon in the IBM world. Therefore, many aspects of network support are still evolving (e.g., network management). In particular, TCP/IP applications typically require a closer cooperation with the underlying network transport function.

2

Network Addressing and Routing

The Internet Protocol layer includes several different protocols operating together in order to route datagrams through the internetwork. The individual protocols that are part of this layer, each discussed later in the chapter, include:

- Internet Protocol (IP)
- Internet Control Message Protocol (ICMP)
- Internet Group Management Protocol (IGMP)
- Address Resolution Protocol (ARP)
- Reverse Address Resolution Protocol (RARP)

IP is the main Internet layer protocol, and central to the flow of data. This protocol utilizes a 32-bit address for both the source and destination when processing datagrams. The IP address must be unique for all of the nodes participating in the internetwork.

As mentioned earlier in Chapter 1, the Internet Protocol provides a connectionless service. The instances of IP spread throughout the internet engage in a best-effort attempt to send datagrams on to their final destination. End-to-end services, such as packet sequencing and flow control, are not provided. If a datagram is lost or stolen, an upper-layer protocol must detect this situation and retransmit the packet. A natural result of this is the need to detect and appropriately discard duplicate datagrams.

ICMP assists in the management of the IP operations, and generates messages describing error conditions in the network. IGMP allows nodes on the same physical network to coordinate their multicasting operations.

ARP and RARP, which are sometimes grouped together forming a sublayer of the Internet layer, provide link support. They allow IP to associate a particular IP address with the corresponding physical link station address.

2.1 Datagram Header

Each datagram, as illustrated in Chapter 1, contains an IP header followed by the data being transported. The content of the data portion depends on the Transport layer protocol in use, and the application. For example, a TCP segment is carried in the datagram between two applications after a connection has been established.

Regardless of the content of the datagrams, each is accepted by IP at the host in one of two major ways:

- The local Transport layer protocol or application passes data down to IP when sending a packet.
- A network connection (e.g., Ethernet) presents a datagram to IP on the host for routing, either to a local application or back out into the network.

In addition, instances of ICMP within the Internet layer can create datagrams for specific errors and problems.

The IP header is, of course, very important to the routing of each datagram. It contains fields which determine the processing by IP and describe the enclosed data.

Version, Protocol, Length, and Checksum

Figure 2.1 illustrates the formatted content of a datagram, featuring the IP header. The header is divided into an integral number of 32-bit words, each consisting of four 8-bit bytes. The TCP/IP standard is based on the "big endian" notation style, where the most significant bit of each field is arranged first.

The first 4 bits of the header designate the version of the IP protocol in use, with 4 being the current level.

The protocol field indicates the content and use of the datagram, and therefore determines its local destination. This provides a type of first-level multiplexing, where datagrams are first routed locally by protocol. There might be a second-level multiplexing, as mentioned above, according to the TCP port number. Note that the protocol destination is logical in the sense that the exact implementation can vary. It might be a unique process, or perhaps a thread within an existing process (where other protocols also operate).

0   31

VER	HDR LEN	TYPE OF SERVICE	TOTAL DATAGRAM LENGTH	
IDENTIFICATION			FLAGS	OFFSET FOR FRAGMENTATION
TIME TO LIVE		PROTOCOL	CHECKSUM FOR HEADER	
SOURCE IP ADDRESS				
DESTINATION IP ADDRESS				
OPTIONS				
DATA				

Figure 2.1 IP datagram illustrating the formatted header.

The exact content of the 1-byte protocol field is reserved by the architecture for the accepted protocols. For example, the values used for the Transport layer protocols are:

■ Transmission Control Protocol (TCP) - 6
■ User Datagram Protocol (UDP) - 17

There are two length fields in the IP header. The first is the length of the header itself, expressed as the number of 32-bit words. The minimum size is 5, but it can be larger if any option fields are included. The maximum header size is 15 words.

The second length field, in the third word, describes the length of the entire datagram (including the header). With 16 bits to work with, the maximum datagram length can therefore be 65,535 bytes (64K). Note that this imposes a size limitation which, in most practical situations, is never approached.

The checksum field is used to assure the error-free transmission of the datagram header. It contains a value which is generated based on the contents of the header using a simple 1's complement algorithm. Note that the data portion can be protected by a different error-detection mechanism, depending on the content, as discussed in Chapter 3.

IP Addressing

As previously mentioned, datagrams flow through the internetwork based on the IP address of the source and destination. The header contains these two addresses, as shown. Some of the techniques and algorithms used to route the data are discussed below. These IP addresses are unique within a particular internetwork.

Type of Service and Time to Live

These two fields can be used to provide a measure of control over the datagram's flow. The type of service field, though not universally used, allows datagrams to be assigned a priority. The bits are defined by the standard, though the corresponding actions and operations taken for each are not.

Time to live was envisioned as a sort of "self-destruct" mechanism, whereby a datagram could be destroyed (i.e., discarded) after spending too much time flowing through the internetwork. The theory is that if a datagram cannot reach its destination by a certain amount of time, it is then assumed to be lost or perhaps looping.

This field was to hold an actual time value, expressed in seconds, which would be appropriately decremented after each "hop." A hop is delineated by an IP instance in a host or router which commonly acts to route the datagram from one network or subnetwork to another. The field would then be analogous to a parking meter.

However, the use of an actual time stamp value in this manner is not practical in most situations. So if used at all, the time to live field is usually just a simple counter, decremented for each hop. In this case, a safe value for the sender to use would be the maximum anticipated number of hops, plus a margin for safety (e.g., twice the expected number of hops from sender to receiver).

Fragmentation

Fragmentation is an IP protocol designed to compensate for the maximum frame size limitation of a network through which a datagram passes. The technique involves splitting a single datagram into two or more smaller fragment blocks, each of which is then routed independently to the original destination. Upon arrival at the target host, the fragments are reassembled by IP before delivery to the local application.

The three fields in the header used to handle fragmentation, all in the second word, include:

- Identification
- Flags
- Offset for fragmentation

This protocol can have an impact on performance, and is therefore a concern to the network designer and operations specialist. Fragmentation, including the use of these three fields, is discussed later in the chapter.

Additional Options

Several different options are available. For example, the Strict Source Route can be used to specify the exact path for the datagram through the IP network. It is therefore in some ways similar to IBM's Source Route Bridge (SRB) LAN protocol.

A maximum of 10 words can be used for the options in the variable length area labeled as OPTIONS. Note that when used at all, the options area must be padded with zeros for alignment on a word boundary. When no options are utilized, the header is five words (20 bytes) long.

2.2 IP Address Space

As mentioned above, a TCP/IP internetwork consists of a collection of interconnected networks. To assure interoperability, each of the internetwork devices sending or receiving datagrams must have a unique IP address. This calls for a method by which to classify and organize the addresses.

The structure of the IP address reflects the nature of an internetwork, and allows for its administration. The address is divided into two parts:

- Network
- Local (i.e., host)

These two elements are combined to form the IP address.

Network and Local Addresses

Figure 2.2 illustrates the split between the network and local sections of the address. The network number must be unique throughout the internet, while the local portion must be unique only within a particular network.

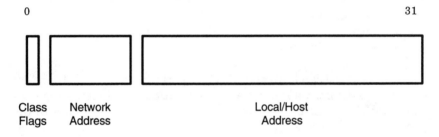

Figure 2.2   IP address divided into network and local parts.

Notice in the figure that there is a section which was not mentioned above: class flags. Each IP address falls into one of several classes, as indicated by these first few flag bits.

Classes of IP Addresses

There are five categories of IP addresses, as shown in Figure 2.3. The first few bits, or class header flags, identify the address class in each case. The first three classes (i.e., A, B, and C) are the most commonly encountered during normal internet operation. Comparing these classes, the difference between them involves where the network-local division is made.

The class A addresses are reserved for very large networks. In this case, there are 7 bits available for the network number, and 24 for the devices in the named network.

Class	Header Flags	Addressing Bits	Description
A	0	Network - 7 Local - 24	Reserved for networks with a large number of devices.
B	10	Network - 14 Local - 16	For medium-sized networks.
C	110	Network - 21 Local - 8	Available for networks with a small number of devices.
D	1110	Network/local split not used.	Used in certain cases for a limited distance multicast.
E	1111	Network/local split not used.	Reserved for experimentation.

Figure 2.3   Classes of IP addresses.

At the other end, the class C addresses are designed to be used by networks that have a much smaller number of IP-addressable devices. The network field is 21 bits long, while the host identifier consists of 8 bits.

Regardless of the class, an IP address can be represented in one of several different ways (e.g., binary, hexadecimal). Most commonly, four decimal numbers are used, each representing a single 8-bit byte (or octet). The digits are separated by a period; an example of "dotted decimal notation" is shown in Figure 2.4.

```
198.17.46.2
```

Figure 2.4   Standard expression of a 4-byte IP address.

Internet Address Assignment

The coordination of the IP addresses is central to the management of a TCP/IP network. These addresses must be assigned in some fashion, allowing for their uniqueness.

Part of the process of connecting to the Internet is reserving a block of IP addresses. The NIC will assign a network address based on several factors, including the size of the user's network. The administration of the local IP address space for the assigned network ID is performed by the local network authority.

For those corporations (or individuals) not connecting to the Internet, such a registration is not necessary. However, in many cases it may still be desirable to register and therefore reserve one or more network addresses for the future.

Subnetworks

With large networks (e.g., class A), the size of the local IP address space can be difficult to administer. In order to help manage the potentially large number of local devices in such cases, the architecture includes the concept of subnetworking.

Through a further division of the local address, a single network can be split into multiple subnetworks. Figure 2.5 contains an illustration of the subnetwork and host addresses.

Subnetworks can be created, arranging hosts and routers according to several characteristics, including their usage and location. It extends the IP routing to allow for more control over both administration and routing. For example, the devices on a physical Ethernet LAN can be assigned to one subnetwork. It is important to note that the subnetworks are not universally maintained, and are visible only within the organization responsible for administering the local IP addresses.

During network configuration, a subnet mask must be created for use by the hosts and routers; an example is included with Figure 2.5. In essence, the mask is a 32-bit template placed over a specific IP address, through a logical AND operation in order to quickly make a routing decision. It contains all 1's for the corresponding network and subnetwork numbers, and all 0's for the host portion. More on the use of subnetworks during IP routing is presented below.

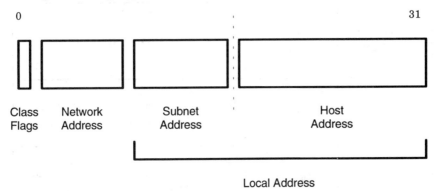

Subnet mask = 255.255.0.0

Figure 2.5 Local portion of a class A address split into a subnetwork and host number, with an example of the corresponding subnet mask.

Broadcast and Loopback Addresses

A small number of IP addresses are reserved by the architecture, each having special meanings and usage. Figure 2.6 contains a list of the major addresses that fall into this category.

In examining the special addresses in the figure, it is clear that two of the class A are not to be assigned: 0 and 127. The loopback address begins with 127, and is used for testing and local interprocess communication. The network ID of 0 is reserved for systems that are just being initialized. Where loopback can be used at any time, the second and third addresses are only available at startup.

The last two in the figure can be used to broadcast a datagram to multiple machines. The first is directed to devices on a named network, while the second is for the current (i.e., local) network.

2.3 Basic Routing Considerations

During normal operation of a network, datagrams are created and flow from one node to another through an interconnection of IP-capable nodes. Each instance of the IP protocol maintains a directory called the routing table with which to make decisions on how to forward the outgoing packets.

Network Portion	Local Portion	Description
127	Any value	Loopback address, used only for testing purposes; never sent over network.
All zeros	All zeros	Can be used during system startup to designate the local host.
All zeros	Specific host	Also used during initialization to target a host on the current (default) network.
Network ID	All ones	Directed broadcast to all devices on the named network; also used with subnets.
All ones	All ones	Broadcast to all devices on the current, local network.

Figure 2.6 Special IP addresses reserved by the architecture.

Hop to Hop Datagram Flow

Among the popular networking architectures, there are different techniques for sending data packets from an originating to destination node. One of the major areas for comparison is whether a complete end-to-end route is established between the two nodes or not.

For example, the SNA Virtual Route (VR) represents an example of a connection which, within the traditional SNA network, is statically predefined. The sending and receiving applications exchange data over sessions which are mapped to the VRs. That is, a VR is established between each pair of communicating nodes in the network before a session can begin; the VR does not change during the lifetime of the session.

The Internet Protocol, on the other hand, is much simpler. In this case, a complete end-to-end link is not used. Rather, IP needs only to decide which node will next receive the datagram (i.e., host or router).

At each stage, a datagram is examined. If the destination network has not been reached, the destination address in the header is compared to the local routing table.

The datagram is enveloped in the local physical transport and sent to the next node for further routing. This is referred to as indirect routing as the datagram is not being sent directly to its destination. Finally, the data arrives at the proper network and is delivered to the local device (i.e., host) - a direct form of routing.

The resulting hop-to-hop path between two nodes can vary dynamically, based on configuration changes and traffic conditions.

One important aspect of the Internet Protocol is that the 32-bit address does not really equate to a host. Rather, the IP address designates a path into or out of a specific host or router. For example, a host may have multiple interfaces, either to the same or different networks, each with different IP addresses. Such a host is called "multihomed."

Routing Tables

Once IP is activated, it maintains a routing table, usually in memory, by which routing decisions can be made. The table is normally initialized from a disk file which the administrator can manually update as needed. During regular operation, the contents of the table can be changed by the operator, or automatically through one of the available dynamic routing protocols discussed below.

Each entry, or row, in the table contains two main values: a destination, and next hop to that destination. When a datagram must be routed, as described above, it is compared to the contents of the table in order to determine the next hop. Figure 2.7 provides a simple example of a routing table, displayed with the "netstat" command.

```
Destination   Gateway       Flags   Refcnt   Use    Interface
127.0.0.1     127.0.0.1     UH      3        52     lo0
149.11.85.0   149.11.20.3   UG      1        147    le0
131.18.25.0   149.11.20.2   UG      2        11     le0
177.100.0.0   149.11.20.2   UG      1        15     le0
203.17.45.0   149.11.20.4   UGD     2        4      le0
default       149.11.20.2   UG      5        18     le0
```

Figure 2.7   Example of the contents of an IP routing table.

The first step in using the table is to determine the datagram's destination address, as extracted from the IP header. It is then compared to the destinations in the table, which can be:

■ Network number
■ Network and subnetwork number
■ Fully qualified destination, including local address
■ Default entry

Examples of these are shown in the figure. The "U" under flags denotes usable, while the "G" means gateway (i.e., router) and "H" is host. The next two columns contain statistics, and the final field is the local interface connection.

If a match in the table cannot be made, the default entry is used. Having such a wild card directive keeps each routing table at a manageable size. In fact, most tables are usually relatively small compared to the total number IP-addressable devices in an internet. It would be impossible to require each host and router to retain the topology of the entire internetwork.

The routing tables are defined manually, but they can also be updated dynamically as mentioned above. ICMP includes such a capability. Also, some of the more advanced algorithms such as Open Shortest Path First (OSPF), which are separate protocols augmenting IP, automatically update the tables based on changing network conditions.

Subnetwork Considerations

The use of subnetworks modifies the routing protocol slightly. In this case, the subnet mask is applied to the destination address in a logical AND operation. This results in a concatenated network-subnetwork field which can then be compared to the table entries as required.

Types of Routing Protocols

The rapid evolution of the Internet has naturally influenced the types of the routing algorithms available with TCP/IP. From a relatively small network, the ARPANET grew into a large backbone consisting of a collection of "core" routers. This core architecture required that networks connect to and rely on the ARPANET backbone.

The core routers each maintained information about every other destination throughout the Internet. The attached networks used non-core routers, and kept only partial routing data. However, due to further growth and the connection of NSFNET, another model emerged.

In order to overcome some of the limitations of the hierarchical core-backbone model, with the central routing authority, the concept of peer backbone networks was accepted. This involved allowing networks to be naturally arranged into autonomous systems, each under one local administrative authority. Autonomous systems could then establish links with each other, thus forming the larger internetwork.

In fact, this concept was solidified to the point of allowing each of the autonomous systems to be assigned a number, registered with the NIC.

As a result, two major categories of routing algorithms evolved:

- Interior
- Exterior

Each is used with respect to the autonomous system boundary. Interior gateway protocols are used by routers within an autonomous system (i.e., usually local to the enterprise), while the exterior gateway protocols are for communication between autonomous systems.

The protocols, most commonly those used within autonomous systems (i.e., interior) can be further classified according to how the routing decisions are made:

- Vector-distance
- Link-state

Refer to the section 2.5 for more information on IP routing.

2.4 Hardware Addressing

Within a TCP/IP internetwork, the IP address is used when routing datagrams between host machines. However, before a packet can actually be transmitted on to a physical network, the destination IP address must be associated with the corresponding low-level, physical address. In this sense, the IP address is more logical, or symbolic, while the physical address is the real address actually used to send the frame. The various underlying network communication protocols used in the typical internetwork (e.g., Token Ring) are not part of the architecture. However, several of the RFC documents contain descriptions of how IP is to be integrated with these standards.

The communication protocols for hardware addressing and routing are considered more fully later in the book, especially when describing the various IBM routers and controllers. Also, Appendix B includes a survey of the popular protocols.

Address Resolution Protocol

The Address Resolution Protocol (ARP), within the Internet layer, provides support for IP-to-hardware address mapping. It is used in the case where the IP address of another device is known, but its hardware address is not. For example, a local host might attempt to send a packet to a host or router on the local network whose IP address is known, but whose physical address is not. In this case, ARP is used to determine the destination's link-level address.

In the LAN environment, for example, ARP utilizes a local (i.e., link-level, not IP) broadcast capability. The IP address of the target node is carried in a special type of request. When the address is recognized by the destination device, a reply is returned, containing its physical address.

Reverse Address Resolution Protocol

As its name implies, Reverse ARP (RARP) operates in a manner opposite to that of ARP. For example, suppose that a host (i.e., workstation) is initialized, and the IP process has access to its local link station (physical) address but not its IP address. This can occur, for example, in the case of a diskless workstation.

Aside from the reverse manner of operating, RARP differs from ARP in the sense that a dedicated RARP server must be installed which is configured to maintain the address mappings. So where ARP does a local broadcast to its unknown IP partner, only one local machine (i.e., RARP server) responds to the client translation requests.

Bootstrap Protocol

The Bootstrap Protocol (BOOTP) is an alternative to RARP, also used with a diskless machine during its initialization (or booting). Both protocols use a broadcast to the server in order to determine the local IP address. However, BOOTP utilizes the Transport layer protocol UDP and IP to send out a datagram. This is possible using one of the special IP addresses (i.e., broadcast) reserved by the architecture.

2.5 Common Interior Gateway Protocols

Several different routing protocols can be used within the backbone IP internetwork. These protocols allow status and topology information to be shared among the IP routers, thus improving throughput and operational efficiency.

Figure 2.8 contains a list of the major routing protocols, both interior and exterior.

Vector-Distance versus Link-State Algorithms

As mentioned above, current interior routing protocols generally fall into two major categories: vector-distance and link-state. They are distinguished according to how routing decisions are made, as well as how the information is propagated and stored by the routers.

The vector-distance protocols are based on some type of simple measurement (i.e., metric) assigned to each destination in the table, usually the number of hops from the local host. In theory, the higher the number (i.e., the greater the cost), the longer it will take to get its the destination. The IP software would obviously select the path representing the least cost (i.e., number of hops). However, this type of algorithm usually does not take into consideration the various link characteristics, such as line speed, and can therefore result in a distortion of its operation. Another distinguishing characteristics is that a node using this type of algorithm will broadcast its entire routing table to neighboring routers on a periodic basis.

The link-state, also referred to as Shortest Path First (SPF), protocols represent an improvement over vector-distance algorithms, and can be used to overcome some of their limitations. More features and sophistication are added, making them suitable for larger networks. One of their major enhancements is a formally defined network topology database at each router. The nodes then send out much smaller update messages, usually limited to network changes (not entire routing tables).

Routing Protocol	Description
Hello	Interior gateway protocol which uses transmission delay rather than hop count.
Routing Information Protocol (RIP)	De facto standard interior protocol first included with BSD; several limitations.
Open Shortest Path First (OSPF)	Part of a new class of link-state interior protocols with growing usage.
Gateway to Gateway Protocol (GGP)	Now historic, GGP was used by the core gateways within the ARPANET backbone.
Exterior Gateway Protocol (EGP)	A widely used exterior protocol designed to connect autonomous systems.
Border Gateway Protocol (BGP)	A newer exterior gateway protocol which is superior in several ways to EGP.

Figure 2.8 Protocols that have been developed to exchange routing information between IP routers and hosts.

Routing Information Protocol

The Routing Information Protocol (RIP) is an old, but widely utilized interior gateway protocol still adequate for many networks. It evolved from the Xerox Network System (XNS) protocol, and was included in the early Berkeley Software Distribution (BSD) UNIX implementation of TCP/IP. The protocol is supported on the host, typically through the daemon process "routed" running in the background.

RIP is based on a simple vector-distance algorithm. Each path to the destinations in the routing table has a perceived cost, which is calculated as the summation of all the hops along the way. The protocol provides for dynamic updates affecting the local routing table, which allows the lowest-cost path to each destination to be selected.

The network is composed of two main types of RIP-capable nodes:

- Active
- Passive

Active nodes, usually implemented as routers, send out route update messages every 30 seconds on their attached (LAN) networks. Both the passive (usually hosts) and the active nodes listen for the RIP messages, and update their own tables as necessary. These messages are constructed from the sender's table, and contain a variable number of entry pairs (i.e., IP address and cost as number of hops). For example, if a new path to the same destination has a lower cost, it will effectively replace the older entry to be used instead. All the routes are specified in each of the messages; those not included in the advertisements after 3 minutes are assumed not to be available and therefore removed from the routing tables.

RIP was placed into widespread usage through the popularity of BSD UNIX before it was thoroughly examined and finalized as a TCP/IP standard. Understandably, it therefore has a few serious limitations. RIP can be unstable, especially in larger and/or rapidly changing networks. A major element in its operation contributing to the instability is the delay in sending the table update messages. This can lead to inconsistent views of the network by the routers.

As mentioned above, RIP uses the concept of cost (number of hops) to each destination. The maximum cost for any destination is 15, after which it is deemed "unreachable." In practice, a hop count of 16 is used to indicate an unreachable destination. As can immediately be seen, this limits the size of a network using RIP. And even with medium-sized networks within the limit, RIP's operation can create problems.

Consider a much-simplified example shown in Figure 2.9, designed only to illustrate the basic problem. Here three networks are joined by two routers. Each router maintains its own routing table which is broadcast on its adjacent local network(s). For example, router 1 broadcasts on networks 1 and 2.

In this example, router 1 advertises a cost of 1 to the nodes on network 1 which need to send to network 2 (as shown by the arrow). Similarly, router 2 advertises a cost of 1 from network 2 to 3. This leads to the cost of 2 from network 1 to 3.

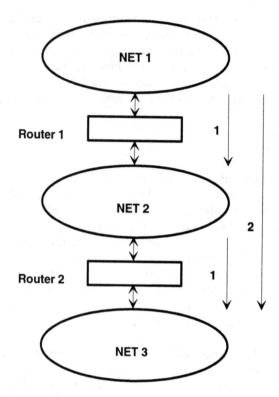

Figure 2.9 Three nodes connected, using the Routing Information Protocol to share routing information.

Suppose a host within network 2 wants to send a datagram to network 3. It will naturally chooses router 2 with a cost of 1. Now imagine that the physical link between router 2 and network 3 goes down. The path through router 2 to network 3 is assigned a cost of 16 (i.e., unreachable), which is broadcast on network 2.

Now the same host in network 2 needs to send another datagram into network 3. This time, however, router 2 cannot be used. However, it appears that a cost-effective path can be used through router 1 ! That is, router 1 has been advertising a cost to network 3 of 2. So the datagram is sent to router 2 - the wrong way!

So it is clear how an unstable condition can arise, since the updates are not immediately broadcast. This will remain until the routers reach a steady-state awareness of the reality of the network's condition. This process is called "counting to infinity," as all nodes must gradually increment the cost to network 3, communicated through the regular broadcasts, until it becomes unreachable (i.e., 16).

Two solutions are used to improve RIP's operation:

■ Trigger updates - requires a participating node to send an update immediately after a metric change has been detected, which speeds up the process.
■ Split horizon - this technique involves removing redundant entries from a node's routing table. For example, in Figure 2.9, router 1 would not broadcast, on network 2 that it knows how to reach router 2 (i.e., network 3). This prevents traffic from be misdirected. A further modification to split horizon is "poison reverse," where router 1 does include an entry for router 2 on network 2, but with a cost of 16 (i.e., not reachable).

While these additions have made RIP more usable, it is still relatively primitive when compared to some of the more recent link-state algorithms.

Open Shortest Path First

Open Shortest Path First (OSPF) is an example of a more sophisticated link-state routing protocol.

OSPF subdivides an autonomous system into several areas, or regions, which are numbered sequentially. Area 0 is designated the OSPF backbone for OSPF in the autonomous system, and must be present and contiguous. Other areas connect to the OSPF backbone; Figure 2.10 illustrates the areas used by the OSPF protocol.

The routers within each area work together to maintain their own regional topology, hidden from the other areas. This topology information resides in a link-state database, an identical copy of which is stored at each of the nodes in the area. The topology database consists of records describing each of the links in terms of an assigned metric; OSPF allows more control in this respect than RIP.

Messages are exchanged between routers which describe changing network conditions. These link advertisements are not complete table updates, as with RIP. Rather, they are more focused on reporting necessary changes. The topology databases at each node can then be updated.

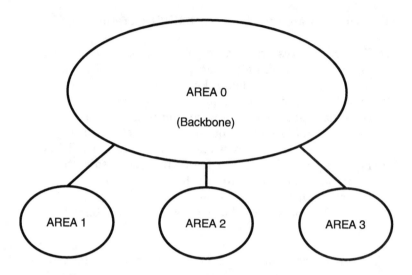

Figure 2.10   Concept of OSPF areas within an autonomous system.

Within a local physical network, there is a further subdivision of functional responsibility. When multiple routers are connected to the network (i.e., a multiaccess network), only one of the routers is elected the designated router. The designated router establishes an adjacency with the other routers, keeping them informed of changing network conditions.

There is a five-step procedure when a network is brought on-line which the participating routers follow. This involves discovering local routers, electing a designated router (and establishing adjacency relationships), synchronizing multiple databases, and building the local routing table.

The routers within an OSPF area share a common view of their area. The areas are linked by border routers within the Autonomous System. Here, only a limited amount of information is necessarily exchanged so as to enable interarea routing. The boundary routers are used to link separate Autonomous Systems.

2.6 Internet Control Message Protocol

The Internet Control Message Protocol (ICMP) is an integral part of the Internet layer. It is used by the hosts and routers in the internetwork to communicate information supporting the transport of datagrams.

Most commonly, ICMP is associated with reporting errors due to routing problems. However, there are 11 different message types that are actively used with ICMP; Figure 2.11 contains a list of the different message types. Note that the two messages, information request/reply (15/16), have been retired and are not shown.

Reviewing the contents of the figure, ICMP is used for a variety of purposes, including to:

■ Support the network management PING command.
■ Report a particular destination as unreachable.
■ Request that a sending host reduce its traffic volume, in an attempt to relieve congestion.
■ Report configuration and route changes.
■ Report IP header parameter problems for a specific datagram.
■ Discard a datagram because its time value has expired.
■ Request a subnetwork mask value.

The ICMP messages are carried in a standard header, and transported as datagrams through the IP network.

ICMP Message Transport

A datagram begins with an IP header, followed by the data portion. In the case of ICMP, this data area contains a precisely formatted data unit.

The exact content varies for each message. However, the first 32-bit word is standard for each. The values contained include:

■ Type (8 bits) - identifies the message, as discussed above.
■ Code (8 bits) - provides further resolution for a specific type value.
■ Checksum (16 bits) - used for transmission error detection.

The "netstat" operator command supports an interface to ICMP, and can be used to review the collected and processed data.

Message Type Field	Message Type
0	Echo reply.
3	Destination unreachable.
4	Source quench.
5	Redirect route.
8	Echo request.
11	Time value exceeded for datagram.
12	Error with datagram parameter.
13	Timestamp request.
14	Timestamp reply.
17	Address mask request.
18	Address mask reply.

Figure 2.11 Different types of ICMP messages available for use.

2.7 Internet Group Management Protocol

The Internet Group Management Protocol (IGMP) is part of the Internet layer. It supports the complexities of multicasting by maintaining and managing a list of group members.

An 8-byte message, included immediately after the IP header, is used to communicate the IGMP requests. The protocol is based on the concept of group membership, where host processes can join and terminate a specific group.

3

Transport Layer

The Transport layer, like the Internet layer, is composed of multiple protocols. Namely, the Transmission Control Protocol (TCP) and the User Datagram Protocol (UDP) provide services to the applications which they support. Each protocol has a different set of characteristics, features, and intended uses.

Figure 3.1 illustrates the position of TCP and UDP, with respect to IP. TCP is a connection-oriented protocol, with end-to-end capabilities such as sequencing and flow control. UDP is connectionless, leaving such features providing reliable transport to the application. In each case, the protocol used during an exchange between two applications is indicated in the IP header within the datagram.

3.1 Data Flow, Ports, and Sockets

The definition of the Transport layer protocols and data formats is an abstraction which must be implemented in the software and hardware in some manner.

TCP and UDP are designed as a set of separate program modules. TCP, because of its complexity, usually executes in its own operating system process. UDP is a much simpler protocol, running as an extension to IP. In both cases, data logically flows between the applications and IP, through the Transport layer.

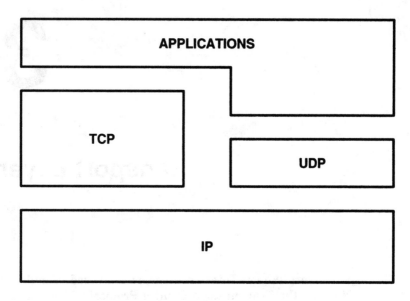

Figure 3.1 The two Transport layer protocols utilizing IP services.

Application Interface to Transport Layer

It is fairly straightforward to see that the Transport layer supports the applications. But how is each application, using one of the protocols, differentiated from the other applications? The answer is through its protocol port number.

Simply put, a port is a mechanism whereby each application using TCP or UDP on a given host is assigned a logical address. These 16-bit numbers identify the applications, and are stored in the TCP and UDP headers during transmission.

Therefore, the three major levels of addressing on the host include:

- Port number - a value identifying the application.
- Protocol number - the Transport layer protocol being used.
- IP address - a path into and out of the host.

When all three values are combined, a path is formed between the local application and the IP internetwork.

Unique Socket Connection

While both Transport layer protocols use the port concept for multiplexing and demultiplexing, TCP adds an even higher layer of abstraction: the connection. A connection is a temporary association between two TCP-based applications. It must be established for data exchange, and then terminated.

There are several different programming technologies available to allow application access to the TCP/IP network resources. The socket interface, developed for BSD UNIX, is the most widely utilized.

The socket concept allows applications to "plug into" the network using a high-level address or handle, requesting services as required (e.g., sending and receiving data). Although widely associated with TCP/IP, the socket interface is actually a generic interface which can be used with several different underlying communications protocols. In fact, one of the parameters supplied when creating a socket address is the networking protocol (e.g., TCP/IP).

After a socket has been created, it is then bound to a local IP address. Remember that the IP address simply designates a specific path out of the host, and that there can be multiple of these connections available. The socket address is a combination of the application port number, protocol, and local IP address. It forms the endpoint of an application link, effectively enabling a socket-to-socket connection.

After a socket has been initialized, it can be used by the application. Refer to Chapter 11 for a more complete discussion of the socket API.

Server and Client Processes

The most common processing model for TCP/IP socket-based programming divides applications into two types:

- Passive
- Active

These roles form the basis for the client/server computing model. A server opens its socket and passively waits for incoming requests. The client, on the other hand, attempts to directly (i.e., actively) establish a connection with one or more of the servers.

Reserved and Dynamic Port Numbers

The client/server model described above presents a problem. How does the client know which port to use for the destination application? The answer is that a block of port numbers are reserved by the Internet administrative authority for use by the standard TCP/IP applications. These "well-known" ports range from 0 to 1023 (i.e., first 1K).

For example, when a local client wants to logon to a remote host application (i.e., TELNET), the TCP port number 23 is used. Note that each number is qualified with the Transport layer protocol. That is, a specific port used for TCP is different than the port used for UDP with the same number. While port numbers for TCP and UDP can at times be assigned the same function, they represent different communication paths.

The remaining ports, 1024 through 65535, are available to be dynamically assigned as required. This happens when a client is activated and must dynamically request a port number. Also, many server processes (particularly user-developed) must be allocated a port. In this case, servers frequently advertise their ports through some type of directory service. For example, RPC-based servers can register their availability with the portmapper application (assigned port 111). Note that through administrative definitions, authorities can establish their own well-known port numbers for local use, as drawn from the range 1024 to 65535.

3.2 User Datagram Protocol

As mentioned above, UDP can commonly execute as a simple extension to IP. An application sends and receives blocks of data called user datagrams.

UDP Header

Each user datagram processed by an application begins with a UDP header. Figure 3.2 presents an illustration of the header.

The ports identify the applications on either side of a single datagram exchange. The source port is optional. However, it must be provided for most UDP implementations where a server accepts requests from different clients, and generates a response.

0   31

SOURCE PORT	DESTINATION PORT
MESSAGE LENGTH	UDP CHECKSUM

DATA

Figure 3.2   UDP header within a user datagram.

The length specifies the number of bytes for the UDP header and data. The checksum field, if used, is generated based on the datagram contents. It is then recalculated at the receiving end for comparison. If equal, UDP assumes that the data arrived without error.

Basic Operation

The raw application interface to UDP is not as clearly specified as the one for TCP. However, the operations provided are fairly simple. The header can be very easily constructed based on known information.

The checksum calculation is also performed. Remember that the datagram checksum only includes the IP header. In the case of UDP (and TCP), the checksum covers the data portion. With UDP, this is the UDP header and data. The exact operation also requires the use of a "pseudoheader", constructed solely for this calculation. Since the operation is virtually identical for UDP and TCP, it is described below in section 3.6.

UDP simply constructs the header, with checksum, and drops the packet into the queue for IP to process and send. The flow is similar in the reverse direction.

3.3 Transmission Control Protocol

An application using TCP has several advantages over one that uses UDP. However, there is of course additional overhead.

Differences with UDP

TCP is a significantly different and substantially more functional protocol than UDP. Its major improvements over UDP are listed in Figure 3.3.

First and foremost, TCP is connection-oriented. It more formally utilizes the socket abstraction model, although the socket API allows access to UDP as well.

Data is passed from the application to TCP as a stream of bytes. Contrast this with UDP, where the application sends blocks. The data is buffered by TCP until enough has been accumulated for a send operation. TCP then constructs a segment, consisting of the buffered data prefixed by a TCP header.

To ensure reliability, each byte of data is identified by a number, assigned in sequential order by the sender. The Sequence and Acknowledgment Numbers are used to guarantee delivery between the two sides. In addition, a windowing concept is used to regulate data flow. TCP can also retransmit data based on internal timers, and must be prepared to identify and discard duplicate data. These protocol operations within TCP are illustrated below.

Basic Interface to TCP

The TCP layer provides six major primitive operations which are described in the RFC, including:

- Open
- Send
- Receive
- Close
- Status
- Abort

There is some freedom in how these services can be implemented. The open request can be active (establishing a connection) or passive (wait for connection requests), as mentioned above. Send and receive allow for the transfer of data. Close and abort are used to gracefully or abruptly terminate the association with TCP and active connections. The status request provides a general-purpose service allowing certain implementation-specific information to be gathered by the application regarding the state of the local and remote environments.

TCP Feature	Description
Connection-Oriented	Unlike UDP, instances of TCP (on different hosts) establish connections on behalf of their applications.
Socket Abstraction	A more complete usage of the socket model (compared to UDP), built on the underlying port and local IP address.
Byte Stream Transfer	Data is transferred from an application to TCP in the form of a stream of consecutive bytes.
Sequencing and Acknowledgment	Each outgoing byte is numbered and must be acknowledged by the receiver to assure delivery.
Flow Control	A sliding window mechanism allows TCP to send data while simultaneously receiving acknowledgments.
Retransmission	TCP uses a technique based on internal timers to initiate retransmission as perceived necessary.
Recognize and Process Duplicates	Due to process problems or delays, duplicate data can be generated; it must be recognized and discarded.

Figure 3.3 Important TCP features not found with UDP.

Finite State Machine Concept

At the core of TCP's internal operation is the concept of a Finite State Machine (FSM). There are 11 primary states which a TCP connection can be in at any given instance. The connection state can change from one value to another in one of a finite number of transitional paths.

Using the FSM model ensures reliable and consistent protocol exchanges and API implementations. The FSM is widely used in system software development. For example, the Virtual Telecommunications Access Method (VTAM), and its control of SNA resources, is also based on FSM theory.

3.4 TCP Header

As mentioned above, data is handled by TCP in the form of segments, which are carried in the IP datagram. Each segment begins with a TCP header. Figure 3.4 contains an illustration of the TCP header.

0   31

SOURCE PORT		DESTINATION PORT
SEQUENCE NUMBER		
ACKNOWLEDGMENT NUMBER		
HDR LEN / RESERVED / FLAGS		WINDOW
CHECKSUM		URGENT POINTER
OPTION VALUES		
DATA		

Figure 3.4 TCP header within a segment.

Many of the header fields have already been discussed. However, there are a few that need more of an explanation.

The HDR LEN field specifies the number of 32-bit words in the TCP header; it can also be thought of as an offset to the segment data.

Also, there are several fields related to data flow, including:

- SEQUENCE NUMBER.
- ACKNOWLEDGMENT NUMBER.
- WINDOW.
- URGENT POINTER.

The use of these, and other fields such as CHECKSUM, are discussed below.

Flags

The header also contains a 6-bit area for flags, allowing information to be exchanged between two TCP processes. Figure 3.5 provides a description of these values.

Maximum Segment Size

Finally, the TCP header includes an area for values used to hold optional configuration parameters for a specific connection. The only parameter supported is the specification of a Maximum Segment Size (MSS). As its name implies, the MSS option limits the size of the segment passed between two TCP machines.

3.5 Connection Establishment and Termination

A connection between two TCP-based applications proceeds in an orderly manner, involving three main data flows.

Three-Way Handshake

Figure 3.6 contains an illustration of the three-way exchange used in establishing a connection. The primary purpose of the procedure is to synchronize each side of the connection in terms of the initial sequence numbers to be used. Remember, one of the features of TCP is the reliable delivery of data. This is done through a technique of assigning the bytes a number sent in each direction. Acknowledgment is made for the range of bytes carried in each segment.

TCP Flag	Description
Urgent data (URG)	The pointer to the urgent data in the header is valid (i.e., in use)
Acknowledgment (ACK)	Signals an acknowledgment, with corresponding value in the header.
Push operation (PSH)	Push operation is requested for the segment, flushing the buffer.
Connection reset (RST)	Used in various manners, to reject a connection attempt or abort a connection.
Synchronize sequence numbers (SYN)	Used to synchronize sequence numbers, especially during connection establishment.
End of byte stream (FIN)	Used during connection termination, signaling various stages of completion.

Figure 3.5 Individual flag bits within TCP header field.

For example, in Figure 3.6 assume that TCP #2 acts as a server, and performs a passive open. The client, TCP #1, then performs an active open, and in the process generates the first data flow shown.

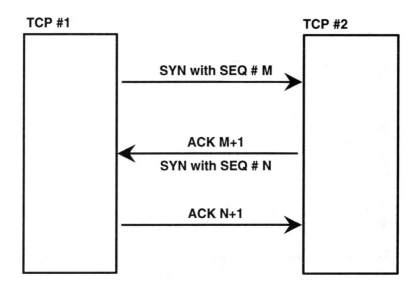

Figure 3.6 Three-way exchange during TCP connection establishment, on behalf of the two applications.

The SYN flag is set in the first datagram, with sequence number M selected by TCP #1. This flow is recognized by TCP #2 as a type of logon request from the other host. TCP #2 returns an acknowledgment number, with the ACK flag set, indicating that the next byte of data it expects should be M+1. So after the second flow, both sides are in agreement that the first byte sent by TCP #1 will be M+1. Also in the second flow is a sequence number N, as picked by TCP #2. The first host returns an acknowledgment number N+1.

So after the third datagram, the two hosts have agreed on the initial numbers to be used during the connection. At this point, the applications are notified of the new connection status, which is open.

Transmission Control Block

As part of the connection establishment process, a Transmission Control Block (TCB) is created and maintained by TCP at either host. It contains a wide range of information, all designed to support the operation of TCP and its protocol operations.

The TCB is implementation-dependent. Although some of the data fields suggested by the RFC fall into the following areas:

■ Local process information.
■ Protocol in use.
■ TCP state.
■ Server or client node.
■ Local IP and port addresses.
■ Remote IP and port addresses.
■ Sequence number information.
■ Flow control window descriptions
■ Queue sizes and local buffer information.
■ Timing and retransmission values.
■ TCP options (maximum segment size).

The TCB is commonly addressable in the system, for example between the application and TCP service process.

Connection Termination

Termination of a TCP connection usually proceeds in manner similar to the establishment, except in reverse order. There are two main ways that a connection is ended:

■ Normal
■ Abnormal (i.e., abrupt)

The normal termination is most commonly used, and involves a precisely defined exchange, similar to the one used during connection establishment.

3.6 Sending Application Data Through TCP

The operation of an application using TCP differs in several ways from one using UDP. Aside from its connection orientation, another area for comparison is the manner data is passed from the application.

Byte Stream to Segments

As mentioned above, an application sends a stream of data to TCP. Once accepted, TCP makes a good faith attempt to deliver the data across the connection to the other side. The data is first placed in a TCP buffer, where it is accumulated for transmission.

At some point, as determined by the buffer sizes at either end, enough data is gathered. The local TCP process then creates a segment, consisting of a TCP header and the data. So the application sends a stream of bytes, which are packed together in segment blocks for transmission within an IP datagram.

An application has some control over the segment creation process. It can invoke one of two options to flush the local buffer:

- PUSH
- URGENT

The push operation causes TCP to immediately create and send a segment, even if the buffer is only partial full. Urgent data, as its name implies, is sent and presented to the remote application. Notice the TCP header field URGENT POINTER, which is used to quickly identify the information in the segment.

Calculation of the Checksum

Another important aspect of segment creation is the TCP checksum. Its value depends on the data passed from the application, as well as certain values extracted from the IP header.

Remember that the IP checksum covers only the datagram header. The reliability of the data portion must be ensured through another means. Namely, both the TCP and UDP headers have their own checksum fields.

The checksum value is computed using a simple one's complement algorithm, in 16-bit increments. The range of data begins with a "pseudoheader," followed by the TCP/UDP header, and finally the data (rounded to a 16-bit boundary).

The pseudoheader is shown in Figure 3.7. It is constructed for the checksum calculation, and then discarded. That is, the pseudoheader is not transmitted with the rest of the datagram.

The two IP address and protocol field values are taken from the IP header. This assures the accuracy of the entire path (IP, protocol, and port).

The ZERO field is reserved, while the length is taken from the TCP or UDP header.

0   31

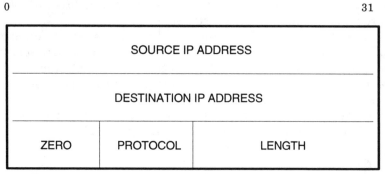

Figure 3.7 Pseudoheader created temporarily for the TCP/UDP checksum calculation.

3.7 TCP Reliable Delivery and Flow Control

TCP includes several protocol mechanisms designed to ensure the
reliable, efficient transfer of data from one application to another. The
most important of these are described below.

Full Duplex Operation

A TCP connection allows a full duplex operation. That is, there is a send-
receive mechanism operating at both sides, at the same time. This fact
plays an important part in how data sequencing and acknowledgment
have been implemented in order to provide reliable data transport.

Each byte is assigned an integer number from a 32-bit counter
which is incremented sequentially. During a send operation, the sequence number field in the TCP header holds the number of the first byte
in that segment. Note that the header also contains a length field,
therefore allowing the range of bytes to be quickly determined for the
segment.

In return, the receiving side acknowledges the receipt of the data.
The acknowledgment number contains the number of the next byte
expected to be received. In effect, this communicates to the sender how
many bytes have already been received (i.e., how many from the initial
sequence number, assuming the counter has not wrapped). This acknowledgment can be "piggybacked" with a send operation flowing in the
opposite direction.

Figure 3.8 contains a simple illustration. In this case, the first
segment contains 50 bytes, beginning with number 451. The next
exchange acknowledges the receipt of up through byte 500 (i.e., byte 501
is expected next). In the same segment, 100 bytes are sent in the other

direction. The third segment confirms receiving the 100 bytes through the acknowledgment number 901.

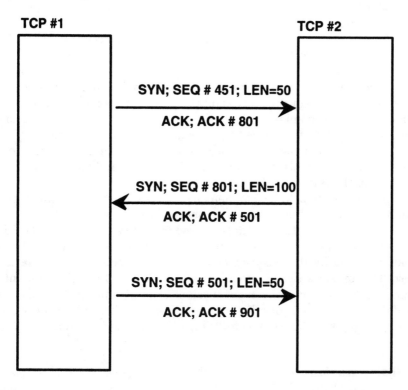

Figure 3.8 Segments exchanged between two applications during a TCP connection.

Retransmission Mechanism

Another aspect of TCP which contributes to its reliability is the concept of retransmission. There are several elements to this protocol operation:

- Estimation of the time needed to complete a round-trip transmission.
- Based on this estimation, a calculation of the worst case amount of time until acknowledgment has been received for the data.
- Setting an internal timer with the threshold value.
- After the timer has expired, the assumption that the data has been lost and must be sent again.

- Initiation of retransmission procedures, usually with multiple retries.
- After each retry, calculate a new timer value (i.e., larger) and set timer.
- After a maximum number of retransmission retries, abort the connection.

The estimated time for round-trip delivery is constantly updated based on the changing network conditions. When a timer is initially set for each new transmission, its value is the sum of this transmission estimate, and a factor derived from its accumulated deviations.

When retransmission has been started, each resend of the same data also includes setting a new timer value (which is adjusted upwards). A count of the retries is also maintained.

Finally, if no acknowledgment has been received after the maximum retry value, the connection is aborted.

One thing to note is the data passed from an application to TCP is buffered even after it has been sent. TCP keeps the data until it has been acknowledged by the receiver, or until the connection is terminated. Also, TCP must be able to recognize and discard the duplicate segments that might arise from the retransmissions. For example, datagrams can be delayed in the network due to congestion, but not lost. In this case, the receiving side can receive multiple copies of the same data.

A Sliding Window

The above discussion illustrates the basic techniques used by TCP to ensure reliable delivery. Another aspect of TCP processing is designed to dynamically regulate the flow of data between sender and receiver. This maximizes the use of the network, and allows the receiver to respond to congestion (i.e., buffer overruns).

Each byte sent must be acknowledged by the other side. However, throughput and response times could be dramatically increase if the sender had to wait for an acknowledgment for each segment before sending the next. The optimal situation is to allow each side to continue sending, avoiding delays where possible.

To accomplish this, TCP implements a sliding window. Network delay can be compensated for by continuing to send new segment blocks, while simultaneously receiving acknowledgments for older ones.

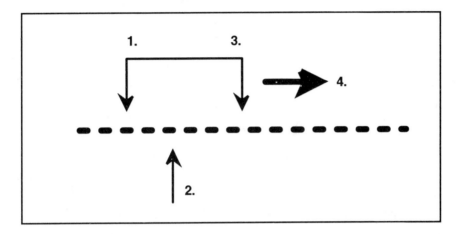

Figure 3.9 Illustration of the TCP sliding window flow control mechanism.

Figure 3.9 contains a simple illustration of the sliding window, from the perspective of the sender. Each of the dots represents a byte, sequentially numbered from left to right. The number 1 represents the current beginning of the window; earlier bytes to the left have already been sent and acknowledged. Number 2 is a point where data has been sent, but not yet acknowledged. No data can be sent beyond the byte pointed to by number 3, the current end of the window. Finally, the window can in effect be slid forward (i.e., number 4) after the next acknowledgment.

Congestion and a Changing Window Size

In addition to efficiently utilizing the network, the sliding window can also be used to respond to congestion. That is, the receiving side controls the sender. It can dynamically change the window size, and can stop the flow of data altogether.

Contained in each acknowledgment, the WINDOW field in the TCP header is a count of the bytes that receiver is able to receive. This number, called a window advertisement, can increase or decrease as needed. However, it cannot contradict a previous advertisement, in effect shrinking the window. But the growth of a window can be stopped. Also, the special case of a WINDOW field of zero is used to close the window altogether.

4

Applications and Services

There is a variety of applications included or associated with the TCP/IP standard which allow resources to be easily shared within an internetwork of distributed hosts. Most of the applications operate using a classic client/server model, as described earlier, and are included with most implementations.

In accessing these distributed applications, it is first important to understand how network resources are named. The Domain Name System can be used throughout, establishing a consistent approach to the organization of names and addresses.

4.1 Domain Name System

The 32-bit IP address provides the basis for how datagrams are exchanged among the hosts and routers in a network. However, it is inconceivable that an end user should be required to use this number when sending and receiving data. Rather, it makes more sense to use names instead of the IP addresses. Simply put, computers work very well with numbers while people prefer text names.

Therefore, a process has evolved whereby a name is established for each IP-designated host. These name-number pairs were originally stored in a "flat" file which was maintained at a central location by the NIC, and distributed on a regular basis.

However, with the exponential growth of the Internet, this simple system became impractical. For one thing, the delay in adding the names, once submitted, continued to increase revealing a bottleneck in the registration process. Also, because the list needed to be sent out to every host, network traffic increased. These, and other problems, made it obvious that a single table was not practical and that a new naming system was needed.

The Domain Name System (DNS) provided the solution. It was created to allow name administration, name-to-address resolution, as well as other functions to be distributed across the Internet. This distributed database approach is better suited to handling network growth than the older central filing system. It scales better, allowing administration to be logically divided across the Internet.

The foundation of DNS is the domain, which is an administrative grouping of host machines. Each domain corresponds to a region or zone in the Internet having a single administrative authority. It may represent one or several networks (i.e., assigned network numbers). Like so many other systems used to establish organization and order, an inverted tree structure is used in the naming standard.

Hierarchical Domain Tree

The Internet domains are arranged in a tree structure, beginning with the unnamed root followed by the top-level (i.e., most significant) branches. The domain zones at the top of the tree can be divided into three primary groups, including:

- Organizational or generic.
- Geographic or international.
- ARPA ("in-addr").

The organization domain branches are probably the most commonly used and recognized. Figure 4.1 contains an illustration, including:

- COM - commercial (businesses).
- EDU - education (universities).
- GOV - U.S. government.
- INT - international organizations.
- MIL - U.S. military (unclassified).
- NET - network support/service providers.
- ORG - nonprofit organizations.

Below the first level shown, the branches of the tree continue. Each level is considered to be a domain (or zone), and is represented by a name formed through the concatenation of each of the levels. For example, the following names describe different levels, all in the same branch of the tree:

- edu
- uci.edu
- ics.uci.edu

Notice that a domain name is formed through the combination of names from the lowest level upwards to the unnamed root. That is, the most significant portion of the name is written on the right.

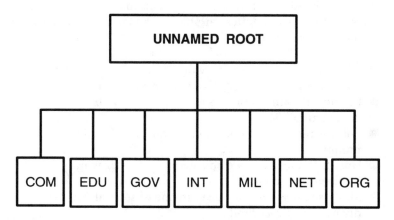

Figure 4.1 The organizational branches of the domain naming structure in the form of an inverted tree.

These nested domains can also be thought of as a set of concentric circles. For example, "ics.uci.edu" is a small circle inside of "uci.edu," and "uci.edu" is inside of "edu." This implies that each of the larger domains is a superset of the lower domains. For example, there are other domains under "edu", such as "ucla.edu".

The geographic domain branches under the unnamed root each begin with a two-character country code, as specified in the ISO 3166 standard. Finally, the ARPA branch is used for administrative data, most notably information which allows for the quick translation from an IP address to a domain name.

One advantage of this tree structure is that domain control is distributed, where each level relinquishes some of its control to the domain below. An authority for each domain in the tree is responsible for administering its domain. Part of this control includes the ability to append new domains below in the tree structure. For example, the owner of "uci.edu" was able to add "ics".

Also, instead of tracking all of the name-address relationships throughout the Internet, each domain needs to be primarily aware of its own domain. The result is an Internet-wide directory.

Information Describing a Domain

But what is the purpose of this directory? It allows information describing certain contents and characteristics of each domain to be stored and accessed by the Internet applications.

There is a variety of data available, in the form of resource records, for each of the DNS domains. The data includes:

- IP address - 32-bit binary value.
- Name server - authoritative server for domain.
- Canonical name - enables a server name to be assigned an alias.
- Pointer record - used for pointer queries (IP address to name).
- Host information - two character strings providing information about the host.
- Mail exchange record - used in one of several ways to divert or redirect mail.

Each of these represents a different record type, and is available through a request-reply operation.

Name Resolution Process

The DNS is implemented through the name server and name resolver. The most commonly used server, at least outside of the IBM world, is the Berkeley Internet Name Domain (BIND), usually running as a process "named." The resolver (i.e., client) can be linked with the application and operates under the covers, usually transparent to the user.

When information is needed by a specific application, the DNS name resolver is invoked through an API call. A request is then formatted and sent to the server using the connectionless UDP. Among other things, the type of information being requested is included in the packet. A reply is generated by the server, and returned to the name resolver using the same message format.

The operation perhaps most commonly associated with the DNS is the translation of a fully qualified domain name into the corresponding IP address. When an IP address must be determined, the name resolver first directs the request to a local name server. If the request is unsuccessful, the search must proceed outside of the local domain. This might eventually involve contacting a designated DNS "root" server. As of this writing there are eight DNS root servers for the Internet.

The root server has much more visibility, and recognizes the highest portion of the domain name. It can either honor the request or point to a server that will allow the search to proceed further. Finally, a name server is located which can provide the translation.

This search procedure can be done on behalf of the name resolver by the local server based on the original request in a "recursive" manner. Or, the local name server can return the IP address of the root name server to the resolver. It is then up to the resolver to carry out the search in an "iterative" manner.

4.2 Remote Logon

A terminal that is directly connected to a host can very easily be used for logon to the local system. A natural extension to this capability is for the same terminal to also be able to access remote systems. These distributed applications, like databases, files, or printers, are resources that can be shared in a primitive manner. The challenge is to define and implement a standard which supports the wide variety of terminal types currently in use by the interconnected hosts.

There are two main protocol standards available for accessing remote applications:

- Rlogin.
- TELNET.

Rlogin was developed for the Berkeley UNIX. It is a relatively simple and stable protocol which continues to be adopted outside of the UNIX community. TELNET, on the other hand, is a more fully functional TCP/IP standard provided with the majority of implementations.

TELNET Connection

TELNET is a general-purpose tool for accessing the resource located across an internetwork in an on-line fashion. It provides flexibility through a negotiation process which is designed to support a wide variety of physical terminal types.

A user first logons on to his or her own local system. The TELNET command is then entered locally with a parameter naming the remote host. After translating the domain name into an IP address (if required), a TCP connection is established with the remote TELNET server through the "well-known" (i.e., reserved) port number 23. With the logon to the remote host, a "shell" application is created to support the terminal user. Data is transported through the network, between the two systems. At this point it appears to the user as if the remote application were actually local.

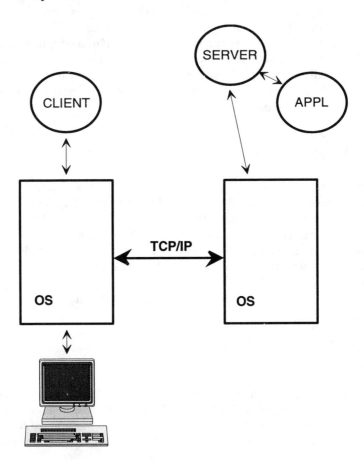

Figure 4.2 An illustration of a remote terminal connection over the TCP/IP internetwork using TELNET protocols.

Figure 4.2 illustrates a typical TELNET session. There are three main "legs" to the data flow during a connection:

■ Flow of data between the local terminal and the TELNET client software.
■ TCP connection between the two hosts.
■ Path from the TELNET server to the shell application, on the remote host.

The large number of terminal types are handled through a consistent standard for client-to-server data exchange which casts the terminal as a logical, or virtual, device.

Network Virtual Terminal

The Network Virtual Terminal (NVT), as its name implies, is a virtual (i.e., imaginary) terminal device. It is used by the client and server in order to establish a consistency for data representation and interpretation. The local terminal data must be transformed or mapped on to the NVT by the client before being sent to the remote server. At the server, the NVT stream is then transformed from the NVT format for presentation to the application.

The NVT assumes an output device (display) and keyboard. The data is initially exchanged as 8-bit bytes, broken into 7 bits of data plus a flag bit. When this flag bit is one, the byte contains an NVT command. Otherwise the byte contains data.

The NVT can assume several different characteristics, as drawn from the actual terminals. When communication begins, each side supports a base subset thus assuring a minimal level of communications. From here, specific options can be negotiated.

During negotiation, NVT commands flow are sent in each direction. Two basic models are used, with respect to the various options:

■ Will and will not (advertisement).
■ Do and do not (request or directive).

These command sequences begin with the "interpret as command" byte, followed by the specific command. After negotiations, the connection is available for data transfer.

TELNET 3270

There are several optional extensions to the TELNET model. One of them is directly applicable to the IBM user: TELNET 3270 (tn3270).

In the UNIX world, ASCII terminals are standard. These utilize the "escape sequences" in the exchanged data streams, allowing the displays to be controlled. IBM, on the other hand, uses the EBCDIC encoding scheme with its 3270 data stream commands for display control.

The TELNET 3270 provides a way for ASCII terminals to access the IBM mainframe applications through an emulation technique.

4.3 Mail Exchange

Perhaps the most popular of the Internet applications is the one providing an ability to send and receive mail messages. This is accomplished using implementations of the Simple Mail Transfer Protocol (SMTP). Because of the Internet's rapid growth, people from all walks of life are now able to exchange SMTP notes.

SMTP Operational Elements

SMTP is a standard application, allowing messages to be packaged and delivered to remote systems. The protocol involves several operational concepts, including:

- User agent.
- User mailbox.
- Message Transfer Agent (MTA).
- TCP connection.
- SMTP formats and protocol.
- TELNET (NVT) protocol.
- Mail exchange (MX) record in the DNS.
- Mail gateways.

For the end user, access to the mail service is available through a user agent. There are a number of user agents available. Each provides a type of front-end editor, usually supporting a variety of functions. Users can compose, edit, send, and receive messages. Other features might also be included, such as address books where symbolic nicknames are used to address mail recipients. The user agent interacts with a local Mail Transfer Agent.

The local MTA, on behalf of the user agent, is responsible for actually receiving and delivering the SMTP notes. To accomplish this, a TCP connection is established with a remote MTA. The SMTP packets are formatted with three simple parts: envelope, header, and message body. The data exchanged between MTAs is based on the TELNET NVT standard.

The local MTA can make a direct connection to the destination MTA on the remote host. Alternatively, mail can be first shipped through a "relay" MTA, which sorts each message and connects to the final destination host to deliver each message. The relay MTA is another example of how a hierarchical organization of functionality can be applied to an internetwork. The notes are finally dropped into a mailbox, usually maintained for each user.

Another consideration affecting SMTP operation is the Mail Exchange (MX) records maintained by the DNS name server. The MX records can be used to redirect mail. For example, if the target host is down, mail can be directed to a backup system. Or, the MX records allow routing of mail to hosts that aren't even directly connected to the Internet.

In the future, the SMTP standard will undoubtedly be updated and enhanced. And in fact, this is already happening. Instead of supporting only text message, a variety of information formats will be available, including graphical images and voice.

4.4 File Transfer

Another important use for TCP/IP is the ability to exchange files. There are two main protocols that can be used to ship files from one host to another:

- File Transfer Protocol (FTP)
- Trivial File Transfer Protocol (TFTP)

FTP is the most widely used and fully functional of the two. TFTP provides a subset of the FTP features, reducing its complexity and resource implementation requirements.

File Transfer Protocol

The major purpose of the File Transfer Protocol (FTP) is to allow files to be transmitted from one host to another. It is important to make this clear because another application, the Network File System (NFS), is used to access data within a remote file. NFS is described below.

The FTP, although rather restrictive, does support a variety of file types and organizations. End users invoke a front-end application which connects to a remote system. From the FTP command prompt, several operations are possible. Figure 4.3 provides a list of the services available with FTP.

FTP Feature	Description
Open-Close Connections	After starting local application, user can open and close FTP connections.
Directory Control	Within connection, the file directory can be changed, listed, and printed by operator.
Mode Changes	One of several different transfer modes can be used, depending on the file format.
Get-Put FIle Transfers	Single or multiple files can be transferred in either direction; monitoring option is available.
Delete Files	Remote files can be deleted.
Help and Information	On-line help is available to the end user as well as local accounting information.

Figure 4.3 Major operations available with FTP.

A connection must first be opened with the remote system using the FTP command. From there several operations are available, as shown. For example, directories can be changed and listed. Entire files can be transferred to or from the local host, or deleted at the remote system.

In carrying out the various user commands, FTP is a bit unusual. Under the covers, two TCP connections, or "bands," between the local and remote machines are utilized. One connection carries command and control information. This session is established when the user first issues the FTP command, and uses the reserved port 21 at the server. To handle the actual flow of data during file transfer, a second TCP connection is made. At the server, port 20 is always used for data.

For example, a RECV command (to receive a file) flows on the control connection to the remote server. Part of the processing on the local machine involves the creation of a "slave" or child process which dynamically acquires a TCP port and waits for the file to arrive. The FTP server accepts the RECV command and creates a process to send the file. This process connects to the newly created process at the user end to transfer the file. Upon completion, the processes at either end can be terminated.

The obvious advantage to this approach is that the server, waiting at port 21, performs a minimal amount of work allowing it to quickly respond to a large number of users. The lengthy and time-consuming data transmission operations are dispatched separately.

One important aspect of FTP use is the concept of an "anonymous" user. That is, in order to use FTP a user must have a userid and password. The logon is performed during the FTP connection process. The situation could greatly restrict the number of users that can access Internet-based information, because each site would have to spend time maintaining accounts. An anonymous FTP site is configured to allow any user access to the system. The userid "anonymous" must be used. In most cases, the user is then directed as to what password to use. Usually this is his or her local userid. Note that this is really a function of the host-specific access control, and not the FTP protocols themselves.

The FTP application is one of the most UNIX-flavored within the TCP/IP suite. This is reflected in both the directory structure used during file navigation and access, as well as in the creation (i.e., fork operation) of separately dispatchable process environments.

4.5 Remote Procedure Call

Most software systems are divided into several programs. In the simplest case, a main routine makes calls to the subroutines, each of which is designed to perform some function. These subroutines can either be directly linked with the application, or separately stored and loaded as needed.

The Remote Procedure Call (RPC) model extends this concept. However, instead of being limited to calling the subroutines on the same host, an application using RPC can invoke procedures on other (distributed) machines.

In approaching the development or use of RPC-based systems, it is clear that there is no single standard. Just as there are perhaps dozens or more different strains of UNIX, there are also several different RPC implementations. While each is slightly different, they all operate in the same basic manner. Of course, some are more widely used than others. The de facto standard embraced by the TCP/IP protocol suite was submitted by Sun Microsystems. Because Sun RPC is general in nature, it also forms the basis for other applications. For example, the Network File System (NFS) uses RPC.

Elements of Generic RPC

There are several major operational elements with any RPC system, including:

- Client main application program.
- Protocol language.
- Protocol compiler.
- Client stub procedure.
- Server (stub) program.
- Server procedures.
- Data representation standard(s).
- Directory services.

Figure 4.4 provides an illustration of the typical RPC environment. As with other TCP/IP applications, a client/server processing model is utilized. Here the connection between systems is application-to-application. Although a message is sent from the client to a server, it represents a request to call a procedure. In this sense, an RPC server is really an "application server."

First, a client application program makes a call to a subroutine procedure which appears to be local. In reality, a "stub" routine is called which acts as an interface to the desired application. The two stub modules must be created by the protocol compiler, as discussed below.

As part of the calling process, the parameters are passed to the client stub in a commonly addressable storage area. The data is then marshaled, a process by which it is transformed into a representation understood by both sides. The message is then transmitted over the network.

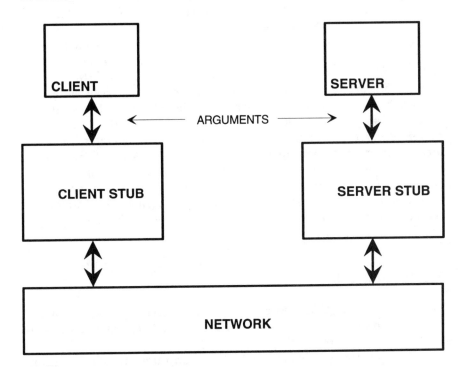

Figure 4.4 Elements of RPC operation.

At the receiving end, a server (stub) receives the request and prepares the local execution environment. The server procedure is scheduled, with parameters recreated from the original caller. Output can be generated by the procedure, which then terminates. The mechanism works in reverse on the way back to the client. The server transforms the data into the common representation format and returns it to the client. Finally, the client stub unpacks the data and presents it to the original caller. One important aspect of RPC operation to recognize is the suspension of the calling (i.e., client) program. That is, the RPC model is usually synchronous in nature, requiring the client program thread to wait.

One area for comparison between the different RPCs available is the protocol compiler and the compiler language. When developing an RPC-based system, the characteristics and operation of the client and server processes are defined using a protocol language. This file is passed as input to the protocol compiler in a preprocessor phase, creating the two stub routines. After this, the actual server procedure(s) and other code can be written, compiler, and linked with the stubs. The data representation scheme used between the client and server depends on the RPC toolset. Each encoding scheme provides consistency for data transfer between the two stub routines.

Finally, a directory service of some type is usually provided. In its simplest form, this involves locating an RPC server on a specific host. With TCP/IP, for example, such a process is identified through an application port number. While some RPC servers have reserved ports, many user-written applications are started and dynamically assigned a port. This situation therefore creates uncertainty as to the port which a server is currently using. Therefore a special application must be included in order to maintain the location of the RPC servers on a specific host. When an RPC server starts, it registers with this database. Each client stub module first contacts the directory service on the target host to determine the location of the desired server program. This framework serves to abstract the RPC application from the networking particulars, such as TCP/IP port number.

Sun RPC with TCP/IP

The RPC developed by Sun Microsystems has been integrated within the TCP/IP architecture. It uses TCP or UDP, although a transport independent version is also available.

Each server stub is assigned a program number. The program, which is accessed through a port, contains one or more procedures. It is these procedures that are called by the client. Also, a version number is associated with each program and provides more resolution for a particular server. Therefore, incompatibilities between client and server code can be avoided.

The External Data Representation (XDR) specification is used in formatting the data shipped between a client and server stub. The portmapper application provides the directory service, mentioned above. Portmapper itself uses RPC, and is access through the well-known port number 111. It includes four procedures:

- Register a server (add to database).
- Unregister a server (remove from database).
- Obtain port number for a specific server.
- Dump the entire portmapper database.

This RPC implementation continues to be enhanced by Sun. In fact, the elements listed (and more) are grouped together as part of Sun's Open Network Computing (ONC) standard.

Foundation for Distributed Processing

The RPC model is an important technology. It is used by several different types of applications and appears to be gaining a widespread usage in the development of distributed applications. While RPC plays an important part in this as the core technology, several other services are required to create the "industrial strength" environment required for production-oriented, scalable applications. Some of these were listed above (e.g., machine directory services).

Framework	Description
Open Network Computing (ONC)	Submitted by Sun, this RPC form is a de facto standard, used with NFS and NIS.
Network Computing System (NCS)	The Apollo/HP standard, NCS provides several advanced features such as multicanonical data representation.
Distributed Computing Environment (DCE)	A "best of breed" standard created by OSF with widespread support and implementation.

Figure 4.5 Popular RPC-based frameworks for distributed processing.

Figure 4.5 contains a list of the three most prominent frameworks for distributed processing. Each of these uses RPC as its core technology, and is finding use by client/server developers. DCE will be especially important to IBM users, as this technology is now supported across all of the major platforms, from OS/2 to MVS.

4.6 Remote File Access

The Network File System (NFS), as mentioned above, was included by Sun along with RPC. It provides the ability to access files and file systems on remote machines as if they were local. Where FTP is used to transfer entire files, NFS supports a wider array of basic file I/O operations. These include the commonly used features of most local files systems, such as reading and writing bytes of data.

Operating System Integration

NFS is divided into client and server functions. Some systems might provide both pieces, but it is also common to support only the NFS client, as with the example of a small PC.

Both client and server functions are tightly integrated into the operation system on each machine, allowing the filesystem semantics to be mapped. That is, a program transparently accesses remote files as of they were local. Normal I/O function calls are used. If the file is allocated locally, there is no need for NFS. However, if the file is remote the I/O request is passed transparently to the NFS client. From there it is shipped to the remote server.

RPC at the Core

Communication between the NFS client and server is based on the Sun RPC, previously described. The UDP protocol is normally used, therefore providing a minimum level of reliability and recoverability. Another important aspect of NFS, closely linked to the use of UDP, is its stateless nature. That is, the NFS server does not keep track of the clients or the requests that are made. Each call to the server is treated as a separate, independent transaction.

The NFS server actually consists of a group of programs. These programs in turn consist of multiple procedures. For example, the RPC server programs include:

- NFS.
- Mount.
- Lock manager.
- Status monitor.

A mount operation must be requested first by a client. This program allows the remote file system to be "mounted," or mapped. After this, normal I/O operations (e.g., read, write) can be carried out using the mainline NFS. The lock manager and status monitor enable the locking of specific parts of an individual file. The portmapper server, not shown, is also required during normal operation.

Network File System

In response to a mount operation, the server returns a handle for the filesystem in use. This value is retained by the client, and returned on future RPC requests. There are a variety of functions available with NFS.

Version 2 (there is a Version 3 in the works) consists of 15 procedures. These routines fall into several categories, including:

- Return the status of a filesystem.
- Read, create, or delete a file directory.
- Look up a file.
- Create a "hard" link to a file.
- Create and access file names by symbolic links.
- Read, create, or delete files.
- Read from and write to files.
- Create, remote, or rename files.
- Get and set file attributes.

Each of the 15 procedures that fall into these categories allow most local file I/O systems to be mapped to remote systems through NFS.

4.7 Security

The principle security system associated with TCP/IP is Kerberos. It provides:

- Authentication - validates user identify.
- Authorization - can be implemented independently, based on a reliable authentication.
- Accounting - the foundation exists such that an accounting or billing system can be implemented.

The basic elements and operation is described below.

Kerberos

Kerberos, like the other applications and protocols that are part of the TCP/IP standard, has continued to be expanded and enhanced. Version 4 is expected to be superseded by Version 5, which is now being proposed as a standard.

There are two major concepts with Kerberos:

- Resource naming.
- Authentication process.

Each client or server must be assigned a name, called the principal identifier. With Version 4, the name consists of three parts: the principal (or main) name, an instance qualifier (usually tied to access privileges), and a realm (or domain). With Version 5, the principal identifier is reduced to two parts: domain realm and remainder (which is flexible in its content). With V5, the Abstract Syntax Notation One (ASN.1) standard is used to define these two parts.

The second concept important with Kerberos is the actual authentication process, whereby a client is granted access to a particular server. Of course, encryption is used to assure security and system integrity.

Servers have a special link to Kerberos, relying on it to help assure client authentication. Each server in effect is "locked up" by Kerberos. Therefore, a client must first get a key, usually called a ticket, before it can access a server. The client first contacts Kerberos, and after an initial interaction, is assigned a valid ticket. The client can then make a request to the server with the ticket. This information is used by the server to validate the identity of the client.

4.8 X Window System

The X Window System (or just X) provides the ability to distribute the operation of a Graphical User Interface (GUI) display. That is, a back-end application can be connected to one or more remote graphical terminals, controlling parts of each screen. The look and feel of these output devices can differ, depending on the programming style used, but is generally similar to the characteristics of an OS/2 or Windows PC (e.g., windows, pull-down menus).

X was developed at MIT based on work that was originally started at Stanford University. It is designed to allow the multitude of graphical display devices from the various vendors to be addressed and controlled in a consistent manner. To accomplish this, the imaginary "X" terminal was invented. Output is passed between the terminal and a remote application based on this generic X terminal model. Applications use a standard library of function calls to manipulate the screen display. At the same time, software at the display supports the particular characteristics of the physical device by mapping the command input and output to the X terminal. In this, and other ways, X Windows can be compared to TELNET with its Network Virtual Terminal (NVT).

X is designed to be portable, flexible, and extensible. It can use interprocess communication when the controlling application is on the same local machine as the display. Or the application and display can be separated with communication provided through a networking protocol such as TCP/IP, with which the X libraries are bound.

Inverted Client-Server Model

The X Window System is based on the concept of a client connecting to a server. However, the role of each is reversed according to what might naturally be expected. That is, the display device acts as an X server, while the background application is the client. Figure 4.6 includes an example of the X environment.

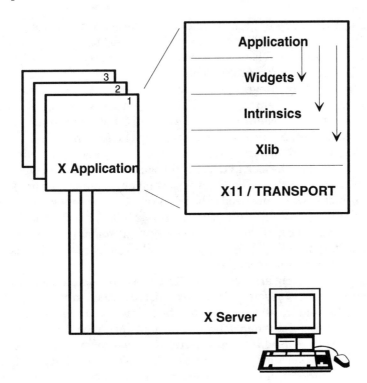

Figure 4.6 An X Windows server with display connected to three client applications.

Here, just as with "normal" client/server systems, several clients can be simultaneously connected to a server. In the diagram, three client applications are connected to the server display. This provides the user with flexibility by allowing access to multiple remote applications.

To understand why X uses this inverted notion of a client and server, consider the function of a server. A server should provide access to a specific resource for its clients. Taking this a step further, it is easy to consider the display itself as a resource. Therefore, each client application can request input (i.e., keystrokes) or request that output be displayed.

The X server itself usually contains a window manager. This allows some of the processing to be offloaded from the client application. For example, a window manager allows window resizing and iconization to be performed locally. Normally, the window manager is resident with the X server, but can be separated to reduce resource consumption (as with a PC).

XLIB, Implementation Styles, and Toolkits

Referring to Figure 4.6 again, it is clear that the application functionality is arranged in layers. This represents how X has been designed.

At the foundation is network communication. This can be TCP/IP, or an IPC vehicle common to most operating systems such as UNIX. The transport is tightly integrated with X as a messaging system. Shown in the figure is the current version, X11. Above this is the core X library, or Xlib. This library contains the lowest level C language functions that can be used by an application in controlling the screen.

On top of the X primitives a particular display style is implemented which determines the look and feel of the windows. Motif and OpenLook are two popular styles. The X Intrinsics layer assembles a set of basic building blocks which are used to build the widgets, or windowing objects (e.g., windows, buttons, pull-down menus, etc.). This functionality is usually shipped as an X toolkit. It allows programmers to quickly build application systems by drawing from a collection of prefabricated windows and displayable objects.

When installing an X-based system, the analyst can use dedicated X terminals. This seems to be an expensive option, since it will most probably be underutilized given the fact that the application code is remote. Of course, this depends on several factors, including the suite of applications to be used. One alternative is to use an emulation package (e.g., under OS/2) which understands and converts the X protocol. This approach allows a user to have the local processing power available with a PC along with the convenience of an X connection. Of course, a UNIX system with a built-in X server is also available.

4.9 Simple Network Management Protocol

The Simple Network Management Protocol (SNMP) was launched in what appeared to be an unassuming manner. It was originally envisioned as a short-term solution to TCP/IP-based network management. OSI protocols, acknowledged as superior, would provide the basis for a long-term product direction.

So far, it doesn't seem to have worked out that way. SNMP was quickly implemented, and in spite of its deficiencies became an entrenched de facto standard. While the OSI specifications lead the way in terms of features and sophistication, SNMP trails along absorbing all that is useful.

Operational Elements

SNMP is an application level protocol which utilizes the UDP Transport layer protocol. A two-way exchange is possible between an SNMP manager (also referred to as the client) and one or more distributed agents (also called the SNMP server).

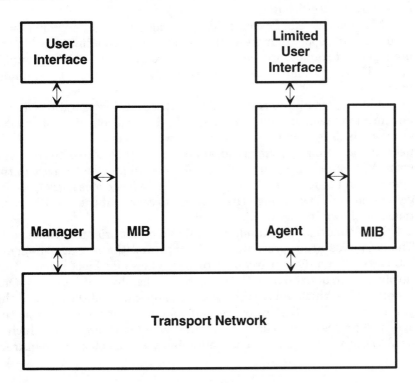

Figure 4.7 Basic manager-to-agent network management framework for SNMP.

Figure 4.7 includes an illustration of the generic manager-to-agent model used with SNMP. The figure represents the logical elements of the framework. These would typically map to a central network management product (e.g., NetView/6000) which communicates with the agents, each imbedded within the distributed networking devices (e.g., modems) or other operating system platforms. In the case where an agent cannot be provided, a "proxy" agent supports the resources outside of the direct manager connection. A proxy agent is very similar to the SNA service point, as implemented by NetView/PC.

The central manager function relies on its agents to report on changing network conditions and carry out commands with two categories of SNMP operations:

- Polling in a request-response fashion.
- Unsolicited event reporting.

Of course a constant polling operation, multiplied by the number of agents in the network, can create a load both in terms of network traffic and operating system resources (i.e., CPU cycles and storage) at the manager. For this reason, the unsolicited reporting of error conditions is usually more efficient.

Many agents can be connected to a single manager or, conversely, an agent can report to more than one manager. In administering the management framework, the concept of a community, or user group, is used. This allows for necessary features such as security to be implemented.

A Management Information Base (MIB) contains definitions for the network management data. A MIB is basically a collection of objects, each of which is used to represent a network resource. To control the network, a manager issues requests to its agents in order to read and write MIB data. Also, an agent is able to send an event report to the manager in the form of a trap. There are five basic messages that are generated and flow through the network to carry out the SNMP operations, as shown in Figure 4.8.

Note that SNMP is fundamentally an object oriented framework. The resources are represented as objects, and the manager-to-agent interactions qualify their request-response flows in object terms. This involves a virtualization of the elements of the physical network. One aspect of this which affects the design and operation of the agent is the gap between an actual resource and its object representation at the agent. A process known as instrumentation must be provided, which is used to update and maintain the data fields of each object as required.

SNMP Data Format	Description
Get Request	Used to obtain information from the agent; prepares for further data access.
Get-Next Request	Similar to the get operation, except executes read based on logical position in the MIB structure.
Get Response	Data returned from the two get requests as well as set operation.
Set Request	Used as a write operation to set a MIB data value.
Trap	Provides a method to report conditions in the network.

Figure 4.8 Basic protocol messages available with SNMP Version 1.

MIB Definition and Registration

A manager and collection of all its agents within a particular enterprise can generally be viewed as using a single MIB. However, there are typically several MIBs involved. Each is packaged as a module, with one or more groups. These MIBs are generally defined in two major ways:

■ Normal standardization process (e.g., RFCs)
■ Vendor (e.g., private)

The standard MIB used with SNMP has evolved, like other aspects of the TCP/IP architecture, to meet vendor and user requirements. The MIB-II specification is now a recommended standard, and should be supported where possible. It replaces the older MIB-I, which now has the designation of historic. The MIB-II model is arranged in a hierarchical tree structure. The highest level serves as the root, splitting to form lower, more specifically defined resources.

In addition to the MIB-II variables, several other MIB groups have been contributed to manage newly emerging technologies. These groups, defined in additional RFC documents, augment the MIB-II standard.

In defining the MIB, a subset of the ASN.1 language is used. Each object is assigned a unique integer identifier, or object ID. Therefore, a particular object in the structure can be described as a chain of integers, proceeding from least to most specific.

The MIB is defined within the broader ISO framework using this naming format. The ISO registration tree, arranged like a MIB, is used to classify and register a wide range of entities and standards on a world-wide basis. There are three main parents in the registration tree: Consultative Committee on International Telegraphy and Telephone (CCITT) (0), ISO (1), and joint ISO-CCITT (2). Under the ISO parent, four major classifications have been established:

- Standards (0)
- Registration authorities (1)
- Member-bodies (2)
- Organizations (3)

The SNMP MIB-II is defined as a part of the registration tree, under the branch formed by the sequential concatenation of ISO (1), Organizations (3), then Department of Defense as an instance under the "organizations" parent (6), and finally Internet (1).

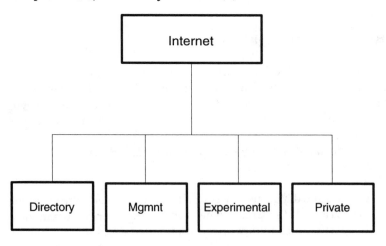

Figure 4.9 SNMP Version 1 MIB definition structure arranged within the ISO registration tree.

Under the Internet, four branches are used to hold the MIB definitions, each used for different purposes in varying degrees of completion. Figure 4.9 includes an illustration of the structure used to hold the definitions for SNMP Version 1 MIBs.

The directory is reserved for future use with the OSI directory (i.e., X.500). Accepted standards fall under the management (MGMNT) branch. The third classification can be used for experimentation. The final branch is reserved for proprietary use, where vendors, developers, or commercial enterprises can define MIB extensions particular to their TCP/IP-based products.

The private branch therefore allows vendors to provide support for their own products which are to be managed by SNMP. Below private (4) is the enterprises (1), under which all of the companies can be registered. For example, the concatenation of internet, private, enterprises, and IBM lead to the area of the ISO registration tree where the IBM-specific definitions MIB are held. The entire path, from the root, is described as:

1 . 3 . 6 . 1 . 4 . 1 . 2

IBM provides four primary MIB groups that are used to extend the capability of SNMP in managing its products. These MIB groups include:

■ IPX Group
■ XNS Group
■ APPN Group
■ Data Link Switching (DLSw) Group

Note that while the ability to define new MIB data by vendors does provide flexibility, it has at the same time resulted in a sort of controlled chaos. Each agent can support a different array of variables, with potentially different ways of managing the same sort of devices.

Referring to the standard MIB-II definitions again, which fall under the management class in Figure 4.9, there are 10 major categories of object data. These include:

■ System - general overall information regarding the system.
■ Interfaces - connections from system to the network.
■ At - address translation information.
■ IP - data supporting describing the execution of the Internet Protocol.
■ ICMP - support for the Internet Control Message Protocol.

- TCP - data regarding the execution of the Transmission Control Protocol.
- UDP - User Datagram Protocol information.
- EGP - data describing the External Gateway Protocol.
- Transmission - general information about transmission algorithms and access protocols.
- SNMP - data supporting execution of the Simple Network Management Protocol.

The formally defined Structure of Management Information (SMI) also contributes to the MIB definition by providing a general framework, or language for MIB construction. For example, it identifies data types, and how resources are named. The SNMP MIB uses scalar values, and simple two-dimensional tables. The data types and capabilities of SNMP MIBs are generally simpler and less robust than the corresponding OSI MIB.

Version 2 Enhancements

A major step toward improving the capabilities of SNMP came with the Remote Monitoring (RMON) feature. RMON represents an extension to the MIB-II, defining interfaces and protocols that allow remote network monitors to collect and forward information. While an important addition to the basic SNMP protocols, RMON is not able to solve the larger problems encountered by users when attempting to use SNMP in an enterprise-wide role. This includes providing a consistent view of remote data across several segments as gather by different agents.

An important revision of the basic protocol arrived with Version 2 (SNMPv2). There are 12 major documents associated with this new version. The enhancements can be grouped into four areas, including:

- Structure of Management Information (SMI)
- Protocol exchanges
- Manager-to-manager capability
- Security

These improvements further extend the usefulness of SNMP. For many organizations, they may be sufficient to adopt the protocol for wider use within the enterprise.

IBM Environment

5

Growth of TCP/IP

Much has changed over the last 20 or so years with respect to data communications and computers in general. At one time, IBM had the market locked up. They provided a kind of one-stop-shopping, supplying everything from computers and terminals to software and support. The newness and cost of this market played into the hands of the large vendors. But even then, the seeds of an unraveling (or at least a reshaping) had been sewn. UNIX was saturating the academic world, being licensed by AT&T at little or no cost. The prices for microprocessors, notably from Intel, continued to plummet with respect to performance. With these and other dynamics, the stage was set for an expansion and redistribution of processing power.

With this growth and dispersion of processing power, there was of course a natural trend toward network computing. Computers, and the users they support, need to communicate. The large-scale, enterprise-capable frameworks included TCP/IP, SNA, and OSI (created in that order). SNA dominated the corporate world, and with IBM's clout was widely implemented. The TCP/IP architecture, on the other hand was viewed (at least by the mainframers) as a "cast out," unfit for commercial use, and a part of the academic and as yet unformed "open systems" worlds.

However, by about the mid-1980s, under increasing pressure from the market and its customer base, IBM began to embrace TCP/IP. And now, TCP/IP within the IBM environment has grown to become a strategic protocol. IBM has gradually lost its proprietary grip and is now following (or being dragged by) the market. In fact, the IBM manual *TCP/IP Introduction* (GC31-6080-04) reads " . . .TCP/IP is the communication protocol of choice for global network access."

In hindsight, it seems that all of this could have been different. Indeed, APPC and APPN are two solid (even superior) protocols that began seeing the light of day in the early 1980s. However, there was a clear failure to implement and promote these standards quickly. This now leaves IBM in a position of coexistence. It fully supports SNA and TCP/IP, as well as a less successful OSI. The IBM strategy revolves around the idea of deemphasizing the actual transport used through the recently announced Network Blueprint. Applications and transport protocols can be selected independently based on their own merits.

5.1 Client/Server Computing

Recently, there has been much interest in client/server computing. The gravitation toward this computing framework by vendors and users alike has been driven by the availability of two key technologies:

■ Inexpensive processing power.
■ Graphical User Interface (GUI).

If one were to graph MIPS according to location within an enterprise today and also 20 years ago, things would look very differently. It now seems that just about every corporate desktop has a 386 or 486 PC. One of the promises of client/server is the ability to better harness these distributed cycles. Of course, the other factor is the GUI capability, as found with OS/2 or Windows. These two advances really go hand-in-hand. Another technological change that has contributed the appeal of client/server computing is the widespread installation of relational database management systems (RDBMS) over the past 10 years. Because of their architectural design, relational databases have a much higher degree of flexibility than the older hierarchical database systems. This has enabled end users and departments to operate more autonomously, accessing data freely with less required systems administration (e.g., compared to IMS).

To summarize, a client/server system allows presentation and perhaps some processing to be performed at the desktop. This front end connects to a back-end server for access to resources. These resources can be files, printers, communication links, but are generally depicted and most commonly implemented as a RDBMS.

IBM made a formal announcement with respect to its client/server strategy in 1990 (refer to announcement letter 290-549) and then again in 1991 (letter 291-469). In some ways, the company again appears to be following (or at least playing catch up). For example, Sybase launched its UNIX-based database server product in 1987. But given IBM's strength across the board, from large systems (e.g., MVS) to the desktop (e.g., OS/2), it is and certainly will be a major player.

Division of Function

Most applications, including client/server systems, can be divided into three major components, as shown in Figure 5.1. A front-end machine provides the graphical interface. Under the covers, a communication link connects the client to one or more server machines. The server provides controlled access to certain resources, such as the data in a relational database.

Client/Server Element	Description
Presentation	User input and output is processing by the user with a GUI technology.
Application Logic	The program logic which forms the core of the system, at the client and/or server.
Resource (e.g., database)	A backend resource, usually depicted as a relational database management system.

Figure 5.1   Main functional elements of a typical client/server system.

There is some flexibility as far as how a system can be arranged. That is, the division between client and server (with respect to the elements listed) can occur at different locations. This in turn determines the exact client/server model used.

Basic Models

In order to assess the market, IBM interviewed a large number of its customers to find out how they were using distributed systems. The findings were published in an *IBM Systems Journal* article (refer to bibliography).

Figure 5.2 lists the major processing models used in distributed processing. With this information, as well as a practical knowledge of many of the products involved, it is possible gain an insight into the characteristics and uses of these models. For example, the X Window System is an example of "remote presentation design."

Perhaps the most flexible of all of these models is the "distributed logic" model. In this case, the client and server connect using an application-to-application link. This "application server" model provides more flexibility than other models, but typically is more complicated to implement and administer.

Systems using a distributed logic model are normally based on some sort of middleware. Middleware is implemented as an API and, among other things, shields the developer from dealing with the underlying complexities of the operating system and communication network. In this sense, this layer of functionality between the application and network can establish a degree of portability between platforms and network transports.

Each side of the link, client and server, will use the same technique (i.e., API) to connect and exchange data. While standards and terminology are still evolving, there are several popular standards that can be considered to be middleware:

- Remote Procedure Call (RPC)
- Advanced Program-to-Program Communication (APPC)
- Message queuing
- Pipes

Of these three, RPC is very commonly used and certainly has a bright future. It forms the basis for several distributed processing frameworks, as described in Chapter 4. These frameworks, such as DCE, should be especially important in the future as the various distributed object computing standards become more commonly implemented.

Processing Model	Description
Nondistributed.	The case reference case where all elements are running on a single machine.
Remote Presentation.	Presentation is distributed between the front and back ends, as is possible with X Windows.
Front-ending.	A PC or workstation handles all presentation locally, and replies on the server for application logic and database (resource) access.
Distributed Logic.	The client performs presentation and part of the application logic, while the server includes the second part of the application and resource.
Staged Data.	A central database server can periodically update one or more regional (or local) servers, targeting data distribution to improve performance.
Resource-centric.	The client application uses the same API to access a resource whether local or remote; distributed data using IBM's DRDA is one example of this model.
Process-driven.	Each of the multiple nodes in the network contain both data and logic, and respond to asynchronous messages for activation (e.g., message queuing).
Multiapplication.	This resembles the process-driven case, with the application always active; foundation for future distributed object computing.

Figure 5.2 Models for distributed processing.

Relationship to TCP/IP

Client/server computing and TCP/IP are well matched. In fact, most of the TCP/IP applications are designed according to the model. This fact has helped to foster the acceptance and use of the client/server model.

And aside from its alignment with client/server processing, there are other factors which assure it a major role in the future. For example, TCP/IP is a widely used protocol. This is especially true within the growing PC/workstation area.

5.2 Uses for TCP/IP

TCP/IP is versatile. Its exact use depends on the needs of the organization. The architecture can be established as the enterprise-wide standard, or it can coexist with SNA (or other protocols). The entire stack might be used, or instead divided with only the relevant aspects applied (e.g., IP routing). In any case, the possible uses and benefits fall into one of several different categories.

Applications

At the highest layer, a variety of applications are included with TCP/IP protocol suite as described in Chapter 4. For many users, it is sufficient to perform a remote logon or transfer a file.

In addition, TCP/IP can be used to create new network-aware applications. Vendors supply such new applications, using TCP/IP as the preferred method for connectivity. In fact, IBM has enhanced its products to include TCP/IP as a transport option.

For the application developer, whether working at a vendor or as an end user, there are several options available. The most prominent programming frameworks include:

- Sockets.
- RPC.

Both operate in a client/server manner, in the sense that the notion of a client and server are implicit in the API itself. There are a variety of other APIs that can be used, as discussed in Part 3.

Data Transport and IP Routing

Another way the architecture can be used is as a network transport, without regard to the application. The Transport and Internet layers, cast as a short stack, can be implemented and treated almost as a commodity. For example, the Networking Blueprint is designed to allow TCP/IP to carry data between two programs using the Common Programming Interface for Communications (CPI-C) API. Another example of this use is with the Data Link Switching (DLSw) protocol, which can encapsulate SNA data across a TCP/IP network. Both of these are discussed later in the book.

Proceeding further down the stack, it is possible to remove the transport layer and only use IP to route datagrams. While IP is an unreliable, "best effort" protocol, its use does have several advantages. For example, IP has been fitted to operate with a wide range of link level protocols. It can be used to encapsulate other types of data, including SNA. This level of integration is especially important for network analysts.

5.3 Comparison to SNA

For corporate America, SNA is still the dominant "industrial strength" networking architecture. However, many users are actively evaluating other protocols. The most prevalent of these, at least for enterprise-wide use, is TCP/IP. Therefore, it is helpful to compare and contrast the two. This is a vast subject area; therefore only a few of the major points are considered.

SNA and TCP/IP are similar (and different) in several respects. It is important, however, to make a distinction between the two diverging SNA models:

■ Traditional SNA.
■ "New" SNA.

The traditional subarea networking model is what many people think of when SNA is mentioned. This embodies the original design, where the host forms the center of the processing universe. While still supported today, IBM is in the process of staging a migration to its Advanced Peer-to-Peer Networking (APPN) model.

The older version does have several disadvantages. However, its reliability and performance can make it easily justifiable by many of the high-end mainframe users. APPN operates in a peer-to-peer fashion by removing the requirement for a central mainframe. In this way, it more closely resembles the TCP/IP internetworking model. And of course the two can coexist. This is especially important for the loyal IBM customers who, as they absorb the various LAN-based devices, want everything under a single networking framework.

Traditional SNA Center

The development of SNA mirrors the evolution of the computer industry in general. Not very long ago, almost all processing power resided at the mainframe. Nonprogrammable terminals, supported by an array of specialized cluster control units, allowed users to logon and access the applications.

The architectural structure of SNA mapped to this early reality and was designed to guide the design of the communication products. A hierarchy was established such that all command and control capability is centrally located. The mainframe software is needed during just about every operation, including session start and termination.

SNA, like TCP/IP and OSI, is arranged in a layer structure. Its protocols are distributed throughout the layers, perhaps more evenly than TCP/IP. The bottom three layers form the Path Control (PC) network, designed to perform internode message delivery. The top layers form the Network Addressable Units (NAUs). These NAUs pair together during sessions in order to allow end user and control data to be exchanged.

This traditional model, with the host at the center, differs from the the TCP/IP architecture in many respects. Perhaps the most prominent is that SNA, in its basic form, specifies the detailed operations within a single network, while TCP/IP is based on the interconnection of networks. SNA recognizes one or more centers. With TCP/IP, however, there is no central computer that all user requests must pass through. Each network, and user within the network, operates independently. Even control and administrative data requested during normal operation is distributed throughout the network.

NAUs, Sessions, and Nodes

There are three types of NAUs, as shown in Figure 5.3. With these, IBM has more formally defined not only user access but also the network's command and control structure.

Network Addressable Unit	Description
Systems Services Control Point (SSCP)	The SSCP is implemented within VTAM on the host. It provides network control and assistance to the other NAUs in establishing sessions.
Physical Unit (PU)	The PU controls a node's physical environment, supporting the local resources with a session to the SSCP.
Logical Unit (LU)	An end user gains access to the network through the LU. Each node usually contains several LUs, such as terminals or applications.

Figure 5.3 SNA Network Addressable Units.

These NAUs send and receive data in a connection-oriented fashion by engaging in temporary sessions. They can be joined in four ways:

- SSCP-to-SSCP.
- SSCP-to-PU.
- SSCP-to-LU.
- LU-to-LU.

The first three are essentially overhead, supporting session establishment and network management. The LU-to-LU session is used by end users to gain access to the network. LUs can take on many forms, such as terminals, PC users, and applications.

In addition, there are several types of LU sessions. Each was created to support a particular hardware or end user requirement. For example, LU type 2 sessions are used between SNA 3270 terminals and the applications that they logon to.

The NAU session is similar to the TCP connection in that it is connection-oriented. However, the connection established between two TCP/IP hosts on behalf of the two application is more basic and flexible. TCP transfers data as a stream of bytes, generally without regard to its form or content. The upper layer applications, such as TELNET, determine the exact nature of the data exchange.

The SNA resources are collected into nodes, each identified by a number. These nodes map to the actual devices used during normal network operation, such as the 3745 communication controller (refer to Chapter 7). The SNA nodes within a traditional network can be broken into two categories: subarea and peripheral. Subarea nodes use a fully qualified network address consisting of subarea number and element within the subarea.

This approach was not taken with TCP/IP. Each "host," whether a PC, workstation, or mainframe is treated equally. Each is assigned one or more IP addresses, and makes TCP and UDP available to its applications. With TCP/IP, any difference between the nodes or attempt to classify them is largely based on the type of applications that run there. For example, one host can contain SNMP agent code, and is therefore part of the network management framework. Another host might include a domain name server application, and therefore support the DNS model in providing name translation. And still another host can function as a file server, using FTP.

SNA and IP addressing are similar, but also differ in several ways. Both are divided into two parts. However, the scope of the SNA address is more narrow, and only valid within a network. The subarea portion refers to an area in the network and the element to an addressable entity (e.g., application). The IP address includes a network address, unique throughout the internetwork. The local portion maps to a host (or router). In this way, SNA includes more address resolution but less of a scope.

Both SNA and TCP/IP use symbolic names which correspond to the underlying addresses used to actually route the data.

Path Control Routing

SNA Path Control routing, as mentioned above, is a function of the lower layers. It serves the NAUs by efficiently transferring session traffic.

Figure 5.4 includes an illustration of the NAUs sitting on top of the PC network. TCP/IP is designed in fundamentally the same way. However, there are several differences in how the transmission of data is performed. The PC network functionality is much more sophisticated and reliable. The top layer, Path Control, includes three sublayers:

■ Virtual Route (VR).
■ Explicit Route (ER).
■ Transmission Group (TG).

Each session is assigned to a VR which provides an end-to-end link with reliability and flow control features (e.g., sequencing). The VRs are logical entities. For routing to take place, each VR must be mapped to an ER. The ERs do not have an end-to-end awareness, but rather transmit data from node to node. Each ER uses a particular TG when transmitting the data across a link, relying on a particular Data Link Control (DLC) protocol and physical link characteristics.

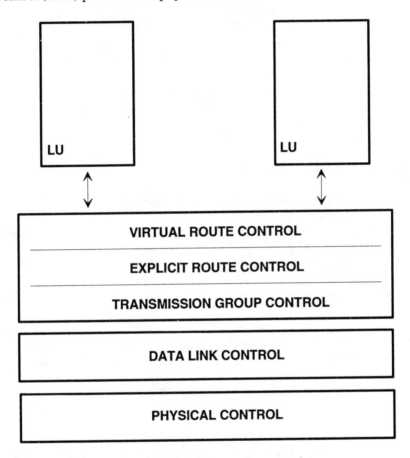

Figure 5.4 NAUs using the underlying PC network to route data.

The subarea nodes use the full network address, and have the full Path Control functionality (including VRs). The peripheral nodes rely on an attached subarea when connecting to a network's backbone. The subarea node's boundary function supports the peripheral nodes, including a translation between the local and network addressing formats.

The routing provided with IP is much simpler and at the same time less reliable. IP has no end-to-end awareness. Each node makes the best routing decision possible based the information it has. When IP must forward a datagram, it examines the routing table and then sends the packet. Any reliability and recoverability features must be provided by the upper transport layer (i.e., TCP) and/or the application. IP is in some ways similar to the ER control function of the SNA path control layer.

While SNA routing is more reliable, it also requires more administrative and operational overhead. All of the routes must be statically defined.

It is clear that routing data through an internetwork will be the topic continued research. This is especially true as SNA traffic is moved on to the IP internetwork backbone.

SNA Network Interconnection

As mentioned, SNA networks are fundamentally isolated. Each is designed to serve the communications needs of a particular user (i.e., corporation). This differs with the TCP/IP internetworking model. However, SNA networks can be joined together with a protocol known as SNA Network Interconnection (SNI).

SNI can be of value to businesses that must share information. For example, a manufacturer can link its network with one or more suppliers.

The setup must be manually configured. Each cross-network session usually consumes a fixed amount of resources (e.g., storage). The addresses in the message headers are then translated as they cross from one network to the other.

APPC Model

The Advanced Program-to-Program Communications (APPC) technology is based on an LU type 6.2 session. Each side, for so-called open implementations, provides a programming interface based on the generic APPC verbs. The Transaction Programs (TPs) then make use of the API to schedule and communicate with remote TPs.

The APPC TPs operate at a higher level than those using the socket API within TCP/IP. This is because of the concept of a TP inherent in the programming model. The socket API is designed to deal more closely with the network and connection operations. RPC, on the other hand, operates above the APPC level (in terms of a layered model). This is because RPC programs have no knowledge of the network or data transmission, while APPC TPs can issue verbs to send and receive data.

APPC is a strategic technology for IBM, designed as the culmination of several other LU session types. It operates both within the traditional model and the APPN framework to provide a general any-to-any connectivity.

APPN Internetworking

As mentioned, APPN is more similar to TCP/IP than the traditional SNA. Using APPN, machines can operate more independently to connect and exchange data.

APPN Feature	Description
Distributed Directories	Dynamically determine, through a distributed search, the node location of a remote LU.
Topology and Route Selection	Allows for the best route to be selected for a session, based on certain user input.
Adaptive Pacing and Transmission Priority	Dynamically adjusts flow based on changing conditions; sessions can also be assigned a priority based on performance objectives.
Intermediate Session Routing	The network node can route session traffic when neither LU is resident in the node.

Figure 5.5 Major features available with the APPN network.

Figure 5.5 provides a list of the major features available with APPN. While its nature is more dynamic and flexible, APPN is still an IBM architecture which is based on the older SNA.

Network Management

The SNA Management Services (SNA/MS) architecture provides the basis for IBM network management. It uses several different data formats and session connections to communicate information, depending on network (i.e., traditional or APPN).

The disadvantages of SNA/MS include those for SNA in general, including its proprietary nature. Also, it is not based on an object-oriented design, as are SNMP and OSI. For example, SNA/MS lacks:

- Manager-agent interaction.
- Object representation for resources.
- MIB as a collection of objects.
- ASN.1 for consistent data definition.

SNA/MS is, however, very well suited to managing SNA networks. It is tightly integrated into the IBM network management products, including NetView.

So while IBM continues to support its own standards, it is also recognizing the importance of SNMP. However, SNMP has its own shortcomings, including the wide variety of enterprise MIBs shipped by the different product vendors. Also, just supporting SNA/MS, SNMP, and OSI can be a problem.

For example, network management applications are typically tied to one protocol or another. One answer is to introduce an API for development which supports a variety of network management APIs. One such standard is the X/Open Management Protocol (XMP). XMP is included with NetView/6000 and should become an important aspect of IBM's ability to provide consistent access to network management data.

5.4 Platform Implementations

With the rapid growth of TCP/IP, IBM has moved to meet the demands of its large customer base by also supporting this important architecture (while also maintaining SNA). In doing so, there are three main areas that have been affected:

- Full-stack host implementations.
- Applications using TCP/IP, both standard and IBM.
- Routing infrastructure.

This chapter presents a brief overview of the six main host implementations of the TCP/IP architecture. Chapter 6 explores each of these in more detail. In addition, several other TCP/IP products are available, some of which are mentioned below.

The products are based on the RFCs available to all vendors and users. Therefore, the IBM products are consistent with what can be expected by an experienced TCP/IP user. However, the standards allow quite a bit of latitude, and for this reason each of the products is slightly different. Also, the unique characteristics of each host environment to some extent determines the use of TCP/IP in that environment. Therefore, while all of the products are very similar, each has its own special uses and application niche.

Large Systems

IBM provides two primary TCP/IP products for its large systems platforms:

- TCP/IP for VM.
- TCP/IP for MVS.

The Virtual Machine (VM) operating system was the first of IBM's major platforms to support TCP/IP. This was in response to the nature of its users and close association with UNIX and workgroup computing. The VM Interface Program for VM allowed a basic TCP/IP capability through a channel attached Series/1. It was included within the announcement letter 284-358 of September, 1984. Following this, IBM solidified its approach with the TCP/IP for VM product.

Following its release of the VM product, IBM introduced an MVS version. TCP/IP for MVS is based largely on the VM product, including an emulation and adaptation of many of the VM-specific technologies, such as the Inter User Communication Vehicle (IUCV) interface.

The VSE environment is supported by a product developed by Openconnect Systems, which is marketed by IBM through its Cooperative Software Program (CSP).

Midrange Solutions

In the context of this discussion, anything not a large system or a desktop platform is considered to be a midrange computer. In this area, IBM supports two main implementations:

- AS/400 TCP/IP.
- TCP/IP as part of AIX for the RS/6000.

In the past, IBM has (and still has) several different AIX implementations, each having TCP/IP support. For example, AIX runs on the RT PC from IBM. Also, the AIX/ESA (large system) operating system also provides support. However, the install base of these is small relative to AIX for the RS/6000, which will be one of the products highlighted in Chapter 6.

Another midrange computer using TCP/IP is the System/88 platform. Again, for many data processing professionals, this machine is outside of the mainstream.

Desktop

Two desktop operating systems include TCP/IP support. The products available include:

- TCP/IP for OS/2.
- TCP/IP for DOS.

Of the two, OS/2 contains more features and can be applied in a larger number of situations. The DOS product can also be used with the Microsoft Windows interface.

5.5 Hardware Support

Along with the product implementations, IBM has enhanced its networking products to handle the TCP/IP traffic. The areas for concern can be divided into two large areas, as shown below.

Routing Nodes

What is referred to here as a routing node includes a wide variety of control units and routers. Figure 5.6 lists the most important boxes that IBM provides.

Some of these are relatively new, while others have been enhanced. The characteristic that is shared by all of them is an awareness of the transport network being used (e.g., SNA, TCP/IP) and the ability to route packets through the network.

Looking more closely at the hardware listed, each can be further categorized according to whether it attaches to a mainframe (to provide host access) or serves as an "outboard" router.

Communication Hardware	Description
3745	Part of a series of front end communication controllers (e.g., 3725) connecting to a host to offload communication processing.
3172	Channel attached control unit providing a connection to the LAN and TCP/IP worlds for the host-based applications.
3174	Control unit which supports 3270 terminals; recently enhanced to support a large and growing list of protocols (e.g., APPN).
6611	A true multiprotocol router designed to handle a variety of transport protocols and link level connections.

Figure 5.6   IBM hardware technology supporting the routing of IP datagrams.

Link Level Protocols

The underlying link level protocols allow the physical devices to be connected, and govern the types of attachments that can be made. Through these protocols, data frames are created and transmitted.

The most important protocols, with respect to IP traffic, include:

■ Token ring
■ Ethernet
■ Synchronous Data Link Control (SDLC)
■ Channel protocols (S/370, S/390)

Of course, there are several other options available. Some of these are receiving a lot of attention because of the high expectations they carry. The appendix contains a brief explanation of these and other link level protocols.

5.6 Coexistence and Integration

Simplicity, where possible, is the best approach to network design. The fewer the protocols used, the better. So it's no wonder that the professionals who are skilled in SNA often regard the current "LAN revolution" with a mixture of reluctance, disdain, and hesitation.

There are several things to consider when building a network that uses multiple protocols. These can be broken into two primary areas: applications and data transport. There are, of course, others as well. For example, the applications in use affect the end users and their capabilities. But from a planning, design, and implementation point of view, these two technical areas are very significant.

Programming Model

The programming model, loosely put, is created and embodied by the API(s) selected for use. An API determines the services provided to the program, and ultimately to the user. And each API is usually tightly coupled to a single network transport.

Major APIs available for creating applications include:

- An SNA-based API, such as CPI-C or APPC
- Socket API, usually associated with TCP/IP
- RPC
- Message Queuing, such as IBM's MQSeries products

And within each of the areas listed, there are more complexities. For example, there are several different RPC implementations. Also, the TCP/IP architecture includes, or is associated with, several programming interfaces. Some of these include:

- X Window System
- Motif
- SNMP Distributed Programming Interface (DPI)
- Kerberos
- Several different socket APIs (e.g., Berkeley, CICS)

So it is clear that a wide variety of APIs exist, and that these can in turn affect the services available to the users as well as the requirements of the underlying network.

Transport Solutions

Another area of concern within a network using multiple protocols is naturally the transport of these protocols. There are several major architectures, such as:

- SNA
- IP (TCP/IP)
- IPX (Novell)
- AppleTalk
- NETBIOS

As networks grow more complex with several networking transports, additional skill is required.

Figure 5.7 contains a list of the methods that are typically used to integrate multiple transport protocols. Encapsulation is a generic technique for sending data from one network to another through an intermediate network.

Multiple Protocols	Description
Encapsulation	A general method allowing data to be packaged for transmission from one network to another through an intermediate network or link.
Multiprotocol Routers	A routing device designed to support a variety of transport protocols, incorporating logic to adapt to and handle different network conditions.
Parallel Networks	The default case where no integration takes place; each network is created and maintained separately.

Figure 5.7 Techniques that can be used in dealing with multiple transport protocols.

There are several types of encapsulation, including:

- Remote bridging
- Network tunneling
- Data Link Switching (DLSw)

Figure 5.8 includes a general illustration of encapsulation. Remote bridging is essentially a technique for extending a LAN by sending frames directly through to another network. One of the concerns here is with the nature of the LAN-to-LAN link. It can take many forms, and usually provides little purpose other than to link the two networks. There can be several problems, such as the poor interaction between products and protocols not specifically designed to work together.

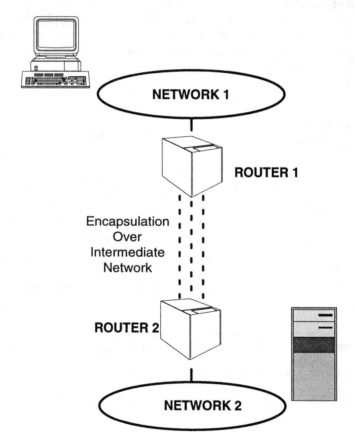

Figure 5.8 Encapsulation of network traffic for transmission through an intermediate network.

With tunneling, the intermediate has more sophistication, usually with its own method for transporting data. It is possible, for example, to accept SNA data and wrap each packet within an IP header. These datagrams use the IP routing capability of the intermediate network. This type of encapsulation can have several disadvantages. Data can be forwarded indiscriminately, or lost due to the deficiencies of the intermediate protocol.

The Data Link Switching (DLSw) standard is a special type of encapsulation created by IBM. Each router has a full TCP/IP stack, allowing connections to be established between the two end nodes. The routers filter traffic (e.g., broadcasts) and guarantee delivery by using the capabilities of the TCP Transport layer protocol (e.g., retransmission). DLSw is discussed further in Chapter 8.

6

Platform Implementations

As pointed out in the previous chapter, there are six primary TCP/IP host implementations within the IBM world. This chapter will present each in a separate section.

It would be impossible to provide a comprehensive description of each product, even with an entire chapter (or book!). Therefore, the goal is to introduce the reader to each implementation, and provide a flavor for the execution environment, installation, applications, and usage for each. Some of the applications will be highlighted and explored in further detail. Also, the appendix includes a summary of the TCP/IP applications and APIs per platform.

6.1 Common Foundation for VM and MVS

Each TCP/IP implementation has been adapted to the characteristics and restrictions of the particular environment. This has determined their internal operation. Of all the platforms, VM and MVS are the most closely related. In fact, the initial VM product was later ported to MVS. Because of this, it is possible to factor out several of the operational characteristics common to each product.

VM Overview

In order to understand the Virtual Machine (VM) operating system, it is first necessary to consider a simple computer. Each "real" machine consists of, among other things, at least one CPU, memory, and disk devices. The operating system controls allocation of and access to these resources on behalf of the multiple applications. The basic operating system therefore provides a virtualization of these components.

VM takes this approach a step further. It allows multiple operating systems to execute, each of which appears to be in control of its own real machine. That is, VM virtualizes the most basic elements of the computer, such as the CPU, memory, and disk files. VM schedules each operating system instance, which in turn can schedule its own applications.

Each of the resident operating systems runs within its own virtual machine, including virtual memory and devices. Access to these resources by the operating system on behalf of the applications is granted by the core VM code, which must trap and redirect calls as required.

The Conversational Monitor System (CMS) is an interaction system tailored to VM. It is IPL'ed like other systems, and is interactive in nature. Also, CMS can be used as the basis for other applications running under VM.

At one time, VM was viewed as a tool to support the migration of users from VSE to MVS, as both systems could be simultaneously supported on the same hardware platform. Then it took on a life of its own, as dedicated users promoted its inherent benefits. Indeed, the development and popularization of VM has resulted in several contributions to computing in general. Some of these include:

- Concept of a virtual machine - reflected in recent hardware advances such as the virtual 8086 mode of the Intel 386 processor which uses a virtual machine.
- Microkernel - a core, but minimalistic, supervisor function reflected in the Mach kernel and Windows NT kernel.
- Multiple APIs - again found with Mach and NT.
- Device independent file I/O - virtualization of physical device, opening the way for sophisticated access methods and file systems.
- REXX - a procedural command list language.

But while there are a large number of VM installations, its usage appears to be waning. This is true if for no other reason than the expense of such a mainframe-based system as compared to the available alternatives.

First VM Implementation

Support for TCP/IP by IBM began over 10 years ago. In September of 1984, the VM Interface for TCP/IP was announced (letter 284-358). It enabled a channel connection to a front-end Series/1 machine or Device Access Control Unit (DACU). The DACU provided an indirect link to networking protocols, such as Ethernet and X.25. Three major application capabilities were included:

- File transfer - with the FTP protocol.
- Sending mail - using the early VMNOTE application as an interface to SMTP.
- Remote logon - through the TELNET protocol.

Following this, the first formal release of a TCP/IP product was announced in April, 1987. Releases 1.1 and 1.2 then followed, with announcements in December, 1987 and July, 1988, respectively. By contrast, the first release for MVS was not announced until September, 1988.

TCP/IP for VM is currently at the V2.2 level. It provides native VM support, and is designed for the VM community at large. This includes workgroup users and the scientific community.

Inter-User Communication Vehicle

IUCV, as its name implies, is a technique which allows VM users to exchange data. It is built on a message queuing mechanism that can be used as:

- An interface between two VMs.
- A method to communicate with the core operating system to request specific services for the VM.

IUCV can be described as language neutral, and has become an important enabling technology used by both IBM and vendor applications. It is accessed from the assembler language, and can therefore be supported in a number of other languages. The protocol is based on interrupts (external), and identifies both a source and target. Figure 6.1 provides a simple illustration.

Here a connection request is made, which generates an interrupt at the server. An accept response is then generated. After this path has been established, the partners can exchange data. Finally, the connection is severed, which can occur for several reasons. For example, one of the virtual machines might be terminated. The partner receives the interrupt for the severed path. Note that a single VM can maintain several connections simultaneously, each identified by path number.

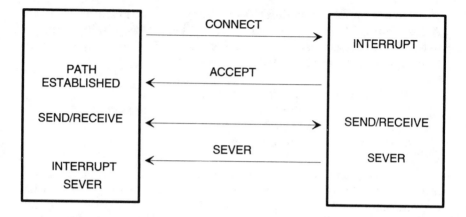

Figure 6.1 An illustration of the interaction between IUCV partners.

There are three macros available for writing the IUCV code directly in assembler:

- IUCV
- CMSIUCV
- HNDIUCV

Figure 6.2 includes an example of the IUCV macro. In this case, a receive operation is executed for the indicated path (i.e., PATHID).

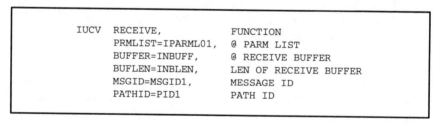

Figure 6.2 An example of an IUCV call.

The VM systems programmer has control over the use of IUCV through the system directory, consisting of userid and other configuration parameters. These can be used to restrict access to the VM servers and CP system services.

Parameter	Description
ACBPOOLSIZE	Activity CBs hold information regarding process scheduling within TCP/IP.
ADDRESSTRANSLATION - POOLSIZE	Each ARP entry is contained in a single CB, translating IP to network address.
CCBPOOLSIZE	Each TCP/IP user, including servers, must have a pool of Client CBs.
DATABUFFERPOOLSIZE	Normal TCP/IP data is held in these buffers - see the small pool below.
ENVELOPEPOOLSIZE	Datagrams and fragments are held here during TCP/IP processing - see large pool.
IPROUTEPOOLSIZE	Each entry in the local IP routing table is contained in a single CB.
LARGEENVELOPEPOOLSIZE	The second envelope pool, normally used to hold larger UDP datagrams.
RCBPOOLSIZE	Applications require Raw IP CBs when directly exchanging raw IP datagrams.
SCBPOOLSIZE	Socket CBs hold information about TCP connections and UDP ports.
SKCBPOOLSIZE	One Socket Interface CB is required to describe a single socket end-point.
SMALLDATABUFFERPOOLSIZE	The second pool for regular data, these buffers are used by the TELNET server.
TCBPOOLSIZE	Transmission CBs hold data regarding TCP connections.
UCBPOOLSIZE	UDP CBs hold information about UDP ports during normal processing.

Figure 6.3 Statements used to define the TCP/IP buffer pools.

Parameter	Description
ARPAGE	ARP table entries are deleted unless revalidated within this amount of time.
ASSORTEDPARMS	An assortment of parameters, which differ by implementation (i.e., VM, MVS).
AUTOLOG	TCP/IP includes a degree of automation, activating processes in the list at startup.
BSDROUTINGPARMS	The ROUTED server builds the routing table based on data about each link.
DEVICE	Used to define a device to TCP/IP - there is a wide variety of types supported.
GATEWAY	The static routes to the named networks or hosts are established.
HOME	Used to associate a home (IP) address with each link.
INFORM	A list of user IDs that will be sent a brief message in the event of a serious error.
INTERNALCLIENTPARMS	The TELNET server, an internal TCP/IP client, is configured with this statement.

Figure 6.4 General TCP/IP customization parameters in common with VM and MVS (part 1 of 2).

IUCV is an improved version of the earlier VM Communication Facility (VMCF). It has the following advantages over VMCF:

- Multiple paths can be declared between VMs.
- Connection-based.
- Address lists are supported which are similar to the socket scatter read/write mechanism.
- Generally socket like.

Parameter	Description
KEEPALIVEOPTIONS	Configures the keepalive option for TCP connections using an internal timer.
LINK	Used with the DEVICE statement to define the connection protocol.
OBEY	The OBEY list contains the users who are able to issue a set of commands.
PORT	A specific user ID/process is associated with a port; additional parm for TELNET.
START	Each of the defined devices can be automatically started.
STOP	Used in the OBEYFILE to dynamically stop active devices.
SYSCONTACT	Allows the configuration of the SNMP object value sysContact.
SYSLOCATE	Similar to SYSCONTACT, defines the device's location; each with 254 max len.
TRANSLATE	Used to augment and replace ARP data for certain devices.

Figure 6.5 General TCP/IP customization parameters in common with VM and MVS (part 2 of 2).

Therefore, if developing a new VM application, users are encouraged to use IUCV over VMCF. And for MVS users, IUCV is important. An emulation of the communication facility has been provided with MVS. This has allowed the TCP/IP for VM product to be more easily ported to MVS.

Fundamental Implementation Differences

Of course, the VM and MVS operating systems are fundamentally different. This fact is reflected in each product's internal operation as well as its installation and definition.

In each case, the TCP/IP functional applications are implemented as a set of processes. With VM, this means a group of virtual machines. In MVS, a set of address spaces (started tasks) are used. Also, VM data is stored on minidisk files while MVS uses datasets.

System Parameter	Description
TCPIPUSERID	The name of the TCP/IP virtual machine; in MVS this is TCPIPJOBNAME.
HOSTNAME	The most specific portion of the fully qualified domain name for the host.
DOMAINORIGIN	Domain name of the host, concatenated with the HOSTNAME parameter.
NSINTERADDR	The internet address of the name server to be used by the local resolver.
NSPORTADDR	The port number of the name server.
RESOLVEVIA	The protocol to be used in communicating with the name server (UDP is default).
RESOLVERTIMEOUT	The amount of time to wait for a response from the name server.
RESOLVERUDPRETRIES	The number of retry operations that the resolver will make with the name server.
TRACE RESOLVER	If included, all queries and responses from the resolver are recorded.

Figure 6.6 List of TCP/IP system parameters, affecting the access to services by local users.

Configuring the Primary TCP/IP Process

With VM and MVS, there is one primary TCP/IP process which must be customized. Each shares a common set of configuration parameters. These are stored on disk, and read at startup. In addition, the OBEYFILE command can be used to affect dynamic, though temporary, changes.

Figure 6.3 includes the statements used to define the various buffer pools, used to hold various TCP/IP-related control blocks and data areas. Figures 6.4 and 6.5 include the remaining parameters common to both VM and MVS.

TCP/IP System Parameters

Both VM and MVS include a set of parameters which enable the local software, primarily the client, to operate. A list is provided in Figure 6.6. Note that the client code on the same system must be able to read this configuration data.

Common Application Support

The VM and MVS products include several common TCP/IP services. These are implemented within virtual machines or address spaces. The applications, most self-evident, include:

- TELNET
- FTP
- SMTP
- DNS
- SNMP
- Kerberos
- Remote printing (LPR / LPD)
- RouteD (RIP support)
- X Window System
- GDDM/XD (conversion between GDDM and X)
- SNALINK
- RPC (Sun standard)
- REXEC
- NCS
- NDB (access to SQL/DS or DB2 database)

There are other consistencies, such as linking the platform's relational database product (i.e., SQL/DS or DB2) to support the applications. This includes, for example, DNS and NDB. Also, each platform shares a common set of network management commands:

- PING
- NETSTAT
- RPCINFO

Of course, there are many other similarities as well as differences between the VM and MVS implementations.

Common Networking Support

Both platforms share network connectivity options, including:

- 3172 Interconnect Controller (with Offload Facility)
- RS/6000 Parallel Channel Attachment (with ESCON support)
- 37xx Communication Controller
- Channel-to-Channel (CTC)
- HyperChannel (Network Systems Corporation)
- 8232 LAN Channel Station (forerunner of 3172)

Most of these technologies are described in more detail later in Chapter 7.

6.2 TCP/IP for VM

TCP/IP for VM product has elements in common with MVS as mentioned above. In addition, several aspects are particular to VM. The overall product is described below, particularly where it differs from MVS. In addition, two application areas are examined in more detail:

- Mail
- Remote Execution (REXEC)

These as well as the other applications are implemented as virtual machines.

Virtual Machines

All of the server applications run in their own dedicated virtual machine, while the clients run in the user VM where they are invoked. Part of the systems programmer's job is to define the server VMs using directory statements before the product is installed.

Figure 6.7 includes an example of the definitions used for the SMTP virtual machine. Each of the machines includes CMS support, as shown with the INCLUDE statement. This defines various spooling devices (e.g., reader), and IPLs the virtual machine when activated. A minidisk is also included.

```
USER SMTP SMTP 4M 4M BG
INCLUDE CMSUSER
OPTION ECMODE
LINK TCPMAINT 591 591 RR
LINK TCPMAINT 592 592 RR
MDISK 191 3380 120 030 VOL001
```

Figure 6.7 CP definitions for the SMTP virtual machine.

The LINK statements provide an association with the data controlled by the TCPMAINT virtual machine. TCPMAINT is central to the operation of TCP/IP under VM. It "owns" the TCP/IP product, providing installation and maintenance, as well as generally supporting the other machines. The disks that it directly controls contain the following data:

- Server specific
- Client specific
- PTFs
- Source and samples
- EXECs

In addition to TCPMAINT, the other important virtual machine is TCPIP. This is the primary process which is configured as discussed in the previous section. It enables basic communications support, and also includes the TELNET server (as an internal application).

Each of the applications listed in the previous section are implemented in one or more of the nearly two dozen other VMs. Note that NFS also runs within a virtual machine, while it is noted below that with MVS this support has been moved directly into the operating system. Just as with the primary virtual machine, each of the application VMs needs to be defined and configured before activation.

In addition to the common communications support, VM can also allow the use of the Integrated Communications capabilities found with the:

- 9370
- ES/9000 (low-end)

Another of the important aspects of the TCP/IP adaptation to the VM environment is the PROFILE EXEC Exit feature.

Profile EXEC User Exit Facility

Each of the server machines is shipped with a PROFILE EXEC file that is executed at startup. There is only one such file to be used for the virtual machine. It controls the customization of the run-time environment through a series of sequential CLIST language statements (e.g., REXX). In addition, TCPRUN EXEC is used to activate each server, usually from the PROFILE EXEC.

Rather than attempt to modify the PROFILE EXEC file, an exit facility is available. The PROFILE EXEC User Exit facility provides a means to extend this initialization mechanism.

A single exit has been established per server machine. For example, SMTPEXIT is used for the SMTP VM. The exit can be called from the PROFILE or TCPRUN exec with one operational parameter specifying the type of call. There are three ways an exit can be invoked:

- PRELUDE
- POSTLUDE
- ABORT

This parameter signals the exit as to the status of the server machine. For example, perhaps it has not yet been initialized (PRE-LUDE).

Mail

The exchange of mail messages has long been a part of VM, such as with the PROFS e-mail product. The SMTP machine shipped with the product extends the user's options. This VM, as with the others, must be configured and activated. There are roughly 30 parameter statements included for the server.

SMTP, as dictated by the architecture, uses TCP port number 25. When started, the PROFILE EXEC invokes TCPRUN EXEC, which calls the SMTP command. During the process, customization can be affected using the PROFILE EXEC Exit facility.

Once up and running, local users can send and receive mail through the use of two EXECs:

- NOTE
- SENDFILE

These are updates to the versions native to VM, supporting both RSCS (i.e., NJE) and SMTP protocols. During transmission, the Domain Name Server or local site tables are used to resolve the name to a destination address.

A machine can also be configured to act as a mail gateway, supporting both RSCS and internet users. The machine must be running RSCS, TCP/IP, and RSCS. The following customization statements apply in this case:

- GATEWAY
- RSCSDOMAIN
- RSCSFORMAT

The SMTPRSCS program implements the gateway function, and must be started. Also, additional customization of the remote RSCS-based machines must be performed. This includes, for example, copying the NOTE and SENDFILE EXECs, as well as hardcoding a pointer to the RSCS-to-SMTP gateway machine. Also, a direct PROFS interface is also implemented through the Extended Mail feature. If not implemented, a limited interoperability using PROFS is still available.

Remote Execution Protocol

VM includes server support for the Remote (command) Execution protocol. The virtual machine REXECD is used as the primary server, waiting for incoming command requests. It relies on one or more slave machines which are used to execute the actual commands. The IUCV protocol is used between machines.

VM accepts incoming commands from REXEC clients. When issuing a command from VM, the parameters used can communicate the following information:

■ Display help information
■ Activate debug trace
■ Host name or internet address
■ Port number of REXEC server
■ User ID
■ Password
■ Command

Figure 6.8 includes an example of the REXEC as directed to another VM system. In this case, the "Q N" command is remotely scheduled.

```
rexec -l guest -p guest -s 512 vml-4 q n

REXECD    - DSC, SNMP      - DSC, SNMPQE    - DSC, RSLAVE1   - DSC
TCPUSR01 - 620, TCPIP     - 610, SMTP      - DSC, NAMESRV   - DSC
GCS       - DSC, VTAM1     - DSC, NETV1     - DSC, PORTMAP   - DSC
OPERATOR - 611, GCS2      - DSC
Ready; T=0.08/0.20 11:25:18




                                                RUNNING   XMS721SE
```

Figure 6.8   An example of the REXEC command used under VM.

The user ID and password are required; the system will issue a prompt if not provided. As a convenience to the user, the NETRC Data file can be used which alleviates the requirement to include these parameters each time. The user will typically maintain the file on the A0 disk (i.e., hidden). It contains three values:

- Machine
- User ID
- Password

In this case, the user can simply issue the command, preceded by the combination of "REXEC" and machine name. The system reads the NETRC file, and creates the appropriate REXEC command.

6.3 TCP/IP for MVS

As mentioned above, the TCP/IP for MVS product is based on the earlier VM product and was first announced in September, 1988. The current level is V2.1.1. In its adaptation to MVS, however, several features and characteristics are specific to that environment. The overall product is first described. In addition, two application areas are examined in more detail:

- Domain Name System (DNS) support
- FTP server

These as well as the other applications are implemented as started tasks (i.e., MVS address spaces).

Connection to Industrial Center

One important fact to be aware of when considering TCP/IP support on MVS is the importance of MVS itself. It is the industrial strength "work horse" foundation for many medium to large-sized corporations. As such, TCP/IP connectivity can be used to establish important links from the distributed PCs and workstations into the corporate center. It should therefore be of interest and importance to the average user.

As the product has been enhanced and utilized, the TCP/IP protocols have been furthered integrated into the MVS environment. Examples of this trend include:

- Network File System (NFS)
- SMTP JES/NJE
- FTP SQL requests with DB2
- CICS socket support

The NFS protocols do not run in a standalone address space, but rather have been shipped as a component of Data Facility Product (MVS/DFP) Version 3 or DFSMS/MVS Version 1. Mail can be accepted and delivered through the JES Network Job Entry (NJE) connection. FTP can be used for job entry, or entering SQL queries. And the CICS socket interface, discussed in Chapter 10, allows CICS-based transactions to connect to internetwork resources.

Multiple Address Spaces

As with VM, the MVS product is implemented horizontally across a collection of process address spaces. The main started task, TCPIP, includes the additional parameters listed in Figure 6.9.

MVS includes a set of address spaces similar to the virtual machines used by VM. Each of the applications must be configured by the systems programmer. With MVS/370, the following started procedures are also included:

■ Termination Notification Facility (TNF)
■ Virtual Machine Communications Facility (VMCF)

MVS also includes the additional networking connectivity:

■ High-Performance Parallel Interface (HIPPI)

Parameter	Description
PRIMARYINTERFACE	Identifies the primary link to be used by the TCP/IP process.
TINYDATABUFFERPOOLSIZE	Buffers holding small amounts of data when supporting offload hosts.
TIMESTAMP	Entries written to the trace and console files can be optionally timestamped.

Figure 6.9 Additional parameters provided with the MVS implementation.

Two of the applications illustrating important aspects of the environment are shown below.

Domain Name Server

As described in Chapter 4, there are two major roles within the Internet Domain Name System (DNS) using a defined name space:

- Name server
- Resolver

The resolver is usually linked in with the client, to provide name support for the application.

An application on the host can access a name server, or the local site tables (described below). If implementing a name server, there are several choices. A primary server, which has authority for the zone and maintains local data, can be used. A secondary server might be used to back up the primary. Both of these must be configured to use DB2. Finally, a caching name server maintains a local cache and relies on a remote name server for unresolved queries. The "caching only" server has no zone authority. Also, it does not require DB2, but rather reads a flat file specified during startup. In each case, resource records (RR), as defined by the DNS standard, are used to define the zone or point to an authoritative server.

Therefore, when using the MVS name server, there are three ways that a translation can be performed:

- DB2
- Cache memory
- Another name server

In any of the cases, the name server must be customized. It runs as address space NAMESRV. One of the parameters passed to the program is the configuration dataset to be used (the other is the module to be used - NSMAIN). Figures 6.10 and 6.11 contain the parameter statements that are particular to NAMESRV.

Parameter	Description
DB2SYSNAME	Identifies the local four-character MVS subsystem name for DB2.
PRIMARY	Used to specify the local zone data for DB2 initialization.
SECONDARY	Identifies a zone transfer request, one secondary server per line.
CACHINGONLY	When DB2 is not used, this line specifies the local dataset to be used.
NEGATIVECACHING	Provides a way to limit the entries that are cached.
STANDARDQUERYCACHE	Improves response time by storing queries and response in memory.
INTERMEDIARYQUERYCACHE	Limits the number of intermediary queries for remote servers in the cache.
INVERSEQUERYCACHE	Manages the number of inverted queries (client answer) managed by the cache.

Figure 6.10   Configuration parameters for the MVS name server (part 1 of 2).

It is useful to consider the steps involved when implementing a primary name server. The major steps include:

- Update the main TCP/IP PROFILE dataset for the FTP ports, 53 for TCP and UDP.
- Make sure that the NAMESRV procedure points to the appropriate configuration dataset.
- Configure DB2 (see below).
- Create a Master Dataset.

- Load the DB2 database from the Master Dataset.
- Complete the configuration.
- Start NAMESRV.

The customization of DB2 is straightforward. There are five members, both Data Definition Language (DDL) and JCL, shipped with SEZAINST (which is built during product installation). First the storage group and single database are created, followed by the two tables and tablespaces. The database is initialized with a zone, and the two programs using DB2 are bound to the database. These programs include:

- NSMAIN - program running as a started task.
- NSDBLOAD - loads database from Master Dataset.

Parameter	Description
LRUTIME	A least recently used algorithm is used to age the entries in the cache.
HOSTNAMECASE	Dictates the case that all queries are translated to for a match by the server.
DOMAINNAMEPORT	The port number used by the name server can be changed for debugging.
UDPONLY	The name server will attempt recursive locate operations using UDP only.
UDPRETRYINTERVAL	The time between retries, after which another authoritative server will be tried.
NORECURSION	Eliminates the use of recursion by the domain name server.
TRACE	Activates a set of up to six internal interface points for debugging.

Figure 6.11 Configuration parameters for the MVS name server (part 2 of 2).

If a name server is not implemented, configuration of the local site table begins with the dataset:

"<site-defined> . HOSTS . LOCAL"

The file contains statements in the standard HOSTS format, describing the immediate hosts, with names and addresses. The utility MAKESITE is then executed, producing two datasets used by the TCPIP address space:

"<site-defined> . HOSTS . ADDRINFO"
"<site-defined> . HOSTS . SITEINFO"

The TESTSITE command can be used to test the configuration data to assure accuracy.

FTP Server

MVS includes both the FTP client and server functions. The server function runs in a separate address space named FTPSERVE. The process used to customize FTP is similar to that of the name server. Three areas of customization exist:

- Main TCP/IP PROFILE dataset.
- Start procedure parameters.
- Configuration parameters specific to FTP.

As with other applications, the ports must be defined. In this case, a pair of control and data ports are used. The started procedure accepts a large number of parameters, as shown in Figure 6.12.

In addition, the FTP configuration dataset read by the procedure includes a variety of different parameters which affect the operation of the FTP server.

After the basic file transfer capability has been established, the server can also be positioned to perform the following functions:

- Generate SMF records.
- Remote job submission.
- SQL queries.

Each of these demonstrates further integration of TCP/IP with the MVS operating system facilities.

Parameter	Description
ANONYMOUS	Establishes an anonymous FTP server for remote clients.
AUTOMOUNT	Allows volumes to be automatically mounted when data is accessed.
AUTORECALL	Through the IBM HSM product, datasets can be automatically recalled.
DATASETMODE	Lower-level parts of address space names treated as part of the directory.
DIRECTORYMODE	Each level of the address space name is viewed as a directory.
INACTIVE	The inactive timeout value in seconds, after which the connection is closed.
NOAUTOMOUNT	Volumes are not automatically mounted when data is accessed.
NOAUTORECALL	Datasets that have been migrated by HSM are not automatically recalled.
PORT	Changes the pair of port numbers used by FTP for control and data transfer.
TRACE	Outputs debug information to the SYSDEBUG DD dataset.

Figure 6.12 Parameters affecting the operation of the FTP server.

6.4 TCP/IP for OS/2

With the decline of the mainframe, OS/2 appears to be a rising star in the IBM product suite. It is the ideal bridge between two worlds, riding the crest of a wave outward from the host center into the realm of desktop computing. The reason for this lies in the nature of the platform itself. First, it is a real operating system with processes, threads, and preemptive multi-processing. Therefore, it can handle (relatively) heavy-duty applications. Second, the Graphical User Interface (GUI) capability allows useful and intuitive applications to be built. It is for this reason that perhaps the most complete set of TCP/IP applications can be found with OS/2. The product also appears to be embracing many of the new standards, such as the Multipurpose Internet Mail Extensions (MIME) in RFC 1521. And many times both the client and server functions are present, including GUI-based display features (i.e., X Windows). Of course, one might say the same things about AIX. But the RS/6000 workstation is much more of a high-end platform, both in terms of features and cost. OS/2 is currently Intel-based (i.e., 386 and above), and is part of a pressured commodity market which appears therefore to have the potential of delivering more function per dollar.

Version 1.0 of the TCP/IP for OS/2 product was first announced in January, 1990. The latest level, V2.0, was announced in August, 1993. In addition to a general overview, this section will present the following features:

■ Networking capabilities
■ Mail

There are a number of options to consider when preparing the product.

Feature Selection and Installation

The product is distributed as a set of components "kits" as listed in Figures 6.13 and 6.14. The base kit contains the TCP/IP stack and many of the standard applications, and is augmented by the other optional kits.

TCP/IP for OS/2 Version 2.0 requires the following software environment:

■ OS/2 Version 2.0.
■ LAN Adapter and Protocol Support (LAPS), included with the Base Kit.
■ Extended Services or Communication Manager/2.
■ A 32-bit ANSI C compiler

The ES or CM/2 products are only needed if extended networking is to be implemented, such as X.25 or SNALINK. Likewise, the compiler only applies if development is to be done.

Component Kit	Description
Network File System	Provides the client and server NFS functions, with interoperability across the IBM as well as other platforms (e.g., NetWare).
Extended Networking	Includes two major protocols to extend the reach of TCP/IP: X.25 and SNALINK.
Domain Name Server	Provides the DNS name server function, as well as a set of support utilities.
Ultimedia Mail/2	Implements multimedia mail based on RFC 1521, with a wide array of data types (e.g., audio).
DOS/Windows Access	A virtual device driver and TCP/IP for DOS programs allowing access to OS/2 services.
Programming	A set of 32-bit APIs, falling into five areas, allowing for the development applications.

Figure 6.13 The component kits available with the OS/2 product, which enhance the Base Kit (part 1 of 2).

There are three primary methods for installing the TCP/IP product, including:

■ Product diskettes
■ Established code server
■ Bootable diskettes

The first is what most people think of with PC-based software. The user installs the system on a single local machine, inserting the diskettes as prompted. The next two involve a remote access and installation. In the third instance, TCP/IP (and NFS) are booted from a set of pre-configured diskettes so as to allow the remote server to be reached (to complete the installation process). These remote installations are based on the IBM Configuration, Installation, and Distribution (El CID) initiative.

In August of 1993, along with the latest V2.0, an installation and distribution program based on User Paks was made available by IBM. Multiple licenses (i.e., 5, 25, 100) of the product can be purchased for use.

Component Kit	Description
X Windows Server	An X Window System server (i.e., display) at the Version 11 Release 5 level.
X Windows Client	The tools required to build X client applications, including APIs and utilities.
NETBIOS	Enables NETBIOS traffic to flow over TCP/IP, according to RFCs 1001 and 1002.
Applications	The Base Kit, with the core TCP/IP, LAPS, and SLIP protocols.
OSF/Motif	The Motif V1.2 client APIs used in developing applications with X.
Asia/Pacific	The Base Kit including DBCS support for the kanji character set.

Figure 6.14 The component kits available with the OS/2 product, which enhance the Base Kit (part 2 of 2).

Configuration of the Base Kit

The Base Kit consists of the TCP/IP protocol stack and applications, including:

- TELNET
- FTP
- TFTP
- REXEC
- RSH
- Remote printing
- SMTP
- LaMail
- NewsReader/2
- TALK
- SNMP
- Routing
- ARP
- PING
- BOOTP
- Portmapper

It serves as a base for the applications and functionality in the other component kits. However, it is not necessarily required, as the optional kits can utilize other products which provide the basic TCP/IP protocol support. Although, in most cases, the Base Kit will be used.

It can be configured using the Configuration Notebook program. Most of the kits are customized using this GUI tool. Also, customization can be carried out manually with the IFCONFIG command. The INETD "super server" is available to help automate the management of the product. For example, INETD starts the servers as needed based on incoming requests.

Networking Options

In many ways, OS/2 is rapidly becoming an important networking hub. This can be seen with the recent AnyNet/2 support, as well as the RouteXpander/2 product.

With respect to TCP/IP, the following capabilities are included with the Base Kit:

- LAN Adapter Protocol Support (LAPS)
- Serial Line Interface Protocol (SLIP)

- Frame Relay
- FDDI

LAPS is based on the Microsoft / 3Com interface to the LAN data link layer: Network Device Interface Specification (NDIS). It is also shipped separately, as part of the Network Transport Services (NTS/2) disks.

Also, two other component kits add options for networking capabilities:

- Extended Networking (X.25 and SNALINK)
- NETBIOS

Each of the kits must be installed and configured before use.

Exploiting the Presentation Manager

The nature of the Presentation Manager (PM), with the Workplace Shell, provides a unique opportunity to enhance the usability of the TCP/IP product. There is a trend toward more fully integrating the applications with the PM, which can be seen by the applications names (e.g., PINGPM).

There are three folders used:

- TCP/IP folder - new with the product, and contains the icons for the PM-based applications.
- Startup folder - holds TCP/IP icon.
- Template folder - allows icons to be duplicated, such as the TELNET client application.

The use of OS/2 GUI capabilities also enables new multimedia applications, such as Ultimedia Mail/2.

Mail Services

There are three applications related to communicating with other users:

- Mail
- NewsReader/2
- Talk

Mail can be broken down further. The standard applications include:

- SENDMAIL
- LaMail/2

SENDMAIL is the standard internet application. It must be configured - the definitions are held in the file SENDMAIL.CF. The main parameters identify the host and domain name. LaMail/2 is an IBM product, integrated with PM, which acts as a user agent front end to SENDMAIL.

The recent Ultimedia Mail/2 is part of IBM's Ultimedia family of products. It is based on the MIME standard, now a draft standard (as of this writing). It requires OS/2 V2.1 and the Multimedia Presentation Manager (MMPM/2).

6.5 TCP/IP for DOS

For system software developers with experience using an operating system such as MVS, OS/2, or NT, the idea of working with DOS has probably never been appealing. On the other hand, it is still widely used and therefore of some importance to the network analyst.

Support for DOS began in November of 1987 with the TCP/IP for PS/2 product, which required DOS V3.0. This product was later withdrawn (September, 1991) with the announcement of TCP/IP for DOS V2.0. The latest level, Version 2.1.1, was recently announced in February, 1994.

Where OS/2 generally provides a wide client and server support for each application, and implements some of the newer RFCs, the DOS version is slanted toward Microsoft Windows compatibility. That is, the applications can be used in DOS mode, or from the Windows shell.

After a basic introduction to the product, the following application areas will be explored further:

- Windows integration
- Networking options
- Mail client

As usual, the reader should refer to the Appendix for a more complete list of DOS-based applications.

Installation

TCP/IP for DOS is similar to the OS/2 product in that it is divided into a base and several optional kits. The optional kits include:

- NFS Kit
- Programmer's Tool Kit
- NETBIOS Kit

The product requires DOS V3.3, and uses the INSTALL program interface to load the kits. After this, the CUSTOM line-mode command is issued to configure various operational aspects, which can be grouped into four major areas:

- Network interfaces and routing
- Domain integration
- Services and applications
- List of applications to automatically start

The TCPSTART.BAT is created as a result, which loads TCP/IP and the applications named during customization. It can be invoked by the operator, or placed in the AUTOEXEC.BAT file.

DOS Applications

DOS, by its very nature, is a primitive operating environment. It implements many of the functions as Terminate and Stay Resident (TSR) programs. While the operating system is geared for client-side support, many of the services also include a server function.

The applications shipped in the Base Kit include:

- File transfer (FTP, TFTP)
- Printing (LPR/LPD)
- Mail
- TELNET
- Remote command execution (REXEC, RSH)
- SNMP agent (not extensible)

Also, several commands are available for configuration and network management.

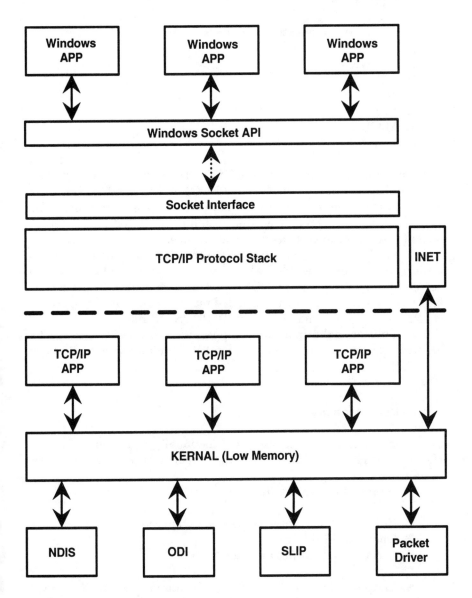

Figure 6.15 An illustration of the internal integration of Windows within the DOS environment.

Windows Support

Many of the applications can be used from the Windows V3.1 interface. They are arranged in one TCP/IP for DOS program group. Both standard and enhanced (i.e., 386) modes are supported.

The following applications can be activated from Windows:

- TELNET
- FTP
- NFS
- LPR
- MAIL
- PING

During configuration using CUSTOM, the user is prompted for input which eventually updates the PROGMAN.INI and SYSTEM.INI files. Figure 6.15 presents an illustration of the active environment. The applications above the dashed line reside in protected mode storage, while those below operate as if in real storage.

The INET program, part running in protected mode and part in real mode, acts as an interface for the Windows applications. It loads a virtual device driver (VxD) named DOS16M.386 during initialization. The latest version of the product has added more control over the operation of INET through parameters in the TCPDOS.INI file.

In addition to the application support for users, two Windows APIs are available (as described in Chapter 10): Windows socket (WinSock) and FTP.

Network Connectivity

The DOS machine is of course less functionally equipped than OS/2. However, this does not diminish the importance of the LAN-based computing issues.

Three interface standards can be used:

- Network Device Interface Specification (NDIS)
- Open Data Link Interface (ODI)
- Serial Line Internet Protocol (SLIP)

Each runs inside of DOS as a TSR. The mainstream LAN protocols can be used, including Ethernet (DIX and IEEE 802.3) and Token Ring.

Another feature related to the network is the option to run TCP/IP for DOS from a LAN server. This allows each workstation user to conserve disk space.

A requester (protocol) is required - examples include:

- DOS LAN Requester (IBM).
- LAN Requester (Microsoft).

- NetWare Requester (Novell).
- NFS client (TCP/IP).

Several operational parameters must be customized at the workstation, to effectively provide the link to the server. This includes, for example, updating the PATH and environmental variables. Most of the files can then reside at the server, while a handful must be unique per user (at the workstation).

Mail Client

Access to mail through TCP/IP is possible when the DOS machine relies on a server running both the Post Office Protocol (POP) Version 2.0 protocol and SMTP. Figure 6.16 provides an illustration.

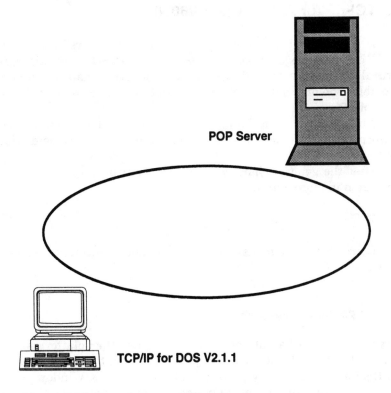

POP Server

TCP/IP for DOS V2.1.1

Figure 6.16   A DOS client relying on a POP mail server.

While POP2 is required, it has now actually become historic, eventually to be replaced by Version 3 in RFC 1460 (now a draft standard).

Part of the configuration includes updating the TCPDOS.INI file. The parameters used include the name of the local user (host) and POP server, as well as the directory to store incoming mail in.

Once active, there are three DOS commands that can be used:

- MAIL - send mail to remote user.
- POPGET - receive mail from the POP server.
- DECODE - decode mail that has arrived encoded.

Mail can be sent to the POP server or forwarded to a second remote machine. It can also be directed to another Windows user.

6.6 TCP/IP for AIX on the RS/6000

TCP/IP, having matured over the last ten to twelve years together with the UNIX operating system (starting with the BSD association), is a natural for AIX. Because of this, the AIX support perhaps more closely resembles the original UNIX implementations when compared to the other platforms.

While IBM has marketed several versions of AIX for different platforms, the RS/6000 workstation is the most relevant and widely used.

After the general characteristics are described, a system area is illustrated in more detail:

- Dynamic routing

There are two daemons available for dynamic routing, as presented below.

Native Application Support

This is too large of a subject area (as are the other platforms) to be described completely. Rather, it is possible to point to the advantages of the RS/6000. It is a very powerful machine, with X Window System graphical capability (in the AIXWindows component).

Daemon	Description
GATED	The preferred of two daemons providing support for interior and exterior routing.
INETD	The "super" daemon, which coordinates the activity of the other processes.
IPTRACE	Enables low-level (network interface) packet tracing for diagnostics.
NAMED	Implements the name server function within the DNS system.
ROUTED	The older, less functional of the two daemons providing RIP routing support.
RWHOD	Broadcasts to connected hosts on a regular basis to share user/network data.
TIMED	Implements the time server function.

Figure 6.17 AIX daemons, supporting TCP/IP, which are managed by the SRC.

The applications are implemented in the foreground (i.e., commands) and as background processes. There are two main techniques for controlling the daemons:

- System Resource Controller (SRC), AIX-specific utility
- INETD daemon

Also, the shell script (command) RC.TCPIP, which participates in the UNIX systems startup, can be used. Figures 6.17 and 6.18 provide a list of the daemons included with the system, according to the method in which they are controlled.

Virtually all of the major protocols are supported. And of course, the user has the added advantage of local proximity to the NetView/6000 network management system (if installed).

Daemon	Description
COMSAT	Used to alert user to incoming mail.
FINGERD	Uses the Finger protocol to provide information about user accounts.
FTPD	Implements the FTP protocol.
REXECD	Provides support for the Remote Command Execution (REXEC) protocol.
RLOGIND	Server implementation for the RLOGIN command from a remote host.
RSHD	Enables remote shell access using commands RCP and RSH.
TALKD	Implements the conversation feature of the TALK protocol.
SYSLOGD	Records and accesses system messages, not strictly part of TCP/IP.
TELNETD	Implements the TELNET server function.
TFTPD	Enables the Trivial FTP (TFTP) function by providing the server.
UUCPD	Coordinates communication between Basic Networking Utilities (BNU) and TCP/IP.

Figure 6.18 AIX daemons, supporting TCP/IP, which are managed by the INETD subsystem.

Network Interfaces

A network interface provides the link between the IP layer and the specific networking protocols. Each interface usually maps to an adapter, which is serviced by a driver for the protocol. The following types of interfaces are supported:

- Ethernet (DIX V2 and IEEE 802.3)
- Token ring
- X.25
- SLIP
- FDDI
- Serial Optical
- Loopback

After installing a new adapter, the operating system will automatically identify and configure the interface, assigning it a name. The interfaces can be listed using the command:

SMIT LSINET

The user can also perform additional customization on each interface. For example, the following attributes are used with the Ethernet adapter:

- NETADDR
- STATE
- ARP
- NETMASK
- BROADCAST

The Network Selection menu of SMIT is used. Also, the TCP/IP command NETSTAT (with the -V option) displays information such as network statistics and the interface to hardware address mapping.

Dynamic Routing

AIX allows for the definition of both static and dynamic routing. There are two daemons supporting dynamic routing:

- ROUTED
- GATED

The routed daemon implements the RIP protocol. The process gated is more recent and well rounded. It includes support for the following protocols:

- RIP
- HELLO
- EGP
- BGP

For this reason, the use of gated is recommended.

6.7 TCP/IP for AS/400

For many users, it's difficult to get a handle on exactly what is happening inside the AS/400. It is a collection of hardware features and operating system subsystems designed to both absorb the previous S/36 and S/38 install base, and to introduce more advanced features. At any rate, the platform is (at least when compared to the others discussed here) a closed system. Assembler language coding is out, and RPG rules. In this world, IBM provides TCP/IP support in the form of the AS/400 TCP/IP Utilities, first announced in September, 1989.

The implementation has lagged the other operating systems, and is generally speaking more primitive. For example, the number of applications supported is minimal. Also, a pool of only 160 data buffers is available for all of the TCP/IP applications at any given time. Since each application uses two per connection, this limits the total connections on a given host to 80. However, the product does provide an adequate base, and as of this writing IBM seems to be planning a set of future enhancements.

A basic overview is first presented, followed by a description of two applications:

- TELNET server
- File Server Support/400

The File Server program provides data access, especially for locally connected PCs.

Execution Environment

The recent "plug and play" PC hardware initiative could have taken its name from the AS/400. The machine is the easiest to use of IBM's major platforms, in terms of installation and administration.

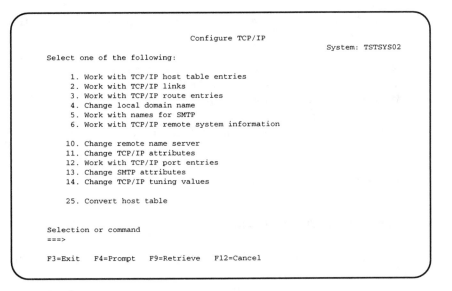

```
                           Configure TCP/IP
                                                   System: TSTSYS02
        Select one of the following:

            1. Work with TCP/IP host table entries
            2. Work with TCP/IP links
            3. Work with TCP/IP route entries
            4. Change local domain name
            5. Work with names for SMTP
            6. Work with TCP/IP remote system information

           10. Change remote name server
           11. Change TCP/IP attributes
           12. Work with TCP/IP port entries
           13. Change SMTP attributes
           14. Change TCP/IP tuning values

           25. Convert host table



        Selection or command
        ===>

        F3=Exit    F4=Prompt    F9=Retrieve    F12=Cancel
```

Figure 6.19 The Configure TCP/IP Menu displayed by the AS/400 user.

The command language (CL) interface provides a JCL-like interface for directing the system's operation at a high level. Internally, the design relies on an object-orientation. The RPG language is most commonly used in a production environment, although C is catching on.

The TCP/IP Connectivity Utilities/400 includes several of the standard applications and services, including:

- TELNET (client and server)
- FTP (client and server)
- SMTP
- Remote spooling and printing (LPR and LPD)

Both the Line Print Request (LPR) and Line Print Daemon (LPD) functions are supported, allowing files to be sent and received for printing.

After installation, the first step is configuration.

Configuration Menu

The command CFGTCP is used to display the Configure TCP/IP Menu. An example is displayed in Figure 6.19. Most of the selection items are self-explanatory.

As can be seen from the menu, the operations generally fall into the following categories:

- Establish and administer network connectivity.
- Define operation parameters for the local host.
- Integrate the machine into the domain name system of the internet at large.
- Configure local applications and manage their performance.

The next step in using the protocols is to activate the subsystem.

Operating the QTCP Subsystem

The TCP/IP applications are started using the Start Subsystem command:

STRSBS QTCP/QTCP

After a minimal delay, this should create a group of jobs. The Work with Subsystem (WRKSBS) operator command provides the means to control the activity for TCP/IP. The jobs can be displayed, and will normally comprise at least eight. These normally include the following:

- FTPSRV1
- FTPSRV3
- FTPS034008
- LPDSRV1
- LPDS225970
- QTCPIP
- QTCPTIMER
- QTMSMTP

The QTMSMTP (mail) job is started with the QSNADS subsystem. Finally, the End Subsystem (ENDSBS) command is issued to quiesce the subsystem activity:

ENDSBS QTCP

One of the applications implemented within TCP/IP is TELNET.

TELNET Server Implementation

The AS/400 includes both the TELNET client and server features. The server, during a connection request, negotiates the following terminal types in full-screen mode:

- 5250
- 3270
- VT220
- VT100

Finally, ASCII line-mode is attempted. Each incoming session is assigned to a virtual device. Of all the customization possible with TELNET, the maximum number of virtual devices must be defined. This is done by updating the system variable QAUTOVRT with the command Change System Value:

CHGSYSVAL SYSVAL(QAUTOVRT) VALUE(40)

Other areas of customization include updating user profiles (e.g., ID and password), mapping tables (i.e., keyboard), and time-out values.

File Server Support/400

The FSS/400 product is an implementation of NFS. Although it generally interoperates with the other IBM platforms, there are a few restrictions introduced in the adaptation to the AS/400. For example, only the server function is provided. Also, direct record access to the platform's data is not possible.

In order to install FSS/400, there are two software requirements:

- OS/400 V2.2 and above.
- TCP/IP Connectivity Utilities/400 V2 and above.

The activation and administration of the product is menu-driven. For example, the following commands are used:

- STRFSS - start the server.
- CFGFSS - perform configuration, including user authorization and working with export tables.

There is no single systemwide root directory in the AS/400. Rather, the following two directories can be exported:

■ /QDLS - document library services (hierarchical).
■ /QSYS.LIB - native AS/400 database file.

It seems likely as IBM pushes its AS/400 to downsizing mainframe users, that the FSS/400 product will become an important option to consider for remote file access.

6.8 Host Resources MIB

Having introduced the SNMP framework for network management earlier in Chapter 4, it now seems appropriate, in the development of the book, to begin discussing specific MIBs in more detail. This will be continued throughout this Part 2, including Chapters 7 and 8.

The MIB-II standard, with RFC extensions, provides a basis for the management of TCP/IP and the network in general. Each of the new MIBs that is created and proposed can be used to manage additional devices or resources.

This chapter has focused on the IBM platform implementations. These are the hosts providing full-stack TCP/IP implementations. So what is the Host Resource MIB, and how does it relate to this chapter?

The Host Resources MIB is part of a trend to expand and mature the coverage possible through the use of SNMP. It provides for management and control of the host as a network resource. The MIB is documented in RFC 1514 as a proposed (elective) standard, and was entered in September of 1993. It greatly expands upon the sparse MIB-II System group subtree, actually requiring support for this established group as well as the MIB-II Interfaces group.

The Host Resources MIB is designed to apply to any host, with independence of the operating system, network, and software applications. To some extent, it overlaps with the work of the Desktop Management Task Force (DMTF), discussed in Chapter 14.

As mentioned above, the MIB has yet to become a full standard, and is not implemented in the IBM world. However, it points to the future as to how host management can be integrated into SNMP, and provides an insight into the work progressing in this area. The Host Resources MIB might be adopted by IBM, or at least serve as a starting point for support of their own.

The Host Resources MIB is placed as a new subtree under the MIB-II definitions. Figure 6.20 illustrates the object ID required to access the MIB. There are six individual groups in the subtree, each numbered sequentially (i.e., 1 through 6), which are briefly described below. The implementation of the first three is mandatory, while the last three are optional.

```
1 . 3 . 6 . 1 . 2 . 1 . 25
```

Figure 6.20   The navigation path to the Host Resources MIB subtree definitions.

System

The System group (hrSystem) contains a total of seven variables describing the local host. The data generally falls into the following categories:

- Time - local date/time, and since last system initialization.
- Initialization - both load device and parameters.
- Usage - number of users and processes.

This group both expands and augments the System group in the original MIB-II standard.

Storage

The second group, hrStorage, is further divided into three sub-branches which describe any of the storage devices located at the host. The supported storage types can generally be grouped into one of several categories, such as:

- Disks
- Real memory
- Virtual memory

There are several types of disks, such as fixed, removable, floppy, and Compact Disk (CD).

A table holds an indexed entry for each logical storage instance on the host. The information contained in each entry includes: description, allocation type, size, and amount used.

Device

The device group (hrDevice) is the largest and most comprehensive within the Host Resource MIB. It identifies over 20 different device types, covering all aspects of a host computer. Some of these include:

- Processor
- Disk storage
- Printers
- Video
- Audio
- Modem
- Tape
- File system

The information in the many tables in this group enables a more comprehensive approach to systems management. For example, disk errors are maintained as well as backup information for each of the installed file systems.

Running Software

As its name implies, the hrSWRun group provides instrumentation of the software which is active on the host. It provides data regarding each piece of software, such as product information and startup parameters, as well as its current status.

Running Software Performance

Limited information on the performance of the running software is provided. This includes:

- CPU usage
- Allocation of real memory

Each entry in the table refers to an entry in the Running Software table in the above group.

Installed Software

The hrSWInstalled group, the last of the three optional groups, includes all software on the host (not just the active applications). Some of the information maintained includes:

- Descriptive product name
- Product ID
- Software type
- Date last modified

This information can be used during inventory and remote management.

7

Host Integration

The TCP/IP networking architecture has been in use for quite a while now. However, it has only recently been completely embraced within the IBM world. This support includes not only the platform implementations described in the previous chapter, but also enhancements to the underlying routing structure.

This chapter presents the major elements and options available when integrating internetwork resources with the mainframe through TCP/IP. The description will include both MVS and VM, but will at times focus on the MVS environment. It is here that features tend to be more advanced, and where the interest of many corporate users lies.

A section is included for each of the mainstream connections and supporting devices. The final section summarizes the remaining connectivity options.

7.1 3745 Communication Controller

The IBM 3745 Communication Controller, with the Network Control Program (NCP) software, performs many functions. Within the past several years, it has been continually enhanced, especially with respect to TCP/IP support.

Features Evolution

NCP Version 6 was announced in September of 1991. Among the enhancements included at this time were Ethernet support, and the ability to transport IP traffic over SNA with the NCP Connectionless SNA Transport (NCST) facility.

After incremental updates in V6.2 and V6.3, NCP Version 7.1 was announced in October, 1993. The new features shipped, with respect to IP routing, included:

- Token Ring support for IP traffic.
- Dynamic IP routing (i.e., RIP).
- APR support.
- Enhancements to the Ethernet Transmission Subsystem.

With V7.1, IP datagrams can now flow over both Ethernet and Token Ring LANs. Also, the many advantages (and some would say disadvantages) of dynamic routing table updates via RIP are included. Also, the Internet layer protocol ARP is now available.

It is most likely, given the growth of TCP/IP, that IBM will continue to upgrade its front end processor hardware and software, including the supporting products. For example, the new NCP performance tool NTune does not yet include support for the IP data.

NCP as an IP Router

The primary function of the NCP is that of a router. In fact, there is a separate internal component which is responsible for handling the following types of traffic:

- SNA
- Internet Protocol (IP)
- Frame Relay

Of course, the focus here is IP datagrams. Figure 7.1 illustrates the three types of NCP internet routing interfaces. They form a type of triad. Two map to physical LAN connections (i.e., Ethernet and Token Ring), while the third allows datagrams to be encapsulated for transmission over the SNA backbone.

The NCP supports both static and dynamic route definition. The IP routes can be defined in three major ways:

- Implicitly - when one of the three interfaces, as shown in Figure 7.1, is defined.
- Explicitly - using the IPROUTE statement, as described below.

■ Dynamically - through a distributed implementation (i.e., host and NCP portions) of the widely used RIP standard.

A Routing Information Table (RIT), consisting of multiple sections, is maintained by the NCP. For example, entries are arranged according to the target host, network, and subnetwork.

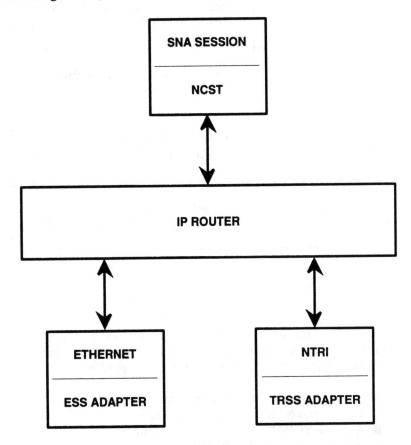

Figure 7.1   Three interfaces used by the NCP's IP Router component.

Overview of Definitions

Several new parameters are used to define the IP support in the NCP. In addition, the standard parameters must also be used, such as GROUP, LINE, PU, and LU. Figure 7.2 contains a list of the new IP-related NCP macros.

IP-Related Definition	Description
IPHOST	Used to define a permanent entry in the ARP table for an Ethernet or Token Ring.
IPLOCAL	A required statement used to define the characteristics of each internet interface.
IPOWNER	Identifies the TCP/IP host which "owns" this NCP for the purpose of routing data.
IPROUTE	Used to define static IP routes to commonly used networks or hosts.

Figure 7.2   Parameter statements used to define the operation and characteristics of IP resources with NCP V7.1.

The exact statements used depend on several factors, including which of the IP interfaces will be installed. However, the resources in the NCP deck are generally defined in the following order:

- Token Ring and Ethernet physical connections, as well as the NCST LUs (GROUP, etc.).
- A single TCP/IP host which "owns" the NCP for routing purposes (IPOWNER).
- Each of the "virtual" IP interfaces corresponding to the connections listed in item one above (IPLOCAL).
- Any explicitly defined IP routes (IPROUTE).

Most of these are optional. For example, if you do not have an Ethernet segment, you won't be defining it. However some of the parameter statements are required, such as the owning TCP/IP host (i.e., IPOWNER). Each will be pointed out below.

Data Link Layer Integration

Support for both Ethernet and Token Ring is integrated with the IEEE 802.2 Logical Link Control (LLC) standard. While the connection-oriented LLC is included (e.g., for SNA traffic over Token Ring), it is the connectionless protocol, or LLC type 1, that is central to IP routing. There are two 3745 subsystems used in supporting the LAN traffic:

- Token Ring Subsystem (TRSS)
- Ethernet-type Subsystem (ESS)

The NCP connects to an IEEE 802.5 network through NCP/Token Ring Interconnection (NTRI), which can handle both SNA and IP traffic on the same physical line. Note that only TIC types 1 and 2 will support the dynamic routing of IP datagrams.

Both major variations of Carrier Sense Multiple Access Collision Detect (CSMA/CD) are supported, and can be transported over the same physical line. These include:

- Ethernet Version 2
- IEEE 802.3

The NCP's Ethernet connectivity has been enhanced with V7.1. For example, multiple lines to the same segment are allowed with dynamic routing, a configuration useful in providing backup. Figure 7.3 illustrates an example of the NCP statements used in defining an Ethernet connection. The INTFACE parameter on the LINE statement is used to associate a LAN attachment to an internet interface, an example of which is shown below.

```
LA7EGRP1   GROUP ETHERNET=PHYSICAL,LANTYPE=DYNAMIC,LNCTL=SDLC
*
*
*
LA7ELNE1   LINE ADDRESS=(1062,FULL),    @ LINE
*
           INTFACE=LA7NIPI1             INTERFACE NAME
*
LA7EPU1    PU   ANS=CONTINUE,           CONTINUE FOR IP
*
           ARPTAB=(500,20),            ARP TABLE
*
           PUTYPE=1                     ETHERNET LAN PU
```

Figure 7.3 An example of the definitions used for connection to an Ethernet LAN segment.

Another recent enhancement is support for ARP. The IPHOST macro can be used to permanently include host entries in the host's ARP table. Figure 7.4 lists the parameters used with this statement, which would be placed after the PU definition for either an Ethernet or Token Ring LAN interface (as shown in Figure 7.3).

NCP Connectionless SNA Transport

Along with Token Ring and Ethernet, the third type of internet routing interface is the NCST facility. These definitions, in the form of one or more LUs, provide the foundation for sending and receiving datagrams over the SNA backbone. The operative word here is "connectionless." SNA is a connection-oriented architecture, while the foundation of TCP/IP (i.e., IP routing) is connectionless. NCST is therefore an adaptation of SNA to IP.

Parameter	Description
HDWADDR	The hardware address, represented as 12 hexidecimal digits, of the attached host.
IPADDR	The corresponding IP address of the local LAN-attached host.
LANTYPE	Used to distinguish between Ethernet V2 and IEEE 802.3 LAN segments.

Figure 7.4 Parameters used with the IPHOST statement.

An NCST LU can be configured to link the NCP in several ways, including to a host or another NCP. This topic is considered more completely in the next section. However, with respect to the required NCP definitions, a connection must be made between an NCST LU and the host (i.e., NCPROUTE).

Figure 7.5 presents interface definitions for the NCST feature. The parameters on the LU statement include:

■ INTFACE - the interface LU, and optional Maximum Transfer Unit (MTU).
■ REMLU - the name of the remote LU and its characteristics, such as modetab and role (secondary LU only).

The INTFACE parameter is very important, and is used together with the IPOWNER and IPLOCAL statements, as well as IPROUTE, in completely defining this internet interface. Figure 7.6 presents the IPOWNER definition, followed by one of the IPLOCAL statements. In this case, the interface over the SNA network from NCST to SNALINK is illustrated; additional IPLOCAL macros would normally be included, one per physical interface.

```
LA7NGRP1   GROUP LNCTL=SDLC,VIRTUAL=YES,NCST=IP
*
*
*
LA7NLNE1   LINE
*
LA7NPU1    PU
*
LA7NSLU1   LU    INTFACE=LA7INCS1,      LU NAME FOR ASSOCIATION
*
                 LOCADDR=1,             FIRST (AND ONLY) NCST LU
*
                 REMLU=(LA2SNATH1)      REMOTE LU NAME
```

Figure 7.5 An example of the definition of an NCST LU.

The interface name (INTFACE) must be consistent among the NCST LU, IPOWNER, and IPLOCAL definitions. Notice that RIP is enabled, according to the PROTOCOL value on IPLOCAL.

In the case of a LAN-based IP interface, the INTFACE values on the LINE and IPLOCAL macros must match.

Static IP Routing

The concept behind static routing is fairly straightforward. All of the IPROUTE definitions follow the final IPLOCAL macro, each line of which defines a static route. Figure 7.7 includes the parameters used with IPROUTE.

```
        IPOWNER HOSTADDR=192.54.2.10 IP ADDR OF TCP/IP HOST
*
            INTFACE=LA7INCS1        INTERFACE NAME
*
        IPLOCAL INTFACE=LA7INCS1,    INTERFACE NAME
*
            LADDR=192.54.2.11,      IP @ OF THIS SIDE
*
            METRIC=1,               COST OF ROUTE
*
            P2PDEST=192.54.2.10,    HOST IP @ - MATCHES IPOWNER
*
            PROTOCOL=RIP            NCPROUTE MANAGES
```

Figure 7.6 Identification of the owning host, with close association with the interface definition (i.e., IPLOCAL).

RIP Support

The NCP includes what is called a distributed implementation of the RIP dynamic routing protocol. The RIP client is defined in the NCP using the NCST facility, while the server is implemented at the host as NCPROUTE. Figure 7.8 contains an illustration.

NCPROUTE at the host maintains the NCP routing tables. The datagrams are sent using UDP, with port 580 defined by default. A single host can connect to multiple NCP clients.

Dynamic IP Routing

The parameters on the IPOWNER statement to some extent control the operation of the NCPROUTE-to-NCST interactions. As mentioned above, this statement is required even if RIP is not enabled. Figure 7.9 lists the parameters included with IPOWNER.

Parameter	Description
DESTADDR	The IP address of the network, subnet, or host of the destination.
DISP	Used to either fix the entry as permanent, or to allow changes through RIP updates.
HOSTRT	Determines whether this is a route to a specific host, or to a network/subnet.
INTFACE	The interface name, which must match a LAN name (i.e., LINE) or NCST LU macro.
METRIC	Consistent with RIP, this value is a cost for the route which ranges from 1 to 15.
NEXTADDR	The address of the next internet gateway, used when sending datagrams on the route.

Figure 7.7 Parameters used with the IPROUTE statement in order to define static IP routes.

The NCP client portion acts as an extension of the host, forwarding information that it receives from its other IP interfaces (i.e., LAN connections). NCPROUTE gathers a variety of data, and sends table updates to each NCP. There are formats defined for use in each direction. For example, the NCP can send to the host:

■ HELLO
■ Interface Status Change

■ Transport
■ Inactive Interface List

In addition to managing the dynamically changing routes, limited support for SNMP queries is available. Routing table queries received by the NCP are passed through to the host for processing.

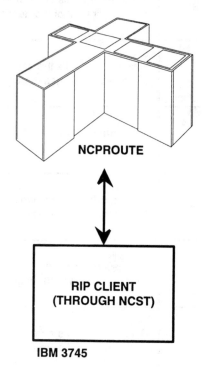

NCPROUTE

**RIP CLIENT
(THROUGH NCST)**

IBM 3745

Figure 7.8 Illustration of the distributed nature of RIP support.

7.2 SNALINK Application Support

The SNALINK application is the host-based counterpart to NCST in the NCP. It allows LU-to-LU sessions to be created in order to exchange IP datagrams over the SNA network. SNALINK has been implemented in the VM, MVS, and OS/2 environments.

Parameter	Description
HOSTADDR	The IP address of the host to which this NCP connects; matches P2PDEST= on a corresponding IPLOCAL statement.
INTFACE	The interface name, which matches the NCST LU parameter and IPLOCAL macro.
MAXHELLO	A limit to the number of HELLO messages sent by the NCP to the host, after which an alert is sent and the NCP pauses for 9 min.
NUMROUTE	Reserves routing table entries in the NCP storage for additional routes.
UDPPORT	The UDP port number used by the NCP and NCPROUTE to communicate RIP routing information.

Figure 7.9 Parameters used with IPOWNER to control interaction with the host (i.e., NCPROUTE).

Configuration Options

The SNALINK applications, including NCST, can be configured in one of several ways. The different types of connections that can be made include:

- MVS-to-MVS
- MVS-to-VM
- MVS-to-NCP

■ VM-to-NCP
■ NCP-to-NCP
■ OS/2-to-OS/2
■ MVS-to-OS/2

Of primary importance, with respect to host integration, are the links with MVS and VM.

Basic MVS Support

The original SNALINK feature, supplied with both MVS and VM, utilizes SNA LU type 0 sessions between nodes. In the MVS environment, a started procedure is used. There are three major areas for customization:

■ TCP/IP configuration definitions
■ Parameters for started procedure
■ VTAM definitions

SNALINK is closely associated with the TCP/IP address space, and relies on a defined IUCV connection to provide a path out into the internetwork. There are four definition statements that are used: DEVICE, LINK, HOME, and GATEWAY. DEVICE and LINK define the IUCV LINK. The HOME definition establishes a set of home addresses, matching a link to an IP address. Finally, GATEWAY determines how the datagrams will be routed.

There are two categories of links. One involves hosts that are connected to other networks, and must therefore handle internetwork traffic. In this case, the SNALINK home IP address is taken from a local host IP address providing the link into the internetwork. SNALINK does not have its own unique IP address. If the host is not part of an interconnection of resources (e.g., standalone), access to the host-based applications is still possible. In this case, the IUCV link is assigned a unique network or subnetwork address.

Another area for customization is the parameters for the started procedure. Figure 7.10 contains a list. These are included on the EXEC statement, and determine the operation of SNALINK.

Parameter	Description
DEBUG	Must be the first parameter, and allows internal tracing of SNALINK activity.
TCPIP	The name of the primary MVS address space used for TCP/IP.
VTAM_APPL_ID	The name of the VTAM LU (i.e., APPLID) that SNALINK will use locally.
MAX_RU_SIZE	The maximum size of an RU that can be exchanged over the network by SNALINK.
MaxSession	The maximum number of SNA sessions that can be created.
Retry	A delay retry value which is specified in hours and minutes.
SessionType	SNALINK can create a single FDX session, or two HDX sessions for each link.

Figure 7.10 Parameters used with the SNALINK started procedure under MVS.

There are two statements which create the connection between the TCP/IP and SNA worlds. The TCPIP parameter determines one end of the link by specifying the name of the TCP/IP address space. The IUCV protocol is used between the SNALINK and TCP/IP address spaces. The VTAM_APPL_ID parameter establishes the other end, allowing SNA sessions to be initiated, the characteristics of which are determined by the product's own BIND image.

The status of the links can be determined using the general-purpose TSO (or CMS) command:

NETSTAT DEVLINKS

The status of the SNA side, in each case, is reflected in the IUCV link status.

MVS LU Type 6.2 Connectivity

The MVS environment also provides an option to use LU type 6.2 sessions, instead of LU 0. In this case, a separate started task, SNALNK62, must be used. The line parameters on the EXEC card of the procedure are removed, and placed in a separate LU 6.2 configuration dataset instead. There are several parameters that can be used, as shown in Figure 7.11.

Operation of the links can be controlled using an MVS MODIFY command. The text buffer is passed to the started task, and can include one of several subcommands:

■ CANCEL - ABENDs the procedure, with a user dump.
■ DROP - terminates a destination.
■ HALT - gracefully terminates the procedure.
■ LIST - displays connection status and usage information.
■ RESTART - restarts connections.
■ TRACE - controls tracing options.

The support for LU type 6.2 communications is consistent with the IBM strategy, at least with regard to the transmission of data across the SNA network.

Parameter	Description
BUFFERS	Defines the buffer pools used to store IP datagrams through three subparameters.
DEST	Associates an IP address to a pair of VTAM LUs (APPLIDs).
LINK	Identifies a LINK statement in the main profile dataset to which the remaining DEST statements apply.
TRACE	Controls the extent and range of tracing performed by SNALINK.
VTAM	Defines the VTAM APPLID to be used in establishing the link.

Figure 7.11 Configuration parameters for the SNALINK procedure using LU type 6.2 sessions (SNALNK62).

NCP Definitions Revisited

The previous section introduced the NCP's NCST facility. The LU macro is used to establish the SNA sessions, using two parameters: INTFACE (local LU) and REMLU (remote LU). Figure 7.12 provides an illustration of how two NCPs can be linked, and the relation of the parameter values in the definition statements. Multiple LUs can be defined per interface, where one is the primary and the others are backup for the NCP.

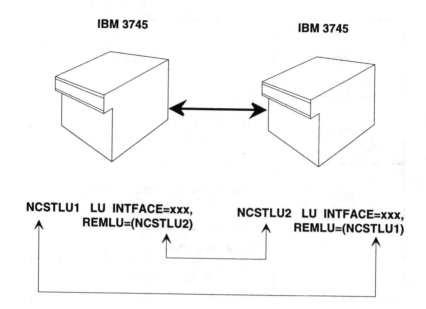

Figure 7.12 An illustration of an NCP-to-NCP session using the NCST LU facility to route IP datagrams.

OS/2 Recently Enhanced

The Extended Networking kit includes the SNALINK application support. It must be installed, along with either the Communications Manager (CM/2) or the earlier Extended Services (ES).

SNALINK includes several files. The customization should be performed using the Configuration Notebook Program, which accesses SNALIP.CFG. This file can also be updated using a text editor, a practice that is generally not recommended. Figure 7.13 includes a list of the parameters included with each line of the configuration file.

7.3 3174 Establishment Controller

The 3174 EC, as with the 3745/NCP, has been enhanced in several areas to take on an expanded role in the enterprise. While it is a solid networking platform, with several features that might be of interest to the network analyst, this section presents its most prominent feature with respect to TCP/IP.

Parameter	Description
IP_ADDRESS	A unique fully qualified IP address of the node in the internetwork.
DEST_LU	The SNA LU name of the destination as an alias (of the partner LU).
TIMEOUT	A value in seconds, after which the session is deallocated.
MODE	The mode name used during session activation; should be set to SNALMODE.
Session Establishment	Session can be established at startup (INIT) or when data is sent (DATA).
LU Definition	Determines whether the LU will be dependent (DEP) or independent (INDEP).
LOCAL_LU	The alias name for the local LU used to connect over the SNA network.

Figure 7.13 Individual parameters contained on each line of the OS/2 SNALINK configuration file, SNALIP.CFG.

TCP/IP TELNET Feature

In addition to the normal 3270 to SNA/3270 host connectivity, the 3174 provides three other operating modes in an effort to support a mixture of both SNA and ASCII terminal devices. These modes include:

- 3270 Terminal Emulation
- ASCII Terminal Emulation
- ASCII Pass-Through

Figure 7.14 includes an illustration of the related internal components. A complete description of the 3174 capabilities in this area has not been provided. Rather, an emphasis is placed on how 3270 and ASCII terminals can be connected via TELNET to a TCP/IP host.

The Connection Manager can be used, through a menuing interface, to configure a TELNET connection. For 3270 terminals, the ASCII emulation function is used to convert the data stream.

7.4 3172 Interconnect Controller

The IBM 3172 IC is a versatile platform for enabling the integration of the LAN-based resources into the host environment. It is fundamentally different from the IBM 6611 NP, in that the 3172 is designed to be attached to a host, acting as a gateway into the LAN world. At the same time, it can also perform a router function when two or more LAN adapters are used.

The 3172 IC was originally announced in October, 1989 along with Version 1.0 of the Interconnect Controller Program (ICP). The 3172 family grew to have three models of varying size and capacity, but only model 3 has survived and is available today. Models 1 and 2 where withdrawn (in December, 1993 and March, 1994, respectively).

This section provides an overview of the capabilities of the 3172 IC model 3, and the ICP software, currently at V3.2. The recent offload support, designed to enhance the performance when the 3172 is dedicated to a TCP/IP network, is also discussed. Finally, network management issues are presented, including access to the SNMP subagents.

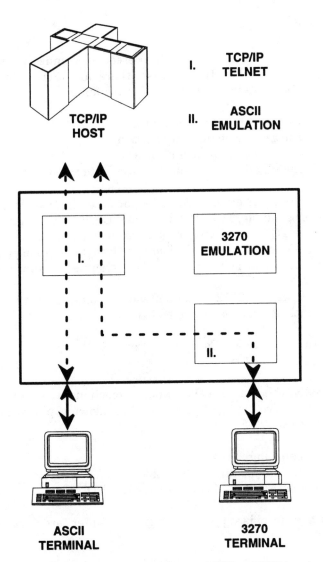

Figure 7.14 The 3174 TELNET feature supporting ASCII and 3270 terminals.

Functional Overview

The 3172 is based on an Intel processor, and must be customized according to its role. In any case, there are four major levels of functionality associated with the 3172, including:

- Host software using the controller.
- Nature of the channel connection.
- Software running within the 3172.
- Network adapters connecting the IC to the network.

There is a variety of techniques for accessing the device. These include, for example, TCP/IP, VTAM, and OSI/CS. Of course, the focus here will be TCP/IP. Moving away from the host out into the network, the next major configuration decision involves the channel protocol to be used. Figure 7.15 includes a list of the channel adapter connections supported.

As far as the 3172-based software is concerned, there are two choices, each of which is described below:

- Interconnection Control Program (ICP)
- Offload facility

Finally, the type of networking connections used depend on the customer requirements. Currently, the following protocols are supported by the 3172-3:

- Token Ring
- Ethernet (V2 and IEEE 802.3)
- Fiber Distributed Data Interface (FDDI)

Each protocol is supplied through an adapter card installed within the 3172.

Interconnect Controller Program

The ICP is broken into two parts: base code (in the 3172) and the Operator Facility (OF/2). The ICP is a general purpose program which can support a connection to the host-based TCP/IP.

Channel Adapter	Description
S/370 Parallel Channel Adapter	The older block multiplexer channel protocol is used with a pair of subchannels for a 4.5 MBps rate.
ESCON Adapter	The Enterprise Systems Connection (ESCON) adapter supporting higher speed links.

Figure 7.15 Channel adapters providing direct host attachment for the 3172 Interconnect Controller.

The OF/2 is used on a separate OS/2 machine in order to generate a configuration for the ICP. It operates in standalone mode or LAN-connected to the 3172. Using the LAN-attached option allows the device to be loaded over the network, rather than through a diskette carried to the machine. A direct connection from OF/2 to the 3172/ICP also has the following advantages:

■ The 3172 can be remotely IPL'ed.
■ The status and configuration can be displayed.
■ Error and trace log features can be accessed.

The OF/2 definition procedures can be divided into several major categories, including:

■ Characteristics of the 3172.
■ Channel connections.
■ Network adapters.
■ LAN gateway functions.

Each 3172 connection from the host requires two subchannels, an even-odd pair. When using ICP V3.2, this path can be shared (e.g., by VTAM).

```
CHPID      PATH=((05)),TYPE=BL

CNTLUNIT   CUNUMBR=640,PATH=(05),
           PROTOCOL=S4,UNIT=3088,
           SHARE=N,UNITADD=((40,32))

IODEVICE   UNIT=CTC,ADDRESS=((640,32)),
           STADET=N,CUNUMBRR=640,TIMEOUT=Y
```

Figure 7.16 An example of the MVS/ESA block multiplexer definitions.

At the host, the 3172 must be defined to the operating system and to TCP/IP. The definitions vary, both between MVS and VM, and within releases of each OS. Figure 7.16 provides a simple illustration of a direct attachment over a block multiplexer (parallel) channel, as indicated by the TYPE value. The speed is 4.5 MBps, as shown with the PROTOCOL parameter (i.e., stream mode, 4.5). A range of 32 address is defined, which is 16 even-odd pairs.

```
DEVICE LCS01 LCS  640 NETMAN

LINK TR1   IBMTR     0 LCS01
```

Figure 7.17 Parameters used to define the 3172 running ICP to the TCP/IP for MVS program.

Figure 7.17 includes the basic definitions used to define the link to the 3172/ICP from the host. In this case, the subchannels 640 and 641 are assigned the device name of LCS01. This is associated with the Token Ring adapter TR1, assigned link number 0 (assigned using OF/2).

Offload Facility

The offload facility was added with model 3, in June of 1992. It is designed for use with TCP/IP V2.2 and above at the host, and can help to improve overall performance.

Offload has the following minimum requirements:

- IBM 3172-3 configured for offload.
- OS/2 V2.0 (recommended)
- TCP/IP for OS/2 V1.2.1 base kit.

Also, either TCP/IP for MVS V2.2.1 or TCP/IP for VM V2.2 (with Offload Feature Diskette) is also required.

As its name implies, some of the TCP/IP functions are shifted to the OS/2 platform, freeing up host cycles. Datagrams can be blocked and deblocked at the 3172 workstation. The Common Link to Workstation (CLAW) algorithm is used, which minimizes I/O interrupts and keeps the dedicated channels continuously active.

Offload Link	Description
IP	Defines a link between the IP instance at the host and on the 3172.
API	Defines a link between socket/Pascal interfaces on the host and the 3172.

Figure 7.18 Description of the two links used in supporting the 3172 Offload Facility.

Figure 7.18 lists the two additional links defined when using offload. The IP link bypasses the transport protocol to directly pass datagrams from the 3172 to the host. This is generally used when the source and destination is not at the host. In other words, when the host is acting as a router. The API link passes application level (i.e., socket API) requests from the host-based application directly to the 3172 Offload server component. The Offload facility processes these requests so as to relieve the host and conserve cycles.

```
DEVICE OFFLOAD1 CLAW 740 TCPIP OS2TCP NONE 20 20 4096 4096

LINK IPLINK01 OFFLOADLINK1 1 OFFLOAD1

LINK TR1 OFFLOADAPIBROAD 192.54.2.12 OFFLOAD1 IPLINK01
```

Figure 7.19 An illustration of the DEVICE and LINK statements used in defining an offload 3172 to TCP/IP at the host.

Figure 7.19 presents the TCP/IP parameters at the MVS host. The DEVICE statement provides a name and subchannel address, as well as read and write buffer information. The LINK statements define the IP and API links mentioned above.

Management Considerations

There are several methods that can be used in managing the IC. These include:

- Operator Facility
- Operator Panel
- SNA
- SNMP and TCP/IP tools

While certain information can be obtained in standalone mode, access via a LAN connection can provide access to data in realtime. This includes configuration and status information, as well as certain operational statistics.

A panel display on the 3172 includes indicator lights, and keys used to enter commands. Of course, the user must have direct, local access to the box.

Integration with NetView was added in June, 1991. Enabled with the Interconnect Enhancement Feature for ICP, it includes:

- Creation and viewing of generic alerts.
- Management of the hardware and software through the Central Site Control Facility (CSCF).
- Request Vital Product Data (VPD) through the Network Asset Manager (NAM) facility.

MIB Table	Description
System Table	Provides general system information, such as hardware and software, as well as location administrative contact.
Trap Table	Maintains the SNMP trap settings, which allows traps to be enabled and disabled by interface.
Channel Counters	A set of variables used to count traffic, both in and out of the 3172, by byte (octet) and channel block.
LAN Counters	Counters for the LAN side of the IC, with variables for errors and discards.
BLK Counters	Statistics on generated by the Blocker task, with bytes blocked.
DBLK Counters	Inverse of the block counters, where a record of deblocking is maintained.
Device Table	The device tables holds information describing the devices for the interface.

Figure 7.20 The enterprise-specific MIB variables used to support the 3172 running ICP.

Management within the TCP/IP world is based on the SNMP and the support tools (e.g., PING).

```
DEVICE RS6KCLAW CLAW 840 HOST PSCA NONE 20 20 4096 4096

LINK RS6KLNK1 IP 0 RS6KCLAW
```

Figure 7.21   An illustration of the DEVICE and LINK statements used in defining a connection to the RS/6000.

SNMP Subagent Support

The 3172 does not include an agent. Rather the concept of a subagent is used. Its exact operation, as well as the variables supported, depend on whether the ICP or Offload Facility is used.

When ICP is loaded and active, the SNMP agent at the host supports the attached 3172 as if it were part of the host. Therefore, all requests must be directed to the MVS or VM agent. Two types of data are available. First, the host includes MIB-II variables, some of which apply to the IC. Second, a set of enterprise-specific MIB variables, tailored to the 3172, are maintained by a subagent at the host.

The enterprise-specific variables fall under the subtree:

1.3.6.1.4.1.2.6.1

Each of the seven tables, as shown in Figure 7.20, is numbered sequentially (e.g., 1.3.6.1.4.1.2.6.1.1).

The operation of the 3172 in offload mode is different. In this case, the OS/2 processor executes the module OFFSNMP.EXE, which performs the subagent function in the 3172. The subagent is not directly addressable, and still must be access through the host. The MIB-II variables are maintained, but the enterprise-specific data is not supported (i.e., with Offload).

MIB-II variables in the following categories are supported by the 3172 subagent:

- Interface
- Address Translation
- IP
- ICMP
- TCP
- UDP

Connection	Description
HIPPI	TCP/IP for MVS can be configured to use the High-Performance Parallel Interface (HIPPI) driver.
HYPERCHANNEL	The Series A devices from the Network Systems Corporation are supported.
X.25	A link to the NCP Packet Switching Interface (NPSI) is available.
CTC	Hosts can be linked through a Block Multiplexer Channel or more recent ESCON connection.
CETI	The Continuously Executing Transfer Interface (CETI) can be used with supported devices.

Figure 7.22 A summary of additional host connectivity options.

The exact response from the IC depends on the nature of the request, and how it arrives. The Offload Facility maintains a basic capability even if the host is not available. For example, the response to a PING request sent to the host's IP address through the 3172 will be responded to by the IC. And this is consistent with other products where the IP function is offloaded, and resides in an intelligent network device or interface card.

7.5 RS/6000 Connectivity

A direct channel connection to the RS/6000 workstation provides an important, high-speed link into the LAN world. Processing can be offloaded to the RISC box, while still allowing for integration with the MVS mainframe.

There are two types of link connections that can be made to the RS/6000, each of which requires a special adapter. The channel protocols include:

- Block Multiplexer (Parallel) Channel.
- Enterprise System Connection (ESCON).

Support for both was added in January and September 1992, respectively, in the form of RS/6000 adapters for each. Both are used to link the mainframe to the AIX operating system. These connections can be utilized by user-written programs, or with TCP/IP applications. Figure 7.21 presents an example of how a block multiplexer channel is defined to TCP/IP at the host. The CLAW algorithm is used to transport IP datagrams.

7.6 Additional Connectivity Options

The previous sections presented the major techniques used to integrate the mainframe with the larger internetwork. There is also a second tier of connectivity options available for the MVS and VM user. Figure 7.22 presents a list.

8

IBM 6611 Network Processor

The IBM 6611 Network Processor (NP) is a versatile platform which can be used to link a variety of network and transport protocols across an interconnection of LANs and WANs. It was first announced, along with the corresponding Multiprotocol Network Program (MPNP), in January of 1992.

The 6611 family consists of three models, providing scalability for the many small to large corporations that are using or considering this machine. Also, the MPNP software, a type of specialized operating system for the 6611, is continually updated and enhanced.

This chapter begins by presenting an overview of the 6611 NP and MPNP. After this, the features and characteristics that are designed specifically to support a TCP/IP network are examined.

8.1 Operational Overview

In the past when using an IBM mainframe, many corporations were able to limit the variety of the networking protocols used to a small number. SNA provided the transport over a limited number of link connection types. In fact, the original architecture logic manual mentions only two data link standards: the Synchronous Data Link Control (SDLC) and channel protocols.

Of course, the situation has changed. The rapidly expanding install base of PCs and workstations has brought with it a potpourri of network protocols. These include standards involving the physical connectivity, data link control, and networking transport. While many of these are based on international consensus (e.g., OSI and IEEE standards), this has not always made things easier for the network analyst.

It is a considerable task to plan, design, implement, and support a network consisting of multiple protocols. Many times, the applications in use drive the networking requirements. This can be like putting the cart before the horse, as network managers are handed the task (after the fact) of making it all fit together.

Whether trying to catch the run-away network train, or given the luxury of designing a new network from the ground up, it is normally preferable to standardize on a single backbone technology. In past times, this consisted of leased lines, connecting the subarea nodes, using SDLC. Some of the more popular backbone protocols in use today, supported by the 6611 NP, include:

- Token Ring
- Ethernet
- X.25
- Frame Relay

This is where the 6611 comes into play. It supports all of these protocols, and more. The NP can therefore be used to "glue together" the pieces of the new enterprise network, adapting to the role as required.

Networking Capabilities

The 6611 is used to interconnect and manage networks which use differing protocols. Generally speaking, it allows LAN segments and WANs to be linked together.

It supports a variety of options for physical connectivity, and the corresponding data link elements. The 6611 can also transport data packets at a higher layer, based on one of several available routing protocols. Therefore, the functions of the 6611 generally fall into one of three different classifications:

- Bridging
- Routing
- Data Link Switching (DLSw)

Bridging and routing are general terms, each covering an array of specific technologies. The operation, in terms of its features and sophistication, can be viewed in relation to the layered network model. The Data Link Switching (DLSw) standard, on the other hand, is one of several specific technologies designed to solve a more general problem. IBM created DLSw, and is now trying to gain popular support for the standard. It is discussed in a separate section below. Briefly, however, DLSw uses TCP/IP (not just IP) to transport various types of data (e.g., SNA, NETBIOS) across an intermediate network between two routers. Among other features, DLSw includes the reliability made possible through the use of a TCP connection.

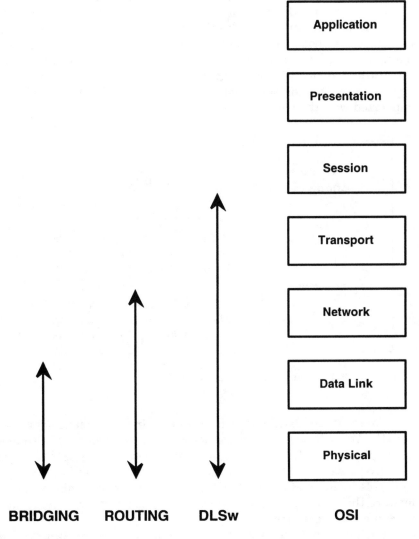

Figure 8.1 An illustration of the three primary functions of the 6611 as compared to the OSI reference model.

Figure 8.1 provides an illustration of the three functions of the IBM 6611, showing the position of each with respect to the OSI model.

Bridging

When linking two LANs together, a "repeater" provides the most basic function. It receives frames from one segment and simply sends them on to the other. Bridging, on the other hand, involves the same sort of concept but provides more sophistication and control over the flow of data. In general, the ability to bridge LAN segments requires more integration, as well as a better awareness of the overall network topology. Figure 8.2 provides a list of the bridging technologies that are supported with the IBM 6611 NP.

Bridging Technology	Description
Source Route Bridging	An IEEE standard used to bridge Token Ring LANs by requiring the sender to completely specify the hop-to-hop route.
Transparent Bridging	An IEEE standard used to bridge Ethernet LANs, where the bridges decide how to forward packets based on filter databases.

Figure 8.2 Bridging capabilities provided with the 6611.

Source Route Bridging (SRB) is an IBM invented technology used with the Token Ring LAN protocol. It allows the frame sender, or source, to completely specify the path to the destination in terms of the bridges that are passed though. Each bridge along the way examines the fields in the Media Access Control (MAC) frame header to determine where to forward the frame next. The packet is sent from bridge to bridge, until reaching its destination.

Each ring and bridge is assigned a number during configuration. The control information in the header forms a list of each of the bridges that the frame is to pass through.

Because the SRB protocol operates at the data link layer, with fields in the MAC header, it can be used regardless of the higher-level networking protocol (e.g., IP). Therefore, it is considered to be protocol independent.

There are two ways SRB can be used:

- Local bridge function - a single 6611 connects multiple Token Ring LAN segments, acting as a central hub.
- Remote bridge function - a 6611 connects to another router to route data remotely.

In the case of remote bridging, the 6611 can operate in one of two ways. If connected to another 6611 (i.e., two 6611 NPs), it takes advantage of the native features of the processor. A 6611 can also link to either one of the following:

- IBM Token Ring Network Bridge Program V2.2
- IBM Remote Token Ring Bridge Program/DOS V1.

In either case, the 6611 must operate according to the Token Ring programs in compatibility mode.

The Transparent Bridging protocol is used with Ethernet LANs. It differs from the SRB protocol, primarily because the source does not specify the path for the frame. The sender drops it into the LAN network, and relies on the bridges to forward the data to its destination.

In order to accomplish this, each bridge (or more accurately, each adapter in a bridge device) maintains a routing table (database). Each of the frames passing through the adapter is examined. Based on this information, the bridge can keep a record of where to forward frames based on their header addresses. The packet will eventually arrive at its destination network for direct delivery.

Routing

Routing protocols operate at a slightly higher level. Rather than relying solely on a physical frame address to exchange data, routing protocols are based on a protocol-specific network address which usually provides a much wider access within the enterprise.

Figure 8.3 presents the routing protocols that are supported with the 6611. At the very top of the list is the Internet Protocol (IP), which of course forms the basis for sending and receiving packets in a TCP/IP network. While the reader might have interest in the other protocols as well, the focus will be on routing datagrams using IP.

Routable Protocol	Description
Internet Protocol	As discussed earlier, the TCP/IP internetworking protocol.
Internetwork Packet Exchange	The Novell protocol, used in its NetWare product, for packet exchange.
AppleTalk Phase 2	The networking structure created by Apple Computer, and extended with Phase 2.
XNS Internetwork Transport	The Xerox Network Systems protocol, initially designed for Ethernet LANs
DECNet Phase IV	The Digital Equipment Corporation's architecture, evolved in phases.
Banyan VINES	The Virtual Networking System protocol, consisting of a full seven-layer stack.

Figure 8.3   Networking protocols that can be routed using the 6611.

IP datagrams are forwarded in a hop-to-hop fashion, over a variety of link level protocols. The routing table contains information which IP uses in deciding which host to forward a packet.

There are primarily two ways to affect the operation of the IP routing function:

- Static definitions
- Dynamic routing protocols

There are options and configuration decisions that are made in both cases.

8.2 Functional Characteristics

The operation of the 6611 can really be divided into two aspects: the Network Processor hardware and its accompanying MPNP operating system. This packaging should not be unfamiliar to the mainframe systems programmer, who has long had to deal with the 3745 Communication Controller and the Network Control Program (NCP).

There are several options available in choosing the NP, largely based on the number of network adapter connections needed. The MPNP software, like the NCP, must also be configured. But the process is different, relying on a separately executable component called the Configuration Program.

Models

Figure 8.4 provides a list of the models currently available in the 6611 NP family. The models 140 and 170 were included with the original announcement in January, 1992. In March of 1993, the model 120 was introduced along with a corresponding upgrade to the MPNP.

Model	Description
120	An entry level model that is configured by the cusomer with one or eight configurations.
140	A mid-range NP which, along with the model 170, is configured by IBM.
170	The most powerful and flexible 6611, which can include all of the adapter options.

Figure 8.4 Selection of 6611 models available.

The installation and use of the two groups, models 120 and 140/170, differ in several ways, including:

- Product positioning.
- Number of network adapter connections allowed.
- Ordering and system installation.
- Physical requirements and placement.
- Cost.

The 120 can be viewed as an entry model, designed for smaller networks with a limited number of protocols. Both the 140 and 170 can be configured to interoperate with a larger number of concurrent connections.

Adapter Connections

Figure 8.5 includes a list of the six adapter interfaces available with all three models. There is an emphasis on providing Token Ring and Ethernet support, especially with the lower-end model 120.

The model 120 NP is ordered and configured by the customer. There is a maximum of two adapters that can be included, in one of eight predefined configurations. To summarize, the model 120 can be order with one Token Ring Network 16/4 adapter or one Ethernet adapter, along with only one of the following:

- V.35/V.36 compatible serial adapter (two-port).
- V422/V449 Serial Adapter (two-port).
- X.25 adapter.
- SDLC adapter (four-port).

The adapters used with the model 120 are not interchangeable with those of the other processor models.

The models 140 and 170 provide more configuration flexibility, with a wider adapter selection available for one machine. The exact support selected depends on several factors, as discussed below. However, the model 140 can include a maximum of four adapters, as selected from Figure 8.5. Any number of each can be chosen, except for the SDLC adapter, of which there can only be a maximum of three (i.e., 12 ports total). The model 170 can include up to seven of the adapters which, like the 140, can be in any combination. The only restrictions for the 170 apply to SDLC (only six maximum) and X.25 (only four maximum).

Adapter Type	Description
Token Ring Network 16/4	The IEEE 802.5 LAN standard, based on a circulating access token, which can be configured at either 4 or 16 Mbps.
Ethernet	Supports the Carrier Sense Multiple Access Collision Detect (CSMA/CD) in the form of either Ethernet V2 or IEEE 802.3 standards.
CCITT V.35 / V.36 Serial	The Consultative Committee on International Telegraph and Telephone (CCITT) standards for serial data transmission.
EIA 422 / 449 Serial	The Electronics Industries Association (EIA) standards for synchronous and serial transmission, with improvements over RS-232.
X.25	The international standard, based on the three lowest layers of the OSI model, which defines the interface to a packet switched network.
SDLC	IBM's Synchronous Data Link Control (SDLC) standard, usually used in connecting to the subarea network through an NCP.

Figure 8.5 Adapters that can be installed with the 6611, providing link level connectivity.

Multiprotocol Network Program

The MPNP software is preloaded on the 6611 platform. It consists of three components, as shown in Figure 8.6.

The Configuration Program (CP) component is the only one of the three not already loaded. Instead, it must be installed on a separate machine (i.e., PS/2 or RS/6000), as described below. As its name implies, the CP is used to configure the operation of the MPNP, and therefore of the 6611 NP as a whole.

Component	Description
Configuration Program	A separately installed component used to configure the MPNP's characteristics.
System Manager	Used by the systems administrator to control the operation of the NP.
Base Code	The core system which provides the bridging, routing, and DLSw functions.

Figure 8.6 Three components of the Multiprotocol Network Program which execute within the 6611 Network Processor.

The System Manager (SM) facilitates the administration of the 6611 and MPNP. For example, security can be set, operational statistics viewed, and functions started and stopped. There is some overlap between the SM and CP functions. For example, parameters values can be changed using the System Manager. However, it is recommended that all configuration tasks be performed using the CP. The use of the System Manager is discussed in more detail below.

The base code forms the foundation for the product's operation. This includes its bridging, routing, Data Link Switching, and SNMP agent capabilities.

The MPNP continues to be enhanced. Although not directly affecting TCP/IP support, it is interesting to note that support for APPN continues to grow.

8.3 A TCP/IP Perspective

In evaluating the various ways to connect the different network protocols, it is important to sort through all of the options. This was first discussed in Chapter 9, with respect to protocol integration.

For example, it is generally possible to include support for IP routing without an implementation of the entire transport stack. Within a multiprotocol network, this can still allow different types of data to be encapsulated within IP datagrams. However, this technique has several disadvantages, including the inability to guarantee reliable delivery from one end to the other.

The 6611 has a more complete support for TCP/IP. Not only does it include the IP routing function, but it also provides the TCP/IP Transport layer. This allows TCP/IP applications to run on the 6611 NP. The support is basically a special function version of AIX, with support for remote logon, command execution, and process creation. All of this, along with the support for a wide range of data link protocol (i.e., adapters) make the 6611 a flexible and sophisticated platform for network integration.

With respect to TCP/IP, these capabilities show up as features in several specific areas, including:

- Static IP routing.
- Dynamic IP routing.
- Ability to support standard TCP/IP applications.
- Data Link Switching.

Each of these areas is described further below. This includes the recent DLSw standard, which relies on a TCP connection to forward data between 6611 NPs.

Applications Support

The 6611 NP can be used to run three of the standard applications, including:

- File Transfer Protocol (FTP).
- TELNET (remote logon).
- Simple Network Management Protocol (SNMP).

The first two applications, FTP and TELNET, are used during system administration. For example, configuration files or program maintenance can be downloaded to a remote 6611. The TELNET application allows direct access to the System Manager.

MPNP also supports the UNIX-style remote login (rlogin) capability, as well as remote command execution using either:

- Remote execution (REXEC).
- Remote shell (rsh).

The function and uses of these commands is explored further in Chapter 12. However, briefly, each can be used to execute a command on a remote system. They are useful where a complete logon is not necessary.

TCP/IP Transport

The two Transport layer protocols, TCP and UDP, are supported. They are required by the applications listed above.

At the Internet Protocol layer, three protocols have been supplied:

- Internet Protocol
- Internet Control Message Protocol
- Address Resolution Protocol

In addition, several dynamic routing protocols, used to link routers and hosts to sharing routing information, have been included as discussed below.

8.4 Basic Installation and Configuration

There is a variety of options available to the user when selecting a 6611 NP for installation. This section presents an overview of the major considerations and administration tasks.

More on the 6611 Adapters

Perhaps the most important aspect of selecting a model involves the number and diversity of the link level and network protocols that are to be used. With a new network, these protocols can be selected based on their merits. With an established network, integration and coexistence become important, and migration can be slow. Of course, another factor closely related to this is the size of the network.

The protocols placed into service correspond directly to the network interfaces available. It is therefore helpful to examine these adapters more closely.

The Ethernet adapter supports both the DIX Version 2 standard, as well as the closely related IEEE 802.3. The Token Ring Network adapter is based on the IEEE 802.5 specification.

Both LAN adapters provide one port. The IEEE standards (i.e., 802.3 and 802.5) rely on the Link Control (LLC) interface, or 802.2. In this case, a native LLC protocol data unit format or the expanded Sub-Network Access Protocol (SNAP) header is used.

Each of the EIA 422/449 and V.35/V.36 cards, collectively known as the "serial adapters," include two ports and provide synchronous/serial data transmission. They can be used to interface to the network through a Data Service Unit/Channel Service Unit (DSU/CSU) or modem. Three protocols are supported:

- Point-to-Point Protocol (PPP)
- Frame Relay
- Token Ring Bridge Program

The 6611 PPP is a composite protocol, largely based on eight RFC documents. It supports a variety of network data (including IP datagrams). The frame format used is similar to that of HDLC, containing addressing and control information as well as a protocol field. Frame Relay is a packet switching standard which improves upon the earlier X.25. The 6611 NP is also compatible with the Token Ring Bridge Program.

One of the considerations for selecting a protocol and adapter type is its support for IP traffic. The protocols implemented in the 6611 which can be used to transport datagrams include:

- Ethernet V2.
- IEEE 802.3 (Ethernet) using SNAP.
- IEEE 802.5 (Token Ring) using SNAP.
- Point-to-Point Protocol (PPP).
- Frame Relay.
- X.25.

The SDLC adapter provides a link into the traditional SNA world through the DLWs standard, and does not directly support TCP/IP at this time.

Planning and Feature Selection

IBM has developed a recommended approach to designing a network which includes one or more 6611 NPs. This involves clearly sketching each 6611 NP and the accompanying links. Each device and its adapter interfaces must be carefully documented and reviewed.

CP Window	Description
Main	The program's main window, which is used to control overall operation of the system as well as to transfer configuration files.
Port Configuration	The adapter slots, and underlying ports, are graphically displayed for configuration.
System Configuration	There are certain parameters that affect the systemwide functions which can be set.
System Management	Management of the 6611 involves assigning a unique name, and specifying how devices will be accessed through the IP network.

Figure 8.7 Four types of windows provided with the 6611 Configuration Program in order to create the configuration files.

The protocols selection process is based on several factors, such as: Maximum Transmission Unit (MTU) or physical frame size, addressing considerations, hop length (i.e., SRB), and speed.

For example, the MTU for an Ethernet V2 segment is 1500 bytes, while that of Token Ring Network (4 Mbps) is 4472 bytes. The maximum speed of the various adapters provided with the IBM 6611 varies, particularly on the interface used in certain cases. Generally, however, the speeds possible can be briefly described as follows:

- Ethernet - 10Mbps.
- Token Ring - 4 or 16 Mbps.
- Serial adapters - 9.6 Kbps to 2Mbps.
- X.25 and SDLC - 2400 bps to 64 Kbps.

Another important factor, mentioned above, is the number of adapters that can be used. The maximum for the models 120, 140, and 170 is two, four, and seven, respectively. Reviewing the network requirements, and deciding upon a design, the next step is to place the order. There is flexibility in the models 140 and 170, while the 120 only comes in one of eight different configurations.

Configuration Program

The base code and System Manager components of the MPNP come preloaded with the 6611. The Configuration Program (CP), on the other hand, is shipped on diskettes and must be installed by the customer. It provides the ability to create a custom MPNP configuration. The CP can be installed on one of two platforms:

- RS/6000
- PS/2

The use of an RS/6000 workstation requires, among other things, AIX V3.1.5, AIXWindows, and TCP/IP. With the PS/2, either Windows V3.0 or V3.1 is used.

The CP has four primary window types which are used during the configuration process, as shown in Figure 8.7. The general procedure to be followed involves:

- Begin by selecting the proper model, such as 170.
- Configure the system management parameters, as required. These include host name, SNMP information, and user ID information (for subsequent logon).
- Configure each adapter, and subordinate port(s).
- Setup the system configuration.
- Save the configuration file.

After this, the file must be transferred to the target 6611 NP. There are two ways to do this: copy it to a diskette or transfer it over the network. Network transfers used for initial configuration can be executed in one of three ways:

- Direct IP connection.
- Modem transfer.
- Use of FTP.

Direct transfer to the MPNP's System Manager is only possible from an RS/6000 box. Also, the modem transfer can be used as long as the Xmodem protocol is supported.

During power up (or through the System Manager function), the MPNP is initialized and the configuration is loaded. The general operation and control of the 6611 NP is carried out using the System Manager, which is described below.

8.5 Datagram Flow

One of the several network layer protocols support by the 6611 is, of course, IP. Each datagram is indirectly routed based on its network ID, or optional subnetwork ID. Once at the target network, it can be directly delivered to the destination host. The administrator has several options available when configuring the 6611 to route IP datagrams, as described below.

IP Operation

Each of the adapter connections must be configured to use IP. At a basic level, this includes three values:

- Enable IP.
- Specify the IP address.
- Enter the subnet mask value.

In addition, there are several other parameters depending on the adapter type. These include, for example, the MTU size and whether the ICMP query (subnet) address mask is supported.

Static routes can be defined when a source to destination pair is commonly used, and perceived to be stable. One disadvantage of static routing is that changes to the network topology, such as unexpected outages, cannot be determined and compensated for (as with the dynamic routing protocols). Still, static routes are useful and can cut down on the amount of network (broadcast) traffic. These routes are defined in terms of a destination address (and mask), at least one "next hop" router, and a preference value. There can be one to three paths (next hops) to a destination, over different protocols. In the case of more than one, the 6611 will attempt to balance the traffic load accordingly. The preference value is used to control route selection.

Routing Protocols Supported

The dynamic routing protocols generally fall into one of two large categories with respect to an autonomous system:

- Interior
- Exterior

Figure 8.8 lists the routing protocols supported by the 6611. The first three listed are interior gateway protocols, used within an autonomous system. The last two are used externally, allowing for the interconnection of autonomous systems through the use of boundary routers.

Routing Protocol	Description
HELLO	This is a very simple vector-distance protocol that specifies the metric in terms of network delays (instead of hops).
RIP	RIP is a widely used standard generally adequate for small to medium-sized networks, though it can suffer from stability problems.
OSPF	This new link-state protocol includes several improvements over RIP though it is not yet widely implemented.
EGP	This is an old protocol, derived from the early ARPANET when the core backbone routers communicated with noncore.
BGP	BGP is the only protocol which relies on a TCP connection to commuicate data, and is designed to gradually replace EGP.

Figure 8.8   The dynamic routing protocols supported by the 6611.

Filter	Description
IP Packet	This is a system-level filter that restricts incoming datagrams according to IP address.
Inbound Port	Operates in the same manner as the packet filter, except at a more specific port level.
Well-known Port	The well-known (software) port numbers can be used as a basis for restricting access.
Export	This filter type determines what routing information is shared with other protocols.
Import	Import filters operate on the receiving end of the data passed through the export filters.

Figure 8.9 Different types of filters that can be defined for the MPNP.

While OSPF is much more sophisticated than RIP, and solves several of the problems and shortcomings associated with its use, it is still not widely implemented. The host platforms use RIP daemons, and do not support OSPF. Part of this revolves around the fact that OSPF is much newer than the entrenched RIP. Also, some router vendors have developed their own link-state protocols, comparable to OSPF, thus further delaying its widespread usage.

Filters

The MPNP can be configured to use one of several types of filters, as listed in Figure 8.9. A filter is a shared definition that the protocols use in determining whether to pass (i.e., forward) or not pass (i.e., discard) a packet or frame. They can be used to control the flow of traffic, such as restricting traffic over a congested route or adapter. Filters can also be used to implement security policies, such as to deny access through the 6611 from certain networks, or to applications on the 6611 itself.

Each filter definition contains a set of generic elements (i.e., fields) which describe the filter in terms of its:

- ID - a unique number within a specified range.
- Type - filters operate in one direction (singular), but can be paired so as to impose a restriction in both directions (dual).
- Access - allow (forward) or deny (discard).
- Direction - inbound or outbound from the perspective of the 6611.
- Address - type of address used (e.g., IP address).
- Mask - applied to address type in determining whether the filter applies.

The exact definition of each filter differs, depending on its type as shown in the figure.

Additional Flow Control

In addition to the use of the basic IP support, dynamic routing protocols, and filters, the MPNP includes additional techniques that can be used to control and enhance the flow of datagram traffic, including:

- IP Priority.
- Transmission Groups.

A three-tier priority value can be assigned to each datagram of a serial port using the PPP or Frame Relay. This value is based on the TCP or UDP port (and corresponding application) being used.

Also, a Transmission Group (TG) can be defined, similar to the SNA TG, for use between adjacent 6611 NPs. This protocol must be enabled at both the IP level, as well as for the two-port serial adapter being used. When operational, the traffic between the processors is balanced by the MPNP across the two connections for optimal throughput.

8.6 Data Link Switching

The Data Link Switching (DLSw) standard was created by IBM, and has been implemented in the base code component of the MPNP. It provides the capability to improve interoperability of the SNA and NETBIOS network traffic.

Support for the DLSw protocol was first announced with Release 1.2 of the MPNP software, in January, 1993. It was then quickly added to the Release 1.1 MPNP as part of the announcement in May of 1993.

Functional Overview

Simply put, DLSw is an architecture which allows a processor (namely, the 6611 NP) to switch between multiple data link protocols. As mentioned above, it currently supports SNA and NETBIOS. Both of these were created by IBM and provide connection-oriented service.

There are two data link control protocols used with DLSw during normal data exchange:

- Synchronous Data Link Control (SDLC) - used over a serial line.
- Logical Link Control (LLC) - the type 2 support of this 802 series protocol is used for connection-oriented service over LANs.

The exact operation depends on the implementation selected: either local or remote switching. Both of these rely on a type of encapsulation, either within the 802.2 LLC frame or within an IP datagram over a TCP connection.

Local Switching

The local switching capability requires a single 6611 and only supports SNA data. Figure 8.10 provides an illustration.

An SNA PU type 2.0 control unit connects to the 6611 NP over an SDLC line as a secondary link station. There is no TCP connection or IP routing involved, and the operation is fairly straightforward. The 6611 converts between SDLC frames used on the serial line and LLC 2 frames used on the LAN.

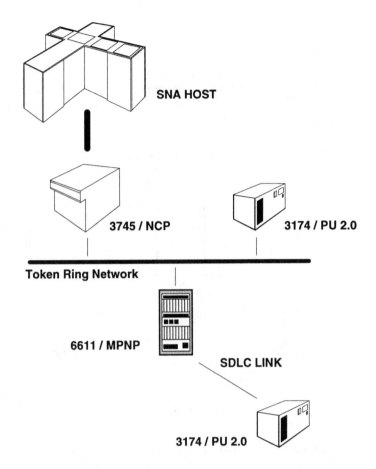

Figure 8.10 Illustration of the 6611 implementing the local switching function.

The PU 2.0 device appears to the NCP and VTAM as a switched device, which can also support other downstream PUs. A MAC (physical) LAN address is assigned to the SNA PU 2.0 (SDLC) device, but is not actually used during transmission. Rather, it serves to identify the PU for the traffic flowing from the LAN-based devices.

When an SDLC frame arrives at the 6611, it is encapsulated within an IEEE 802.2 frame for transmission on the attached LAN. Although not shown in the figure, traffic flow from the 6611 onto the LAN can be destined for a directly adjacent device, or for a remote network. In the later case, bridging can be used with up to the normal seven hop limit allowed with SRB.

Remote Switching

Remote switching builds upon the data link encapsulation used with local switching. It includes several new features, the most important of which is the ability to ship data frames between 6611 NPs over an intermediate IP internetwork. Therefore, in its simplest case, remote DLSw requires a pair of 6611 processors.

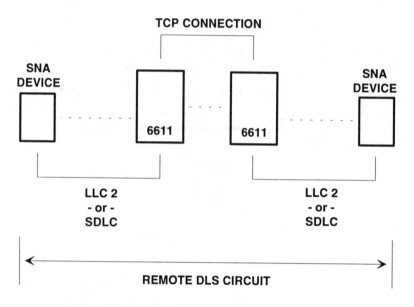

Figure 8.11 Illustration of the 6611 implementing the remote switching function.

As with the local DLSw, SNA devices can be connected over SDLC serial lines. They can also use the LLC LAN protocol. NETBIOS, on the other hand, is only supported on the LAN through LLC.

Figure 8.11 provides a simple example of the configuration of a network using remote DLSw. The two 6611 NPs are considered to be "partners," and work together in linking the two LANs shown.

There can be more than two 6611 processors connected. A part of the configuration process involves specifying what 6611s will communicate with which other NPs. A group of 6611 NPs can be grouped together forming a Virtual Ring, which is assigned a unique number by the systems administrator.

The Switch-to-Switch Protocol (SSP) defines the architecture and data flows which support the interaction of 6611 processors implementing remote switching.

SSP Architecture

In March, 1993, IBM documented the SSP standard as informational RFC 1434, making it available to the Internet community. Also, the DLSw working group, which consists of IBM, Cisco, and other vendors, is working to establish DLSw as a TCP/IP standard.

In addition to the support for SDLC-to-LLC conversion, DLSw also improves upon the LAN bridging protocols (e.g., SRB). This is done by offloading some of the LAN's operation and control to the 6611 NPs at either end. In between, they are linked over a TCP connection which carries the LLC traffic for all of the devices that have established connections.

Each end-to-end connection, from a device in one LAN to a device in another passing through the 6611-to-6611 TCP link, is called a circuit. The circuits are managed by the 6611 NPs on behalf of the users at either end of the TCP connection, over which the data flows. There can be a maximum of 2048 circuits setup per 6611.

SSP Protocol	Description
Connect	Used to establish a connection between a pair of switches (e.g., 6611 NPs) and then a pair of end-user systems.
Link Restart	An end-to-end connection can be restarted, which terminates the existing link preparing both sides for the start of a new connection.
Disconnect	Once initiated, the disconnect procedure terminates the connection and also the circuit.

Figure 8.12 Three major protocol suites included with the SSP architecture which support remote switching.

The SSP includes the exact protocol exchanges to be used by the NPs in controlling the establishment and flow of LLC data. These protocols fall into three categories, as shown in Figure 8.12.

Problem Solved	Description
DLC Time-outs	Regular 802.2 LLC type 2 service uses timeout values, to trigger retransmission, the operation of which can be inadequate for larger networks.
Acknowledgments for DLC Frames over WAN Links	Acknowledgment frames must normally pass through the entire WAN, from end-to-end.
Flow Control and Congestion	DLSw in the 6611 can directly control the flow of data frames to and from the adjacent data link LAN connections.
Broadcast Control Used for Searching	Broadcast are frequently used, as with NETBIOS, and can be a significant source of network overhead.
SRB Hop Counts Limitations	The SRB bridging standard is limited to seven hops, which can be extended through DLSw.

Figure 8.13 List of bridging problems and deficiencies that are alleviated through the use of Data Link Switching.

Operation of the SSP is based on the concept of a finite state machine. A circuit can be described by one of three "steady" states:

- DISCONNECT
- CIRCUIT_ESTABLISHED
- CONNECTED

In addition, there are eight other pending or reset states used to describe brief periods of transition during connection establishment and termination.

It is not possible to give an exhaustive explanation of the SSP operation. To summarize, however, each LAN device uses well-established procedures in order to establish an LLC 2 connection. This works differently for SNA and NETBIOS. For example, SNA devices start out in LLC 1 (connectionless mode) by sending TEST or XID frames to initiate the connection set. The data frames in this search mechanism are intercepted and processed by the local 6611, which attempts to locate the requested partner. During this early phase the circuit is first created (state of CIRCUIT_ESTABLISHED), and then the LLC 2 connection (state of CONNECTED).

Benefits of Data Link Switching

There are obvious benefits that come with the DLSw protocol, including the support for SDLC-to-LLC integration. In addition, several problems and deficiencies of normal LAN bridging with SRB are alleviated. These are summarized in Figure 8.13.

In understanding these benefits, it is important to realize that a fundamental characteristic of the protocol involves terminating the LLC2 at the 6611 NP. This allows the 6611 to extend and control the operation of the adjacent LAN. For example, there can be up to seven SRB hops from each side, thus doubling the effective range of this bridging protocol. Also, the NP can apply congestion and flow control. For example, acknowledgments do not have to flow the entire length from one end of a connection to the other. Under the proper conditions, they can be generated by the 6611 itself, a process known as "spoofing."

8.7 Network Management Considerations

The management of network devices, particularly a node such as the 6611, is an important concern for users. The management of a 6611 NP can be carried out primarily within three frameworks:

- SNMP (for TCP/IP).
- SNA/MS (for SNA).
- System Manager component of the MPNP.

This section will present an overview of the SNMP-based approach, which was introduced earlier in the book. The 6611 NP's connection to and use by the network management products, such as NetView/6000, LAN Network Manager, and LAN NetView, is discussed further in Chapter 14. The System Manager component is presented below.

RFC Number	Description
1229	Interface Extension
1231	Token Ring
1232	Data Services 1 (DS1)
1243	AppleTalk
1253	Open Shortest Path First (OSPF)
1269	Border Gateway Protocol (BGP)
1284	Ethernet
1286	Source Route Bridging
1289	DECNet
1315	Frame Relay
1354	IP Forwarding
1389	Routing Information Protocol (RIP) V2

Figure 8.14 RFC documents which augment the MIB-II definitions.

MIB Groups

The 6611 acts as an SNMP agent, which can connect to a management platform such as NetView/6000. Consistent with its role, it maintains information regarding its configuration and usage within several MIB definitions. In addition to allowing this data to be read by the manager, the 6611 can also generate SNMP traps.

The MIB data supported by the 6611 is drawn from three sources:

- MIB-II standard (RFC 1213).
- Extensions to MIB-II through RFCs.
- Enterprise-specific MIB definitions.

MIB-II forms the basis for the organization of the management data. The extensions, either RFC or enterprise-specific, are collected together into "MIB groups." Figure 8.14 contains a list of the RFCs which extend the MIB-II framework. Note that most of the enterprise-specific data is supplied by IBM, but does include MIBs from other vendors (e.g., Banyan).

Another way to organize the definitions is according to broad functionality. In this way, not only the RFCs but also the enterprise-specific data can be included. Figure 8.15 presents such an organization of the MIB groups for the IBM 6611.

Overview of SNMP Support

The SNMP Version 1 standard is supported by the 6611. Of the five protocol operations, only "set" is not supported. The SNMP configuration activities fall into several different areas, including:

- System
- Community
- Trap
- T1/DS1 and DSU

The 6611 can also generate traps, either generic or specific. The specific traps fall into one of several areas:

- IBM 6611
- Frame Relay
- Transparent bridging
- Border Gateway Protocol (BGP)
- Point-to-Point Protocol (PPP)

Functional Grouping	Description
System Management	Provides information with respect to the management of the system itself, such as system identification and utilization.
Interface Management	Includes data describing the interfaces and also enterprise-specific information such as the MPNP filters.
DSU/CSU Transmission Media	This broad category includes information about the media, such as Token Ring, Ethernet, Frame Relay, and the PPP.
Protocol Management	These groups cover the higher-level protocols, such as TCP and IP, as well as routing protocols like APPN, RIP, and IPX.

Figure 8.15   Four major groups of all the MIB data, as drawn from MIB-II, RFCs, and enterprise-specific definitions.

These traps can optionally be converted into SNA alerts if sent to NetView/6000.

8.8 System Manager

The System Manager (SM) component of the MPNP is an important tool used during the administration and management of an 6611 NP. It provides a menu-driven, text-based interface from a local or remote terminal.

There is a relation between the SM and Configuration Program (CP) components. For example, SM is used to specify the hosts that can connect to the 6611 in order to perform CP-related functions (i.e., configuration hosts). Also, some of the CP parameters can also be updated by the SM, although this is generally not recommended.

Types of Access

There are two access paths into the SM function:

- EIA 232 serial port.
- IP internetwork.

Generally speaking, IBM service personnel utilize the serial port in order to provide installation and diagnostic support. The administrator at the customer location will normally logon through the IP network.

An ASCII terminal can be directly attached to the serial port for onsite access. As an alternative, a modem can be attached, therefore supporting the ability to dial in from a remote location.

There are two ways that the IP network can be used to logon:

- TELNET
- Rlogin

Regardless of the type of connection, the user must enter an ID and password at the prompt. With a successful logon, the System Manager main menu is displayed. There are two categories of user IDs: controlling (administrator) and viewing.

In addition to a normal logon, FTP is also supported and allows files to be transferred to (and from) the 6611. The REXEC and RSH command interfaces, as discussed in Chapter 12, are also supported.

Main Menu

There are several options available from the main menu. Figure 8.16 contains a summary. Each of these can be selected by positioning the cursor and pressing the <enter> key.

8.9 RouteXpander/2

The RouteXpander/2 (RXR/2) Version 1.0 product was first announced in September, 1992. It shares several characteristics with the 6611, and at the time was envisioned as a "feeder node" for the more powerful Network Processor. More recently, IBM enhanced its RXR/2 offerings by announcing an entire family of related products. These products position the OS/2 workstation for improved association and access to the other networking systems devices, such as the 3745 and 3174.

Option	Description
Operations	Used to control the general operation of the 6611, including use of filters, routing protocols, file transfer, MIB data, and shutdown procedures.
Problem Determination	Supports a wide variety of information, such as processor data, system statistics, dumps, and the operation of the trace facility.
Configuration	Provides general configuration capabilities, such as the maintenance of user IDs and passwords and application of configuration changes.
Software Installation and Maintenance	Can be used to receive and list software updates, as well as apply or reject the maintenance.
Hardware Maintenace	Ability to list installed devices and their characteristics, as well as access and update the Vital Product Data (VPD).
System Manager Help	Help can be accessed on-line by the operator regarding all aspects of the use of the System Manager, listed by functional category.

Figure 8.16   A summary of the selections available from the main menu of the System Manager.

RXR/2 Version 1.0

RouteXpander/2, as its name implies, expands the routing capability available to the OS/2-based applications. It provides an entry-level platform that can be used within a bridge or router network. This includes a DLSw link to the backbone 6611 NP.

RXR/2 requires the following additional software:

■ OS/2 V2.0 and above.
■ Network Transport Services/2.

RXR/2 also supports several optional programs, depending on the applications being used, including TCP/IP for OS/2.

A major benefit is the ability to isolate higher-level protocols, which deal with a Token Ring network, from the complexities of Frame Relay (as well as other future protocols).

Product	Description
RouteXpand/2 Version 1.01	An enhancement to the original release, with support for IPX traffic over Frame Relay as well as the Ethernet transparent bridging protocol.
RouteXpander/2 Version 2	Based on the V1.0.1 product, V2 includes an improved Presentation Manager (PM) interface as well as three support programs (below).
RXR LNM Support/2	Provides various features which enhance the operation of the Token Ring network, as well as monitoring for the bridging functions.
RXR X.25 Support/2	Supports multiple virtual circuits over one physical link when accessing the packet switched network.
RXR Multiport Support/2	An enhancement which allows the RXR/2 V2 product to be used as a concentrator for downstream connections to RXR/2 V2 and FR Token Ring/DOS.
X.25 Xpander/2 Version 1	Standalone support for X.25 networks at a lower-cost entry level, with a published API supplied.

Figure 8.17 Products announced as part of the RouteXpander/2 Family.

Family of Products

The product family announcement as of March, 1993, included several products, as shown in Figure 8.17. The original product was enhanced (i.e., V1.0.1). In the next version, the functionality has been separated into optional support products, which operate with RXR/2 V2.

9

Networking Blueprint

The Networking Blueprint is designed to bring order to the networking chaos brought on by the multitude of products and protocols. It will also certainly be used as a vehicle by IBM in an attempt to maintain control of both the network-aware applications and the underlying transport network.

The blueprint was unveiled by IBM in March of 1992 through, among other things, its statement of direction to support the Berkeley socket API over SNA; this was included in the VTAM V4.1 for MVS/ESA phased announcement (announcement letter 292-168). Six months later it was more formally announced (letter 292-476).

The Networking Blueprint is targeted at users who must support multiple networking protocols. Its primary goal is to allow the applications to be insensitive to the underlying network, so that virtually any transport can be used regardless of the API. In the early stages, however, its support will be focused on SNA and TCP/IP.

9.1 Goals and Benefits

The primary goal behind the Networking Blueprint is to provide a structure for coexistence of the various network transport protocols. Users should be able to select applications and transports separately. And ultimately, the number of networking protocols can be reduced.

A Method in the Madness

In approaching the Networking Blueprint, it is important to recognize three fundamental forces affecting IBM's strategy. First, applications have traditionally been tightly tied to the underlying transport. That is, when using a particular communication API, it is assumed that the matching network transport will be used. For example, most products which use an SNA API (e.g., APPC) will communicate across an SNA network. Also, an application using the Berkeley socket API will be served by a TCP/IP network.

The second factor is the large number of transport protocols which are now being widely implemented. At one time, the SNA network was the only game in town. Slowly, however, other protocols have been developed and implemented. There are now four to six primary transport protocols (e.g., SNA, TCP/IP), and perhaps a dozen or more others. This situation is further complicated by the large number of link level protocols in use.

Finally, many IBM customers are at least looking at downsizing. This can frequently involve scaling back, or perhaps even eliminating, investment in mainframe technology.

Extrapolating a bit further, it is easy to see that the different transport architectures are competing for dominance in corporate America. They compete on their relative technical merits and cost of implementation. Some of the decisive factors include:

- Which protocol is most reliable? What is the cost of this reliability in terms of resource consumption?
- Which is most efficient?
- Which is most widely supported so as to provide a variety of products (e.g., routers)?
- Which is easiest to manage and has the most options for management support?
- What skill set is required to install and maintain the networking products?

In addition, the transport protocols compete based on the variety and quality of the applications that they bring with them. For example, the TCP/IP protocol includes a large number of standard applications that many users have grown accustomed to. These include, for example, SMTP (mail) and FTP (file transfer). In addition, vendors frequently supply applications tied to one protocol or another. The Novell Netware product is the most widely used Network Operating System (NOS), and uses the Internet Packet Exchange (IPX) protocol. Finally, end users can develop their own applications based on an API or supporting software (e.g., TP monitor).

Therefore, pressure is being felt by IBM on several fronts based on the three factors listed above. Applications are frequently installed on nonmainframe, non-IBM platforms. This is especially true in the growing LAN arena. Sometimes these applications add auxiliary functionality, and other times they are designed to replace mainframe applications as customers begin downsizing. Many of these new applications do not rely on SNA; they have their own communication requirements. So the new applications drive the networking needs and requirements.

At the same time, these multiple protocols can create a nightmare for the network analysts and support staff. Each has its own support requirements. There is often a desire to simplify network operations by reducing the number of protocols in use.

And herein lies the rub. Not only might customers choose non-IBM (or at least non-SNA) applications, but there might also be pressure to eventually remove their SNA networks. Consider the case where a set of UNIX (i.e., TCP/IP-based) applications are brought in. With this move, TCP/IP usage could grow. If there is a recognizable trend away from SNA, the network manager could decide to standardize on TCP/IP instead of SNA.

A partial solution has been put forth by IBM in providing a wide support for TCP/IP. While this might maintain their platform viability within that market, it does not alleviate the competition in the network. The risk of losing SNA dominance is still there.

So the Networking Blueprint was created as a method for solving this problem. Users will ultimately be able to select the applications and network transports independently, each based on their own merits. The blueprint includes the following key aspects:

- Decouple applications from the network.
- Provide end-to-end connection capability.
- Systems and network management.
- An evolutionary path to emerging technologies.

The Multiprotocol Transport Networking (MPTN) architecture was subsequently introduced as the primary (but not the only) method for accomplishing the goals of the blueprint.

Decouple Applications from Network

The most important objective of the Networking Blueprint is to make applications independent from the network. The theory is that customers should be able to create or purchase applications without regard for their communication needs.

This will be done by identifying a set of programming interfaces and networking transports to be supported. The two can be mixed and matched. Some of this has been tested and documented before by the Internet pioneers. For example, TCP/IP can be used to transport NETBIOS (RFCs 1001 and 1002) and OSI (RFC 1006). The networking blueprint, in the form of the MPTN architecture, supports a sort of protocol conversion function to accomplish this goal.

This strategy should alleviate the pressure between the application and network groups because of the fact that applications are normally tied to one transport.

The benefits can be summarized as freedom to select:

■ Applications
■ Networking transports

This has side effects as well. For example, users can keep their SNA applications in place regardless of the protocol. Also, if any protocol can be used, the possibility exists to reduce the number of protocols.

Reduce Number of Protocols

While there will be more work needed to implement the Networking Blueprint products, the potential advantage is that the number of transport protocols will be reduced.

It appears that more work now will (might) result in less problems later. IBM is trying to capture all of the protocols into one framework, at which time it can gain control and direct the market as it sees fit. This situation is analogous to the runaway horse. The hero must chase after it, and after getting a hold, can then slow it down.

Of course, this scenario assumes a widespread acceptance of the various blueprint elements (including MPTN). This seems dubious, given IBM's track record in such large-scale frameworks. However, it is still very possible.

And once reduced, what will the remaining transport protocols be? One can only guess. The official line is "any that the user wants." It seems likely that SNA will be strongly suggested. Or perhaps the newly emerging high-bandwidth protocols, such as the APPN follow-on dubbed High Performance Routing (HPR), will be used.

9.2 Layered Network Model

The blueprint for how the consolidation and integration will be provided is naturally depicted as a layered model. With this model, the various elements can be isolated and highlighted.

Figure 9.1 illustrates the view of the network, as see through the eyes of the IBM architects. There are four main layers. In addition, systems and network management functions are included.

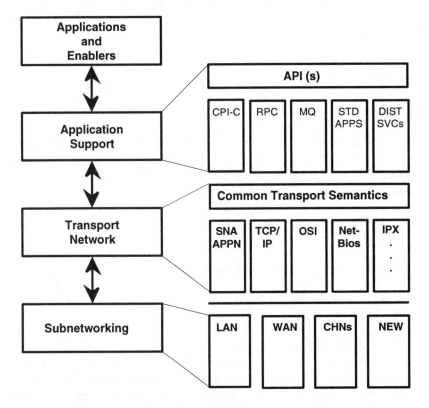

Figure 9.1 Elements of the Networking Blueprint illustrated as a layered structure.

The previous discussion focused on the ability to mix and match the application interfaces (i.e., APIs) and the network transport. While this is the primary focus of the framework, it also allows for independence in other areas, such as the Subnetworking layer and the systems management backplane.

Application and Enablers

The top layer represents the applications which utilize the network. This includes applications as well as enablers. Application enablers provide a higher-level service such as access to a database management or transaction processing system, messaging capabilities, printer services, or telephony.

Both the applications and the optional services access the network through an API best suited to its needs. For applications which evolved from the TCP/IP model, this would normally be a socket or RPC API. For SNA applications, this could be an APPC API.

Application Support

The application support layer provides, as its name implies, support for the applications. It provides one or more of the commonly used interfaces. As shown in the figure, this includes APIs such as APPC and RPC.

The number and content of the vertical slots at this level can vary, depending on user needs and implementation details. New application protocols can be added as required.

Transport Network

The transport network is actually composed of two parts:

- Common Transport Semantics (CTS).
- Transport networking protocols.

The CTS sublayer enables the establishment of a common method for addressing the various transports. Each application uses the API most appropriate. CTS then compensates, where necessary, in order to map the data flows on to a different transport network. It can be useful to think of CTS as a kind of protocol converter, although this is not totally accurate. It provides other functions, and also introduces its own commands and data headers.

Initially, four transports are supported:

- SNA
- TCP/IP
- OSI
- NetBIOS

In the future, other protocols will undoubtedly be supported. These include, for example, DECnet and IPX (i.e., Novell).

The Multiprotocol Transport networking (MPTN) architecture provides the bulk of the CTS implementation. MPTN is described below.

Subnetwork

The subnetworking layer corresponds roughly to the lower three OSI layers. It includes the common link level communication capabilities, such as Token Ring, that are commonly used by the transport layer.

In the future, the number and sophistication of these protocols will most probably increase in size. This will be especially true as new, higher-speed technologies become widely used, such as Asynchronous Transfer Mode (ATM). It is also likely that new protocols in the subnetworking layer will affect the higher-layer protocols.

Systems Management

Systems and network management is obviously an important aspect of the modern communication network. Consistent with the OSI specifications, where this capability can be embedded within each layer, the Networking Blueprint includes a systems management backplane.

In addition to the support of the standard network management protocols (e.g., SNA/MS and SNMP), additional functionality is required. For example, a record must be kept to provide a correlation between application and transport, as well as between network connections through an MPTN gateway (a type of node, described below).

9.3 Multiprotocol Transport Networking Architecture

MPTN enables the creation of the Common Transport Semantics sublayer. As such, it is a significant part of the overall Networking Blueprint.

The MPTN architecture was formally announced in March of 1993. It defines several operational aspects of CTS, including MPTN commands and inserted headers. The name AnyNet was later coined for the products which implement the MPTN functionality.

Common Transport Semantics

The theory behind CTS is not unique to IBM's Networking Blueprint. Other groups, such as X/Open, have been actively involved in developing similar specifications. The X/Open Transport Interface (XTI) is one example of a "competing" framework.

As explained above, the CTS sublayer within the MPTN architecture, allows applications to transparently access a variety of transport networks. An application's use of a particular transport can be classified in one of two ways:

- Native
- Nonnative

An application using a native network implies that it is using the protocol designed for its API. For example, the native network for an APPC application is an SNA network. A nonnative network implies that a switch has been made, in effect pairing an API with a different transport. In the case of the APPC application, this might mean sending the same data over a TCP/IP network.

Functional Distribution

Thus far, most of the discussion has focused on supporting the applications. This would imply an MPTN software capability on all of the hosts involved (at least those accessing a nonnative transport). There are actually several types of MPTN nodes, including:

- Access node
- Gateway node
- Address mapping

Each of these nodes is discussed below. Briefly, however, the access node allows an application to access a nonnative network, while a gateway can be used to bridge unlike networks. The address mapping function can be placed at either the access or gateway node to assist in linking the addressing structures from one network to another.

MPTN Services

The MPTN framework is drawn from the features of SNA, TCP/IP, OSI, and NetBIOS. Because of this, it includes two main types of services:

- Connection-oriented
- Connectionless

The ability to provide these services in a transparent manner across several transport protocols is dependent on four main features. Figure 9.2 lists the primary functions of MPTN.

MPTN Function	Description
Compensation	This feature allows the requirements of the transport provider to be matched to the transport user (application).
Address Mapping	A database which maintains pairs of addresses designed to support requests from the Access and Gateway nodes.
Gateway Routing	A function of the Gateway node which enables data packets to be exchanged between unlike network transports.
Gateway Routing to Native Networks	An instance in the gateway node used to access a native network, where no compensation is required.

Figure 9.2   Main functions provided by MPTN.

The concept of compensation basically involves translating or mapping from one transport to another. It is most natural to think of this function as being closely associated with an application at the host, but a gateway node must also include this capability to join two unlike networks. In fact, compensation together with gateway routing, either nonnative or native (items 3 and 4 in the Figure 9.4), are used to create the MPTN Gateway node. The address mapping function is needed to support mapping between two different transports.

An application, or transport user, relies on the Access node with its compensation function to exchange data over a nonnative node. The Transport Layer Protocol Boundary (TLPB) forms a boundary between the application and the Access node functions. A variety of verbs, specified in more or less a generic fashion, are arranged into six groups, as illustrated in Figure 9.3.

TLPB Verb Category	Description
Initialization	A transport user first makes itself known through a call describing its characteristics.
Address Binding	After initialization, a transport user registers itself with an address.
Connection Setup	As with the socket API, a passive listener and an active call model is used.
Connection Termination	These verbs are paired logically with setup in order to terminate a connection.
Connection-oriented Data Transfer	After a connection has been established, reliable, in-sequence delivery is possible.
Connectionless Data Transfer	These verbs allow datagrams (packets) to be exchanged without connection setup.

Figure 9.3 Categories of the Transport Layer Protocol Boundary verbs.

MPTN Data Formats

In order to provide a completely transparent solution for the applications being supported, the MPTN architecture includes its own data formats. These fall in one of two categories:

- Commands
- Data headers

The commands operate in a typical request-reply fashion, and are used by the distributed MPTN elements. The headers are inserted into normal user data to carry and communicate special MPTN information.

MPTN Data Format	Description
MPTN_Connect	This packet is sent over a transport in order to establish a nonnative network connection.
MPTN_Datagram	The structure used to carry the actual user data over a nonnative transport network.
MPTN_DG_OOB_Data	An "out of band" technique for directing data to flow on a separate, alternative path.

Figure 9.4   Data formats used in MPTN-based communication.

For example, there are several data formats used by MPTN when establishing a connection (connection-oriented service). Figure 9.4 contains a list. The out-of-band format can be used, for example, in the case when expedited data must be sent.

9.4 Types of MPTN Nodes

The MPTN architecture defines three types of nodes, as mentioned above. Each of these shares a set of common MPTN capabilities.

Common Elements and Structure

Figure 9.5 contains a list of the functions common to the MPTN nodes. The Common MPTN Manager (CMM) forms the generic core of the MPTN processing on each node, while the Protocol Specific MPTN Manager (PMM) deals with a particular protocol. There is additional functionality, depending on the node type.

Common Element	Description
Common MPTN Manager (CMM)	A set of commonly used functions designed to support the TLPB and PMM interaction.
Protocol-Specific MPTN Manager (PMM)	Within the Access and Gateway nodes, the PMM interfaces to a specific transport.
Transport Layer Protocol Boundary (TLPB)	Provides a set of services to the transport user in supporting a variety of APIs.
Transport Provider	One of several underlying transport networks which the customer might use.

Figure 9.5 Common internal elements to the MPTN nodes.

Access Node

The Access node, as its name implies, allows access to the network. Its chief characteristic is "compensation" which provides the independence between the API used by the application and the underlying transport network.

Figure 9.6 provides an illustration of the internals of the MPTN Access node. The TLPB forms a boundary with each of the transport users (i.e., applications). The connection is managed by the CMM, with data funneled through the PMM instances.

Also shown in the figure is an address mapping function, which is described below.

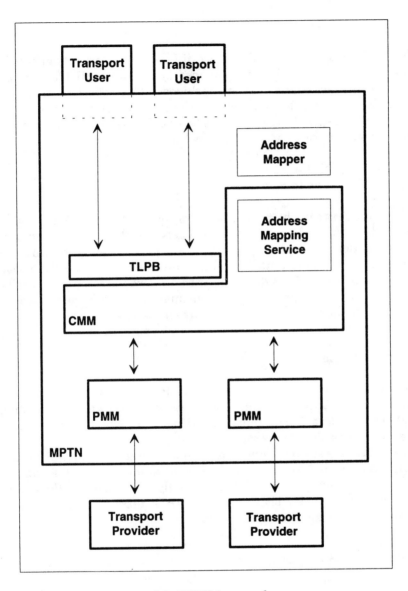

Figure 9.6 Internal structure of the MPTN Access node.

Transport Gateway

The MPTN Gateway node allows two different transport networks to be linked together. In addition to compensation, two other MPTN functions (as drawn from Figure 9.2) are included. This collection of MPTN capability provides flexibility in how the gateway can be positioned.

The Transport Gateway allows two configurations, with respect to the transport networks, to be used by the applications:

- Nonnative-to-nonnative.
- Nonnative-to-native.

In the first case, both end users reply on the Access node capability to access what for them is a nonnative network. The gateway contains compensation for each of the networks, plus Gateway routing. A nonnative-to-native gateway provides Gateway routing and compensation for the nonnative side, along with Gateway access to the native network. The transport user in the nonnative network uses an access node, while the application in the native network does not.

Address Mapper

One of the problems of linking applications with unlike transports involves addressing. Each transport network has its own way of sending and receiving data. For example, TCP/IP uses the 32-bit IP address while the SNA relies on its network address.

The Address Mapper function is fundamentally a database containing the address pairings, from one transport to another. It has flexibility in how it can be implemented, but is usually a part of either the Access and/or Gateway node. The distributed MPTN functions make requests of and receive responses from the Address Mapper.

9.5 Usage Scenarios

There are several ways that MPTN, or AnyNet as it is now called, can be used. Within a single network, it provides flexibility in allowing several different types of applications to communicate. As discussed above, AnyNet products can also be used to link transport networks, thereby further extending the reach.

The examples below give a good introduction to how MPTN can be configured. They move from simple to more complex.

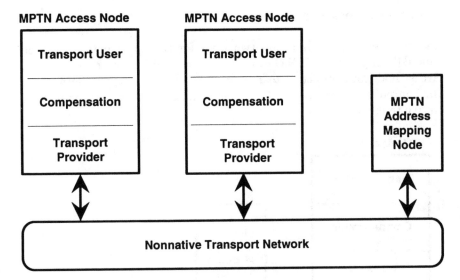

MPTN Access Node

- Transport User
- Compensation
- Transport Provider

MPTN Access Node

- Transport User
- Compensation
- Transport Provider

MPTN Address Mapping Node

Nonnative Transport Network

Figure 9.7 Two transport users connecting through MPTN to a nonnative network.

Native Network Access

It is instructive to first begin with the case where MPTN is not needed. In this case, as has been the case in the past, each application is coupled to the transport. This is referred to as native network access.

For example, two APPC applications on different hosts will communicate through an SNA network. Of course, this implies that each type of application requires its own network. Interoperability is impaired, and expense can increase because of the multiple, parallel networks.

However, even after an AnyNet product has been installed, native network access is still possible. That is, MPTN protocols can be selectively applied.

Nonnative Network Access

The next type of use for MPTN, and also the most natural, is nonnative access. This implies that both transport users connect to the network through the Access node functionality. Their APIs match, but the underlying network does not.

Figure 9.7 contains an illustration of nonnative network access. Here two applications connect through a nonnative network, with compensation provided through the MPTN function in the Access node. An Address Mapping node is also required for address management.

Protocol Conversion at Gateway

As described above, there are two ways for transport networks to be linked through the MPTN Gateway node. Both users can rely on a local Access node for connection to a nonnative network. Or, one connects to the nonnative network while the other communicates with the transport native to its API.

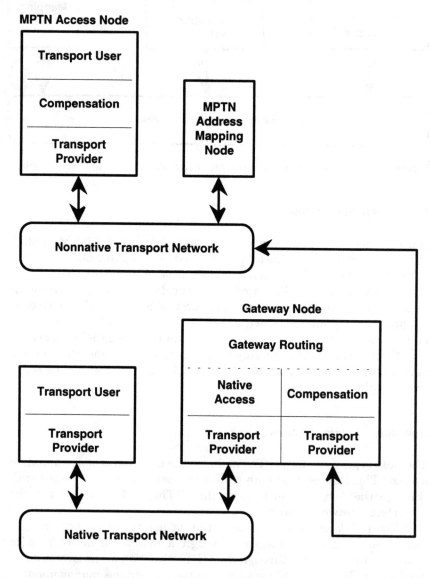

Figure 9.8 A nonnative transport user connecting to a native application through the MPTN Gateway node.

Figure 9.8 provides an illustration of this second case. Here, a transport user in the Access node communicates nonnatively through the gateway. A translation is performed, with a compensation element, and the information is routed to the other network. From here the partner application has a more direct access to the data without the need for MPTN.

9.6 MPTN Implementations

MPTN as an architecture has flexibility as far as how and where it can be implemented. It first became part of the VTAM product under MVS. Since then it has also been implemented under OS/2. The products are now part of the AnyNet family, focusing initially on supporting SNA and TCP/IP.

AnyNet for MVS/ESA

On March, 25 1992, IBM announced its intent to provide a sockets over SNA capability. This was part of the VTAM V4.1 for MVS/ESA phased announcement letter. Of course, this gave the appearance that such support would be included in VTAM V4.1. In September of the same year, the Networking Blueprint was announced.

Then in March of 1993, the MPTN architecture was formally announced, along with its first implementation. The VTAM V3.4.2 for MVS/ESA product includes an optionally orderable priced feature initially called MPTN. The name has subsequently been changed to AnyNet.

The MPTN feature provides two functions:

- APPC over TCP/IP
- Sockets over SNA

This allows the API independence targeted in the Networking Blueprint and MPTN architecture.

At the same time, support is also provided for OS/2. It is shipped with VTAM, and must be downloaded from the host. This feature was later packaged as a separately priced product called AnyNet/2.

AnyNet for OS/2

The AnyNet/2 product is based on the MPTN feature available with VTAM V3.4.2. It includes the same two primary MPTN capabilities as

AnyNet/MVS. In fact, it has been tested for compatibility. Providing this type of communication capability by IBM for both MVS and OS/2 in some ways can facilitate their use in a multiple protocol network. And OS/2 is naturally suited to acting as a front end to MVS-based applications.

Shortly after that, in October of 1993, the AnyNet/2 Sockets over SNA Gateway product was announced. This was a further step in implementing the MPTN architecture.

This product performs the MPTN gateway node function. It allows nonnative socket applications, which utilize SNA as a transport network, to connect to native socket applications through TCP/IP. For example, a host socket application interfaces with the Access node function in order to transmit its data over SNA. The session terminates with OS/2, which transforms the data to flow on an attached TCP/IP network. From here a socket application is connected natively.

Future Directions

It seems likely that both the number of AnyNet implementations and their uses will grow.

Several IBM product groups have in fact stated their intent to implement the MPTN architecture, including:

- AIX SNA Server/6000
- AS/400

Also, some of the entrenched IBM mainframe products will be tailored, as required, to use AnyNet. One example of this is the IMS/ESA Transaction Manager V4.

9.7 AnyNet/MVS Sockets Over SNA

While it is not possible to describe each of the AnyNet products, it will be helpful to at least discuss one. Of the two possible connections mentioned above, the sockets over SNA function in the MVS/ESA environment has been selected. A brief explanation of the operational elements is presented below.

Implementation Overview

Before beginning, it is important to ensure that the software requirements are met. These include:

- MVS/ESA SP Version 3.1.3 or higher
- VTAM Version 3.4.2 with MPTN (AnyNet)
- IBM C/370 Library V2 (PUT 9107 or higher)

The AnyNet feature for MVS/ESA can be installed using SMP/E. Once unloaded, there are several steps that must be performed to complete the implementation, including:

- Define two MVS subsystems.
- Create the internet-to-LU Mapping table definitions.
- Define the SNA network interface.
- Configure the sockets over SNA product.
- Update the VTAM definitions.

Sockets over SNA uses two subsystems, and actually runs as a separate address space. This provides flexibility and guarantees functional separation. For example, any native TCP/IP socket users on the same host are unaffected by and unaware of the AnyNet applications.

Figure 9.9 illustrates the structure of sockets over SNA. Each socket user is served by the internet-LU mapping table, which provides a basic translating between the socket and SNA addressing schemes. At the base, LU type 6.2 (i.e., APPC) sessions are used to transport the data through the SNA network.

There is a wide variety of parameters specific to the sockets over SNA address space which are stored in the ENVVAR data set. A detailed discussion of each value is beyond the scope of this book. The interested reader should consult the product documentation.

The VTAM definitions to be created consist primarily of an Application ID (APPLID) and MODETAB entry. A Cross-Domain Resource Definition (CDRSC) must also be supplied as needed.

Activation and Use

Before an application can be used, it must be recompiled and link edited. Only the C language is supported; sockets over SNA includes header files. If any of the TCP/IP application protocols will be used, the TCP/IP for MVS product libraries will also be needed.

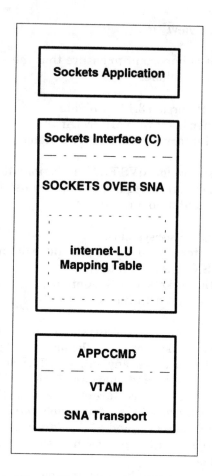

Figure 9.9 Structure of the AnyNet sockets over SNA feature in an MVS/ESA environment.

After the product is installed and the applications are ready, the started task can be activated. At this point, two utility programs can be used:

- SXMAP - provides management of the internet-LU Mapping Table.
- IFCONFIG - assigns an IP address to a specific SNA interface.

Use of the sxmap utility is described below.

Internet-LU Table

The internet-LU table provides the mapping between the internet and SNA addressing worlds. Each entry consists of four values, as shown in Figure 9.10.

Table Value	Description
Internet Address	A fully or partially qualified version of a 32-bit IP address used by TCP/IP.
Address Mask	A 32-bit value which is used to control the entry selection and LU name generated.
SNA Network ID	The Network ID used to describe an SNA network.
LU Name Template	A pattern used as the basis for how the remote (target) LU name is selected.

Figure 9.10   Four values used with the internet-LU Mapping Table entries.

When a socket application initiates a connection request, it supplies the IP address of the remote host. Sockets for SNA receives this information, and using the internet-LU table, generates an SNA LU name. This LU name is then used under the covers to establish an APPC session.

The systems programmer is responsible for matching the IP addresses used by the application to the target LU names. Based on this information, the internet-LU Mapping Table must be updated with the sxmap (TSO-based) utility. The sockets over SNA address space then performs the translation for each request, based on the table.

The algorithm used to select an LU name is complicated. The table is scanned based on the IP address provided and the address mask in each entry. The closest address with the most nonzero bits (i.e., longest mask) is selected. From here, the LU name is generated using the LU name pattern and the remaining mask bits.

Implementation and Management

10

Application Development Options

There are several options available to the application developer, each with its own set of characteristics. The selection of one API over another depends on the nature of the application being created. The available interfaces can generally be arranged into four major categories:

- Part of TCP/IP protocol suite.
- De facto standard.
- Creation by an independent party, with a strong association to TCP/IP.
- Vendor-specific API or extensions.

This chapter will present the major programming interfaces and development options that can be used within the IBM environment. Refer to the appendix for a brief summary of API support by platform.

10.1 Primitive Interfaces

One of the first things to realize about TCP/IP development is that there really is no standard interface to the transport protocols. The TCP RFC indicates that six primitive services are to be "exposed," but does not specify an exact API.

Filling this vacuum, the socket interface, first introduced with the Berkeley Software Distribution (BSD) version of UNIX, has come to be regarded as the de facto standard. However, several other interfaces providing access to network resources through TCP/IP are available on the various IBM platforms and should also be considered.

Programming Interface	Description
Buffer Space Available	Connection buffer space is now available for use with TcpFSend.
Connection State Changed	The new state of a connection, and reason for change, is provided.
Data Delivered	Indication that data has arrived in local receive buffer.
Receive Error	A previous receive operation has failed, with no data delivered.
Send Response	A notification of the result of a previous TcpFSend operation.
Ping Response	Provided when a PING response (or timeout) is received.

Figure 10.1 List of notifications that can be registered by an application in the AS/400 environment (part 1 of 2).

Pascal API

While the socket interface is widely used, there are other TCP/IP access points. One of these is the so-called Pascal API, which is supported by:

- VM
- MVS
- AS/400

Programming Interface	Description
Resouces Available	Local resources are now available to honor a previous open request.
Timer Expired	A notification that the time value on a SetTimer value has expired.
UDP Datagram Delivered	A UDP datagram has been received and placed in local buffer storage.
UDP Datagram Space Available	Space is not available to handle a UdpSend operation.
Urgent Pending	Indication that a very important message has arrived for the connection.

Figure 10.2 List of notifications that can be registered by an application in the AS/400 environment (part 2 of 2).

While there are differences between these three implementations, each operates in the same basic manner. The programming model is asynchronous in nature, and revolves around the concept of notifications. That is, the programmer makes a call that usually returns immediately, even through the process is not yet completed. At various points in the application, the underlying system software will furnish events to the program, in the form of Notification Records. In fact, part of the structured model used in developing such as application involves registering for the various events. The GetNextNote API call is then used to retrieve each notification. Figures 10.1 and 10.2 provide a list of the notifications that can be registered when using the AS/400 Pascal API.

The flow of a typical TCP/IP application using the Pascal API can be summarized as follows:

- Start communication service.
- Establish set of notification events.
- Create connection with partner.
- Exchange data (i.e., send/receive) with local TCP/IP support software.
- Examine status of data exchange operation.
- Terminate the connection.
- End association with communication service.

The data exchange and return code operations are paired together (items 4 and 5), and must frequently be issued multiple times by the application.

Several data structures are used throughout. In addition to the Notification Record mentioned above, the Connection Information Record (CIR) is important. The CIR is analogous to the Transmission Control Block, and holds information describing each of the connections.

While this API is one of several options in the VM and MVS environment, it is the only interface currently available with the AS/400. In this sense, TCP/IP support with the AS/400 has lagged the other platforms. For example, TCP and UDP access is supported, but not (raw) IP datagrams. One bright spot of the AS/400 support is that RPG programs can indirectly make use of TCP/IP services by calling Pascal subroutines, thus facilitating integrating.

Language-Independent Interfaces

Each interface is generally tied to a single language. For example, the socket API has been implemented using the C language. And the Pascal API naturally uses Pascal. In addition to these, VM and MVS support what might be called "language-independent" interfaces. Another way to classify them is low level, because they rely on assembler language access.

These interfaces, both discussed earlier in Chapter 6, include:

- Virtual Machine Communication Facility (VMCF)
- Inter-User Communication Vehicle (IUCV)

VMCF was introduced earlier, and has been largely superseded by IUCV. Both use assembler language, where each application handles external interrupt notifications.

Both of these are supported as part of the TCP/IP environment in MVS. In this case, IUCV is presented as a high-level socket API.

10.2 Socket Support

The socket interface has become a popular and widely implemented model which applications use to access the network resources. There are primarily three socket APIs found within the IBM products:

- Berkeley (BSD)
- Windows (WinSock)
- CICS for MVS

The BSD version is, of course, the basis for the socket interface itself. Each of the IBM platforms (except the AS/400) supports Berkeley-compliant sockets. Chapter 11 describes the OS/2 implementation. In addition, two other interfaces included are presented below.

Windows Socket API

The Windows shell from Microsoft has grown to have an enormous popularity. While Windows PCs can run in a standalone fashion, frequently they are networked together, usually with one or more local LAN servers. In linking these machines, the end user and developer have several networking options from which to select. One of these is TCP/IP connectivity.

Access to TCP/IP from Windows-based applications is possible using the Windows socket interface. This interface provides a consistent programming standard, regardless of the underlying TCP/IP stack. That is, several vendors supply TCP/IP implementations for Windows. These vendors, as well as other interested groups, joined to create the WinSock API.

For the most part, this API follows the BSD standard. However, specific enhancements were necessary given the characteristics of the Windows operating environment. That is, Windows is basically a shell for DOS, and utilizes a message-driven programming model. Therefore, the Windows Socket API can be divided into two major areas:

- Standard BSD API call.
- Extensions which allow integration into the Windows environment.

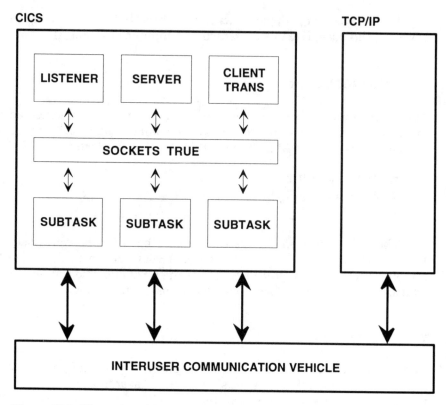

Figure 10.3   Illustration of the CICS/ESA for MVS socket support.

These groupings together form the API, which is assigned a version and release identifier. The WinSock API provided with the IBM TCP/IP for DOS product supports V1.0 and the more recent V1.1.

CICS Socket Interface

Another important socket API, at least for the mainframers, is the CICS/ESA implementation on MVS. This further extends the reach of the networking protocol into the IBM world.

The CICS socket implementation is an enhancement to the CICS product. It allows CICS-based applications (i.e., transactions) to access TCP/IP resources as both a client and server. The TCP/IP for MVS product is required, and establishes communication with the CICS address space through the emulated IUCV facility. Cobol, assembler, and C language programs can be written to utilize the socket interface.

Module	Description
EZACIC00	The Connection Manager, used by the transactions CSKE and CSKD to enable and disable the socket interface.
EZACIC01	The Task Related User Exit (TRUE), which forms the foundation of the socket support in the CICS environment.
EZACIC02	The Master Server (i.e., Listener), running as transaction CSKL, which waits for incoming connection requests.
EZACIC03	The attached subtask program designed to pass data between the transaction and the underlying IUCV interface.
EZACIC04	A utility function which converts data from EBCDIC to ASCII format.
EZACIC05	A utility program which converts data from ASCII to EBCDIC format.
EZACIC06	A bit mask manipulation program, used to convert characters to a bit string for use with the socket SELECT function.
EZACIC07	The C language interface program.

Figure 10.4   List of modules comprising the CICS socket interface (1 of 2).

There are three main types of applications that run as transactions within CICS:

- Master Server, or Listener.
- Server.
- Client.

Each of these issue calls that must be transformed by a stub module, for transmission over an IUCV path. Figure 10.3 provides an illustration of the CICS socket environment.

The CICS transactions make calls to the socket API, which pass through a stub module (EZACICAL). This stub then interacts with the Task Related User Exit (TRUE) facility. TRUE enables the CICS environment to be extended, without corrupting its basic operation. Also, each CICS subtask using the socket interface is supported by a separately attached MVS subtask, as shown. This subtask directly interfaces with the IUCV functions, passing data to the TCP/IP address space.

Figures 10.4 and 10.5 provide a summary of the modules shipped with the CICS product in supporting the interface. Among them are several utility routines and sample programs.

The basic operation depends on whether the application performs a client or server role. The client, which actively connects to a remote server, functions in basically the same manner as would be expected. An application acting as a server must depend on the Master Server, which listens for incoming requests. Part of the request will include the name of the transaction ID to be scheduled as the server. The Master Server helps to effectively create an environment where the server appears to be permanently resident and active.

10.3 Remote Procedure Call

RPC was first discussed in Chapter 4. It is a versatile tool for creating distributed applications, and is actually based on the client/server processing model.

The use of RPC has several advantages. In essence, it allows the application and communication portions of a system to be separated. In this way, development is simplified as programmers can concentrate on the business (application) logic. At the same time, however, the overall design and implementation of a system can become more complicated. The complexity of procedure placement, as well as issues with the protocol language and compiler must be addressed.

Module	Description
EZACICM	The Connection Manager mapset containing all of the BMS maps used when enabling and disabling the interface.
EZACICAL	The Resouce Manager call stub which passes the socket call by invoking the TRUE function.
IUCVMULT	Used by the attached subtask module (EZACIC03) to maintain information regarding the IUCV paths.
EZACICSS	A sample program which illustrates the operation of a server, by accepting incoming client requests.
EZACICSC	A second sample program which interoperates with the Master Server (i.e., Listener) program shipped by IBM.

Figure 10.5   List of modules comprising the CICS socket interface (2 of 2).

Another area for consideration is the diversity of tools available. As mentioned in Chapter 4, there are three major RPC-based models that can be used to create distributed systems:

- Open Network Computing (ONC) model from Sun Microsystems, and included as a part of the TCP/IP protocol suite.
- Network Computing System (NCS) framework, advanced by HP/Apollo.
- Distributed Computing Environment (DCE), as created and licensed by the Open Software Foundation (OSF).

The RPC as part of Sun's ONC has been the most widely implemented, across each of the IBM platforms (except AS/400). It consists of nearly 100 API calls, which can be arranged into several major categories, as shown in Figure 10.6.

API Category	Description
Authentication	Create and destroy authentication information, in the form of handles.
Client Specific	API calls specific to the client side of the logical connection.
Server Specific	API calls specific to the server side of the logical connection.
Port Mapping	Registering, unregistering, and querying the program-to-port mappings.
External Data Representation	The standard for data definition and transmission syntax.
Informational	A limited number of calls used to gather details affecting RPCs usage.

Figure 10.6 A summary of the major categories of API calls included with the TCP/IP standard (Sun Microsystems) RPC.

The more advanced NCS standard is now available within the VM, MVS, and AIX environment (it had been available with TCP/IP for OS/2, but was removed as of the latest release). DCE appears to be taking a very prominent position with respect to IBM's strategic plans. For this reason, it is presented more completely in a separate section below.

10.4 Graphical User Interface

Within the TCP/IP world, the X Window System GUI is widely implemented and most closely associated with the networking protocol. As illustrated in Chapter 4, this includes a basic underlying Xlib as well as various toolkits and widget sets.

X Window Roles

X is based on a client/server model, with the roles inverted according to what is normally expected. Stated simply, the server is the display terminal while the client is the back-end application using the display.

The server can take many forms, including dedicated X terminals. Within the IBM product line, AIX, OS/2, and DOS (through third-party software) can act as a display server.

Widget Set	Description
Athena	A simple set of widgets which was created by MIT for use with X Windows.
Motif	An adaptation of the OSF Motif style to the X Windows system.

Figure 10.7   Widget sets included with the X Windows system platform support.

The X client has been implemented in VM, MVS, OS/2, and AIX. It allows applications to be developed which communicate with and control remote X (server) terminals.

X Client Applications

The first decision that needs to be made when creating an X Window System client application is which platform will be used. Several factors can be involved, including platform availability and cost, implementation features, and integration with legacy applications.

Although this is not always advisable, the developer can write to the low-level Xlib specifications. While allowing a high degree of control, this process can be tedious and time consuming. As an alternative, two primary widget (i.e., graphical object) sets are available as shown in Figure 10.7.

Integration with GDDM

In recent years, IBM has promoted its Graphical Data Display Manager (GDDM) product as an alernative to X Windows. It runs on both VM and MVS, and supports the creation and manipulation of graphical images for display on the special IBM 3270 terminals (e.g., 3179G). While GDDM is fundamentally incompatible with the X Window System, IBM has provided integration between the two environments.

An X to GDDM interface (GDDMXD) is available on two of the client platforms:

- VM (GDDMXD/VM)
- MVS (GDDMXD/MVS)

Each of these is installed and configured as a part of normal product installation. They operate in fundamentally the same manner, transforming GDDM to X Windows API calls. While able to support most types of applications, there are a few limitations for both the application's design and use of the display.

To be used, GDDMXD must first be enabled. This is accomplished with a CLIST (MVS) or command (VM). Also, as part of customization, the target X display must be identified using a TSO or CMS variable. IBM has provided problem determination capabilities (e.g., trace), which are particularly useful during early stages of the interface's deployment. In practice, however, IBM's support of GDDMXD is rather limited.

FTP API	Description
DOS FTP	A set of API routines for use by DOS-based programs.
Windows FTP	Equivalent to the DOS API, this set is designed for use with Windows.
OS/2 FTP	An API provided with the TCP/IP for OS/2 product.

Figure 10.8   Three file transfer APIs available within the IBM environment.

10.5 File Transfer

The ability to transfer files among hosts within the internetwork is, of course, an important and widely used capability. Normally, operators access these functions through text mode FTP commands. A user will "FTP" to a remote site, and then proceed to change and list directories, and send or receive files.

IBM also enables these functions to be accessed through a set of API routines. Actually, there are three APIs as shown in Figure 10.8. One is used by OS/2 programs, and two are available for DOS. Both of these environments are front-end clients, which points to the fact that their inherent graphical capabilities can be integrated with the file transfer operations.

All three operate in the same basic manner. The APIs mirror the FTP commands normally provided with an FTP implementation. Figure 10.9 provides an example of an API call designed for the Windows environment.

The parameters shown in the figure include:

- HOST - host where FTP server resides.
- USERID - user's logon ID.
- PASSWD - corresponding password.

■ ACCT - the account (optional).
■ DIR - new working directory.

This API call is used to change the working directory on an active session from an application running under Windows.

```
WINftpcd(host, userid, passwd, acct, dir)
```

Figure 10.9   An example of an FTP API call for the Windows environment.

10.6 SNMP Distributed Programming Interface

As described in Chapter 4, the SNMP standard is implemented at the application layer and uses UDP as the transport protocol. It is based on the concept of one or more agents reporting to a central manager.

Each agent presents the local resources to a manager in terms of its MIB definitions. These MIB variables, and the agent function itself, are normally "hard-coded," and therefore difficult to update or enhance. It is often necessary to replace (i.e., recompile) the agent in order to make any change in its functional characteristics or the nature of the resources supported. For example, when a MIB group or set of variables is to be added, the entire agent must be updated, reinstalled, and then reactivated.

This inflexibility, of course, has several drawbacks. It can slow the support of new network resources managed through SNMP. Software interoperability at the agent is also reduced.

In order to address these problems, techniques have been developed for creating SNMP "subagents." These are separate programs which associate themselves with the local agent. In this way, the SNMP agent can be dynamically extended, a process which does not interfere with its normal functions and features.

There are two major standards used in creating and supporting SNMP subagents:

■ SNMP Multiplexing (SMUX) protocol
■ SNMP Agent Distributed Programming Interface (DPI)

The SMUX protocol, which is supported by AIX for use with the System Monitor/6000 product, was published in RFC 1227. It is now historic, with its implementation not recommended. SNMP DPI is the preferred subagent standard which is implemented in the VM, MVS, and

OS/2 environments. There have also been indications that SNMPv2 will evolve to include this type of capability, although status of such an enhancement is unclear at the time of this writing.

Functional Overview

SNMP DPI was created by IBM, and first published in RFC 1228 in May, 1991. These specifications form the basis for current implementations, and describe the basic protocol operations and data formats. However, this RFC is now obsolete. Version 2.0 of the SNMP DPI was published in March, 1994 in RFC 1592. It is now in an experimental state, and represents the next major revision of the protocol.

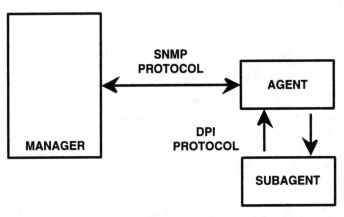

Figure 10.10   An illustration of the DPI subagent within the standard SNMP framework.

DPI provides flexibility, effectively allowing the agent's MIB to be extended. Objects can be dynamically added, deleted, and replaced, without the need to recompile the agent itself. Instead, the subagent executes externally, connecting to the agent in a predefined manner.

Figure 10.10 presents an illustration of the framework. The SNMP DPI protocol is used between the agent and subagent. A variety of defined data units are used to communicate specific information and events. The manager interacts as usual with the agent using the normal SNMP protocol, and has no knowledge of DPI or the subagent.

DPI mirrors the operation of SNMP in that two basic operations can be used. First, when the agent receives a request for an object maintained by a subagent, it passes the request through. Also, traps can be created by the subagent. Both responses to the solicited requests as well as the trap messages are passed to the manager through the local agent.

The use of SNMP DPI creates a level of abstraction, where the sub-agent code is not required to deal with the complexities of ASN.1 or the SNMP data formats (both introduced in Chapter 4). This, as well as the possibility of quick enhancements and product integration, should help to speed the standard's acceptance.

Operational Elements

There have been some changes from specifications that were originally published. Some of the details presented below apply to the current version 2, although the general concepts are common to both.

The first step necessary to use SNMP DPI is for the agent to support the protocol. The major aspects of this support include:

- Support of DPI MIB group.
- Implementation of a DPI-compliant API.
- Connectivity to the subagent(s) through an advertised TCP or UDP port.
- Ability to maintain information regarding the sub-agent, such as what MIB variables it is responsible for.
- Function as a type of a protocol converter, exchanging data between the SNMP manager and the DPI sub-agent.

The DPI MIB maintained by the agent includes the TCP and UDP port numbers over which subagent connections will be accepted. Once activated, the subagent dynamically selects a local port and sends a normal SNMP get request to the agent (at port 161) to determine the DPI port. At this point, the subagent can establish a TCP connection with the agent. Individual MIB variables or subtrees can be registered with the agent, which will then cause requests to be funneled to the subagent.

Application Interface

The API implemented is strongly suggested by the features provided and the original RFC (which includes an API). However, the exact application interface can vary, and depends on the agent and characteristics of the platform.

Figure 10.11 presents the function calls which make up the current MVS SNMP DPI implementation.

DPI Routine	Description
fDPIparse	Used to free a "parse tree," the representation of a request created by the subagent with pDPIpacket.
mkDPIregister	An object identifier, in dotted decimal format, is used to create a request packet for the agent.
mkDPIresponse	This function creates a response packet, indicating the results of a previous request.
mkDPIset	Used to create a portion of the parse tree from input including object ID, type, and value.
mkDPItrap	Both generic and enterprise-specific traps, in the form of DPI packets, can be created.
pDPIpacket	Accepts a DPI request and generates a parse tree as output, for use by the subagent.
query_DPI_port	This API call is first used by the subagent in order to determine the agent's DPI port number.

Figure 10.11 A list of API calls available with the MVS implementation of the SNMP DPI standard.

The "query_DPI_port" function allows the subagent to determine the port over which the agent will accept requests. After registering the MIB variables, requests arrive in the form of packets, which must be parsed by the subagent.

The agent can send the following requests to the subagent:

- GET
- GET_NEXT
- GET_BULK
- SET
- COMMIT
- UNDO
- UNREGISTER
- CLOSE

Likewise, the subagent can generate requests, such as OPEN, REGISTER, TRAP, UNREGISTER, and CLOSE.

Updates with Version 2.0

The version 2.0 specifications include changes and enhancements which generally strengthen the protocol. To summarize, the major updates include:

- The exact API specification has been removed, allowing implementation flexibility.
- Improved security.
- Confirmation flows for requests, as well as dynamic inquires.
- Improved performance.
- Support for SNMPv2.

Of course, the protocol is still in the experimental state and could change further as it moves through the standardization process.

10.7 Distributed Computing Environment

The DCE standard from OSF is an important RPC-based framework for the development of distributed applications. It is a descendent of the earlier NCS architecture. DCE is relevant to the TCP/IP user in general because, in its basic form, TCP and UDP provide both the connection-oriented and connectionless transport, respectively.

For the IBM user in particular, DCE will almost certainly be of major importance. This is because virtually all of the platforms have (or will have) support for DCE. This includes the six primary TCP/IP platforms presented in this book (Chapter 6). Therefore, it seems very likely that many IBM users will begin to encounter DCE in the near future.

Still some people point to the fact that DCE is not yet in widespread use. It is important to realize, however, that the acceptance of any new technology takes time. Also, IBM seems to be pushing DCE (i.e., perhaps a bit prematurely) in response to competitive pressures. DCE will serve as the foundation for future advances, such as distributed object computing (i.e., Distributed System Object Model, or DSOM). Also, in spite of any type of perceived "lukewarm" reaction, the use of DCE does have several fundamental advantages, especially for those with a large number and variety of heterogeneous computing resources. It is an industrial strength framework for the delivery of distributed applications. And it has been designed to interoperate with several (de facto) standards, including DNS, X.500, and Microsoft's own RPC-based (i.e., domain) processing model.

As an architecture, DCE is rather complex. Of course, it helps if the user has had previous RPC experience, especially with ONC, NCS, or Microsoft RPC (very similar to NCS and DCE). Figure 10.12 contains a list of the component parts of the DCE architecture.

A Collection of Cells

The most important concept with DCE, at least from an administrative point of view, is that of the "cell." A cell forms the most basic unit of system organization and administration.

Each enterprise using DCE is divided into one or more cells, the exact size and boundaries of which are defined by the systems administrator. DCE, therefore, is a scalable architecture. The cell boundaries usually revolve around either organization or geographic considerations.

Although it has a rich and evolving set of specifications, the user need not implement all of the services listed in Figure 10.12. However, each cell requires as a minimum:

- Remote Procedure Call (RPC)
- Cell Directory Services (CDS)
- Security Service (SS)
- Time Service (TS)

During installation, the machines within the cell must be configured to point to these key services.

DCE Component	Description
Remote Procedure Call	RPC forms the core of DCE, and is used by the distributed applications and system services.
Threads	Optional POSIX-compliant support for the creation and management of threads within a process; can improve concurrency and RPC throughput.
Directory Service	Repository of resources defined to the local Cell Directory Service (CDS) and the Global Directory Service (GDS).
Distributed Time Service	Enables the control of DCE machines through an international standard for timing synchronization.
Security Service	Allows for authentication and secured access to the resources in a DCE environment.
Distributed File Service	Files can be accessed and shared across the enterprise through a global naming standard.
Diskless Support Service	PCs without local disks can be IPL'ed and configured over the network.

Figure 10.12 Component parts of the DCE architecture.

RPC as a Foundation

DCE is not an application, but rather (as pointed out above) a set of services that together provide an environment within which to build distributed systems. RPC is the most important operational element of the framework. It is used not only by the applications built on top of DCE, but also by the DCE services themselves.

The basics of RPC were presented in Chapter 4. Architecturally, the DCE RPC is very similar to that of NCS. Each interface (or program) is assigned a globally unique ID, called the universally unique ID (UUID). The UUIDs are generated by a utility (uuidgen).

The Interface Definition Language (IDL) is used as input for the protocol compiler, which creates the client and server stub modules, as well as other output (e.g., header files).

Part of the responsibility of directory services is to work with both the client and server elements to ensure that a logical "binding" can take place during RPC processing.

11

Socket Interface for OS/2

The socket programming interface has been mentioned throughout the book. It is the de facto interface standard for applications accessing the underlying TCP/IP transport network.

This chapter begins by exploring the history and characteristics of the socket model in more depth. Then an implementation is examined. Specifically, the API and programming environment provided with the TCP/IP for OS/2 V2.0 product will be discussed.

11.1 History and Evolution

The concept of using a layered model to organize and describe a networking architecture came about with the ARPANET and early TCP/IP specifications. Of course, research in this area had been active before that time, especially at companies such as IBM (which unveiled SNA at about the same time as the introduction of TCP/IP, in 1974).

An important aspect of the layering approach has been that networks and their specifications no longer revolve solely around physical transmission. There is now a logical networking element, which can be designed to support a variety of underlying network protocols. This allows larger, enterprise-wide networks to be constructed. In the case of TCP/IP, the 32-bit IP address, and corresponding routing protocols, provide this capability through link level network independence. Indeed, IP is designed to form the basis for a large virtual internetwork spanning multiple networks, each of which perhaps using different link level protocols.

Of course, applications (and users) must ultimately be able to access the transport network. A programming interface is normally provided. With TCP/IP, there is no standard interface defined by the architecture. In its place, several API sets have been published for use. The two most widely used of these include:

- Socket interface
- Transport Layer Interface (TLI)

The socket interface has become the de facto standard, with virtually a universal acceptance. The TLI interface, as associated and provided with the early versions of UNIX from AT&T, is more flexible (e.g., mapping to the OSI transport layer) but frequently not available.

Association with UNIX

One of the milestones along the way toward the rapid acceptance of TCP/IP was its implementation within the Berkeley Software Distribution (BSD) version of UNIX in 1983. It is largely because of this event that UNIX and TCP/IP have been closely associated. Indeed, both are key elements of what would later be popularized as the open systems movement.

The characteristics and content of the socket API were naturally influenced by the UNIX programming environment. Accessing data from a disk file involved using a well-established, but limited, set of API calls. During file open processing, a file descriptor (integer) is returned for use in the subsequent read and write operations.

Taking it a step further, accessing data from a local disk drive is analogous to accessing data from the network. Conceptually, both are functionally similar. Therefore, the designers of the socket model started from the UNIX file I/O model. Both derive from the basic processing model.

However, it quickly became obvious that the network I/O had a larger set of requirements. There were all types of considerations, such as support for network-wide naming, types of service (e.g., connectionless), and the changing nature of the transport as well as physical transmission capabilities.

Therefore, the socket API was enhanced and made more general in order to deal with the complexities of the network. It essentially allows a process-to-process connectivity, where the programs can be distributed throughout the network. Certain aspects of the UNIX file system were kept, such as the numeric description or handle.

Socket Abstraction

The socket abstraction represents an end point of a two-way communication link. It allows an application to "plug into" the network to exchange data. A socket pairing can be established between two applications. A connection formally exists in the case where TCP is used. Also, the socket API can be used with UDP but in a connectionless fashion, placing more of a demand upon the applications themselves. Figure 11.1 presents the values that uniquely define a TCP connection between two socket-based applications.

```
{ protocol, local-address, local-process, remote-address, remote-process }
```

Figure 11.1   Set of five values which describe a unique process-to-process socket connection.

One of the most important aspects of the socket model, which can be ascertained from the figure, is its generic nature. That is, the socket interface is designed to be transport independent. While the API remains the same, the underlying networking can change. This has the advantage allowing the transport details to be hidden from the application. However, developers using the API are still aware of the network in several ways. For example, data must be explicitly sent and received by the program. Contrast this to the RPC programming model, where even the transport of data at a high level is not handled by the application.

Some of the transports that have been used to carry socket data include:

- TCP/IP internet.
- Xerox PUP internet.
- AppleTalk network (Apple Computer).
- UNIX file system.

In fact, part of what is declared during the sequence of startup API calls is the type of transport address (i.e., addressing family) to be used. The TCP/IP for OS/2 product only supports the TCP/IP internet family. In this case, the IP address is used for the local and remote addresses as shown in Figure 11.1. The Transport layer protocol port numbers define the process end points. And for any connection, the protocol being used must be the same for both sides (e.g., TCP or UDP).

Another important concept to recognize about the TCP/IP socket API is that implementations can vary. That is, BSD serves as a model and is followed very closely. However, a socket API on one platform might be slightly different from that of another platform. This includes the nature and content of the API calls, as well as things like the C language header files.

Access to the TCP/IP Transport Network

A socket interface can access the TCP/IP network in several manners, as illustrated in Figure 11.2. Either of the two Transport layer protocols can be used. In the case of accessing the Internet layer, both the IP and ICMP protocols are typically available.

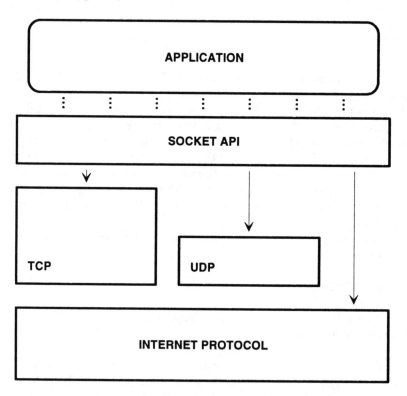

Figure 11.2 Illustration of the socket interface used to access the network through TCP or UDP Transport protocols, or directly to the IP and ICMP protocols through the system.

The exact representation of a socket, both local and remote, depends on the addressing family being used. To enable the support of the variety of transports listed, sockets are named and addressed in a universally accepted manner.

A socket descriptor, similar to the UNIX file descriptor, is used by the application when referring to the socket. This handle is simply an integer value referenced on subsequent calls. Under the covers, the characteristics of the particular network transport dictate the local and process addresses that are used. To allow for and promote a variety of addressing schemes, the "sockaddr" structure is used. This data area begins with a 16-bit field which first identifies the addressing domain used, followed by up to 14 bytes of data. The exact format and content of this second section depends on the transport.

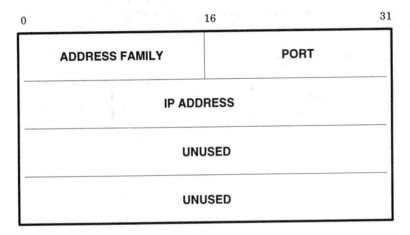

Figure 11.3   Representation of a TCP/IP socket through the sockaddr structure.

Figure 11.3 provides an illustration of the sockaddr structure as used with a TCP/IP socket. In this case, the TCP/IP internet addressing family has been selected. As expected, the port number and IP address are included. The final 8 bytes must be set equal to zero.

11.2 Processing Model

The designers of application interfaces make explicit and implicit assumptions regarding how the APIs will be used by the programmer. For example, at its core APPC assumes a peer-to-peer interaction, where either side can initiate a conversation. Also, the data is exchanged as logical records (versus a byte stream).

The socket model used with TCP/IP is based on a client/server model. While APPC (and other interfaces) can be adapted to the design of a client/server application, the concept is built right into the socket model.

Client/Server Applications

While client/server has recently moved into the mainstream, it has been a part of TCP/IP for quite a while. In fact, the majority of the applications operate in this fashion. A common configuration is shown in Figure 11.4. One application will act as a server, passively waiting for new connections. Each server is usually persistent, allowing a number of clients to establish connections at the same time.

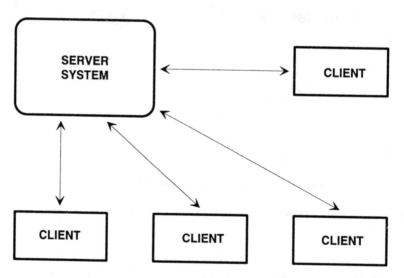

Figure 11.4 Multiple clients connected to a single server.

The client sends a request, which is processed by the server. The ability to act within this request-response model is one of the foundations of TCP/IP socket-based applications.

TCP versus UDP

There are several differences between TCP and UDP, as discussed earlier. TCP is connection-oriented, and allows applications to exchange data as a stream of bytes across the transport network. UDP is connectionless, and enforces the transmission of individual datagrams between applications, one per sent operation.

The use of TCP allows a clearer division to be made between the client and server functions. With UDP, the distinction is still there, but not as well defined.

TCP is based on the concept of a connection which predisposes the socket to operating in a certain manner. There are also differences in the functions used. For example, the server will issue the "listen" API call to allow connection requests (from clients) to be queued for processing.

With UDP, there is no connection. Therefore, both the IP address and port number of the remote partner are usually extracted from the datagram and made available to the receiver. This information must then be used when sending a reply. This model can be used in the most general case of one server connected to multiple clients. UDP also can support a direct one-to-one pairing between socket applications. In this case, the applications are not required to continually respecify the partner's addressing information.

TCP Interface

The RFC documenting TCP includes six basic services that each implementation should provide. It is primarily upon these interfaces that the socket API is built.

While the socket is an abstraction used at the application layer, the implementation-dependent Transmission Control Block (TCB) is maintained by TCP. Each TCP connection is described by a unique TCB, which contains a variety of fields. While the exact content of the TCB is not specified by the standard, it will usually include information regarding the operation of the socket and the management of the connection. Refer to Chapter 3 for more on the TCB and its contents.

Distributed Applications on Heterogeneous Platforms

Both the socket interface in general and TCP/IP as a specific transport were designed to be platform independent. The implementations of each were designed to be adapted for integration into the local operating system environment.

This has meant that a wide variety of hosts now support TCP/IP sockets. Enabling this distribution of processing across an array of heterogeneous platforms involves several considerations, including:

- Ability to locate remote server machines through the use of a universal naming standard.
- Support for different styles of data representation on the individual hosts.

The first of these is typically, though not universally, handled through the Domain Name System (DNS) with a name server. If a name server is not available, then vendor specific schemes might be used. Finally, local definitions for the name-to-address translation can be made available (i.e., HOSTS file in OS/2, discussed below).

Data representation and interpretation is an important area of communications affecting interoperability. Each processor has its own way of storing and manipulating data. At a basic level, the data within each field can be arranged in one of two ways:

- Big endian - most significant byte first in field.
- Little endian - least significant byte first in field.

The TCP/IP architecture is based on the big endian style. Hosts with processors not founded on this approach must support conversion between the so-called "host byte order" and the standard network byte order.

Some of the socket calls require parameters in network byte order. If a host does not use the big endian style, the application must provide a translation. A group of functions included as a part of the socket interface support this translation between host and network byte order.

11.3 OS/2 Implementation

The socket API, along with several other 32-bit APIs (as mentioned in Chapter 6), is included as a part of the Programmer's Kit for Version 2.0 of the TCP/IP product. It must be installed in the OS/2 environment before being available for use.

Processing Environment

OS/2 is an elegant, fully functional operating system. It supports 32-bit virtual addressing within multiple processes. The dispatching of threads is carried out by the kernel in a preemptive fashion.

File	Description
HOSTS	Holds information describing hosts, such as name to address mapping, passed through the hostent structure.
NETWORKS	Holds information describing networks and routing, passed within the netent data area.
PROTOCOL	Contains protocol information, by number, which is passed in the protoent structure.
SERVICES	Standard services and port numbers are defined and accessed through the servent data area.
RESOLV	Used as the root of a DNS lookup, in that the name server is defined.

Figure 11.5 OS/2 files holding configuration data which directly affects the operation of the socket programs.

OS/2 has been compared to UNIX and also to MVS. As a practical matter, all high quality operating systems share many characteristics. While OS/2 is indeed similar to UNIX, it is also different (and superior) in many ways. The most immediate difference is its native GUI support. Also, each OS/2 process can have one or more threads. However, many versions of UNIX, even today, allow only a single thread per process.

In particular, there are differences between the standard BSD socket interface and the one supplied with OS/2; this topic is examined later in the chapter.

Installation and Use

There are four primary libraries directly related to application development: two DLLs and two corresponding import libraries. The two DLLs are:

- SO32DLL - Socket library functions.
- TCP32DLL - TCP/IP network library functions.

Support has been integrated with the C Set/2 compiler and tool kit. When developing a program, it must of course be compiled ("icc" command) and linked ("link386"). Before this is done, however, the socket libraries must be included in the OS/2 configuration file (CONFIG.SYS). This allows the executable images, DLLs, import libraries, headers, and help files to be located.

Configuration Libraries

In addition to the normal libraries included, supporting execution and development, there are also several files which determine the local configuration. Figure 11.5 includes a list of the libraries affecting the configuration of TCP/IP; these are comparable to those used with a UNIX implementation.

Each of these can be accessed through socket API calls, as discussed below. In each case, a data area is used to hold each file entry during a read or update operation.

11.4 API Calls by Functional Category

There are over 60 API calls supported with the OS/2 socket library. This section presents the API calls, organizing them into functional groups.

Socket Setup

This class deals with setting up the local socket, as shown in Figure 11.6. The first two are used at both the client and server. SOCK_INIT is an IBM invention that must be issued first in order to perform initialization particular to the OS/2 environment.

The SOCKET call returns a unique socket descriptor; an example is shown in Figure 11.7. The three types of data transmission map to TCP, UDP, and IP as shown.

Socket API	Description
SOCK_INIT	First API call, which is used to initialize OS/2-specific socket data areas.
SOCKET	Creates the socket endpoint, and returns a (small integer) socket descriptor.
BIND	Associates a socket with a specific local address (IP and port).
LISTEN	After binding to an IP/port combination, the server listens for connection requests.

Figure 11.6 API calls used for socket connection setup and initialization.

The BIND function associates the socket, through its descriptor, with a local address as held in the SOCK_ADDR structure (i.e., the protocol port and IP address). In particular, the server uses this call to communicate through a well-known or otherwise predefined port. A client can optionally use this function to explicitly bind to a local address before requesting a connection.

LISTEN is again used by the server. It specifies the length of a queue to hold incoming connection requests. When this queue is exceeded, additional requests are discarded.

Socket Management

There are a number of calls that can be grouped under the category of socket management; Figure 11.8 includes a list.

```
s = socket(domain, type, protocol)

where:

    "s" is the socket descriptor (output)

    "domain" is the addressing family (AF_INET for TCP/IP)

    "type" is data transmission characteristic
    (stream (TCP), datagram (UDP), raw (IP/ICMP))

    "protocol" is the transport protocol, which is redundant
    and determined by the "type" in the case of TCP/IP.
```

Figure 11.7   Example of the SOCKET API call.

As its name implies, ACCEPT is used to accept a connection request from a client. The CONNECT call, on the other, actively initiates a TCP connection request, and is issued by the client. Also, it has a slightly different function when used with UDP instead of TCP. In this case, CONNECT associates a local socket with a specific remote socket. While a connection is not really established, it can "lock" the sockets together such that subsequent send and receive operations are not required to continually specify the remote socket address.

The SELECT call is especially useful when multiple connections, through different sockets, are being used. The caller can monitor activity by waiting on a variable number of sockets. In each case, four types of events can satisfy the call:

- Read - data to be read.
- Write - data to be written.
- Exception condition - a pending condition requiring attention.
- Timeout - expiration of a time value, as provided with the API call.

Also, there are two versions of select supported: BSD and OS/2-specific. They perform essentially the same function, although the manner in which the parameter values are constructed differs.

There are two calls relating to error information. SOCK_ERRNO retrieves an error number from a previous socket call. PSOCK_ERRNO is used to write a message (e.g., as received from SOCK_ERRNO) to the standard error device (log).

Socket API	Description
ACCEPT	After issuing LISTEN, the server can then accept client connection requests.
CONNECT	WIth TCP, this call is used by the client to establish a connection to a server.
SELECT	Used to monitor several sockets for pending events.
SOCK_ERRNO	Returns an error value from a previous socket call for processing.
PSOCK_ERRNO	Used to write a socket error message to the active error device.
SOCLOSE	Used to close a socket, and free the resources associated with it.
SHUTDOWN	Closes the connection, possibly in one direction only, depending on argument.
IOCTL	A remnant from the UNIX file I/O model, providing control over a variety of socket, transport, and network characteristics.

Figure 11.8 API calls used for socket management.

Socket API	Description
RES_INIT	Reads the RESOLVE file to determine the default name server to be used.
RES_MKQUERY	Used to construct a query in the RES data structure, for use by the name server.
RES_SEND	Sends the request to the name server, and receives reply in target buffer.

Figure 11.9   API calls used for name resolution through the DNS.

Both SOCLOSE and SHUTDOWN are used to terminate a connection, although the later provides more flexibility and control.

Finally, the IOCTL function is used with UNIX file I/O and is also supported in the socket API. It allows for the control of the socket "I/O channel." This includes the socket itself, as well as the underlying transport and network characteristics. For example, a socket can be placed in nonblocking mode. This causes any other API routines that would normally wait to continue program execution instead. Also, the IP routing and ARP information can be accessed, as well as the network interfaces.

Domain Name Server

Traditionally, domain-related (i.e., host name to IP address mapping) information has been stored in one of two locations: a local sequential file or DNS (name server). Within the socket API, there are two corresponding subsets that can be used to access this data:

- Explicit resolver function.
- Direct access to the HOSTS file.

Figure 11.9 contains a list of the API calls included with OS/2 used to explicitly issue a request to the name server. Part of this involves determining its location, as shown with the RES_INIT call. Also included with this group are DN_COMP and DN_EXPAND, used to compress and expand a domain name during formulation and retrieval.

The HOSTS file can also be read in determining host information. This file is technically considered to be a part of the configuration files, listed below. However, there is some overlap with respect to the DNS.

Specifically, the following two API routines can be used to request translation:

- GetHostByName - returns IP address.
- GetHostByAddr - returns host name.

Both will first try to use the domain name server, if available. If not, the HOSTS file is searched on behalf of the caller. Also, there is another group of calls, discussed below, used by a program to directly read through the HOSTS configuration file.

Accessing Configuration Files

Of the five configuration files listed in Figure 11.5, four can be directly read through the socket interface. These include:

- HOSTS
- NETWORKS
- PROTOCOL
- SERVICES

For each file, five calls are available. They are used to sequentially open, read, search, and close the target file. Figure 11.10 presents the calls used with the SERVICES file.

As with the other files, access to the SERVICES file is through a standard control block, in this case called "servent." The fields in this data area, of importance to a developer, include:

- Name
- Alias (if used)
- Port number
- Protocol to be used

Socket API	Description
SETSERVENT	Used to open the SERVICES file, and rewind the read pointer to the beginning.
GETSERVENT	Reads the next entry from the SERVICES file, placing the data in a SERVENT data structure for use by the application.
GETSERVBYNAME	Used to search the file by a provided name until a match occurs.
GETSERVBYPORT	Used to search the file by a provided port number until a match occurs.
ENDSERVENT	Closes the SERVICES file.

Figure 11.10 API calls used to access the SERVICES configuration file.

The SERVICES file describes the standard services that are locally implemented. These include applications, such as SMTP and FTP, that are a part of the TCP/IP protocol suite as well as user-written applications.

Internet Address Management

A set of six functions are included for use with the internet address. These provide a convenient method for handling these addresses, such as their conversion between different representations. Figure 11.11 contains a list.

Socket API	Description
INET_ADDR	Transforms a network address written in dotted decimal to internet format.
INET_LNAOF	Breaks apart the host address to return the local network address.
INET_MAKEADDR	Builds an internet address from a network and host portion.
INET_NETOF	Given an internet address, provides the network number portion.
INET_NETWORK	Constructs a network number from the dotted decimal representation passed in.
INET_NTOA	Transforms an internet address to dotted decimal notation.

Figure 11.11 API calls used to access and transform internet addresses.

Exchanging Data

Figure 11.12 provides a list of the interface routines used to send and receive socket data. These can be divided roughly into those to be used by connected (i.e., connection-oriented) sockets where a stream of data is exchanged, and those dealing with datagram blocks over a connectionless transport (i.e., UDP).

Another special case of a send operation, though not part of the socket API itself, is the REXEC API call. This is issued in order to forward a command to a remote host for executive.

Socket API	Description
READV	What has been called a "scatter" read, in that data is read and placed into an array of buffers.
RECV	Used to receive data over from a connection-oriented socket, using TCP.
RECVFROM	Used to receive a datagram from a socket using connectionless UDP.
RECVMSG	Receives a message from a socket, which is placed in the structure "msghdr".
SEND	Provides the ability to send data through a connected socket.
SENDMSG	Allows messages to be sent, as anchored in the data structure "msghdr".
SENDTO	Used to send a datagram over a socket using the connectionless UDP.
WRITEV	Allows data to be written during one operation from a collection of buffers.

Figure 11.12 API calls used for data exchange between socket programs.

Socket API	Description
GETHOSTID	Returns the 32-bit (IP) address of the local host, in host byte order.
GETHOSTNAME	This API call returns the local host name, set to be the domain name.
GETPEERNAME	Given the number of the connected socket, returns the name of the remote host.
GETSOCKNAME	Returns the local address used for a socket with the specific socket descriptor.
GETSOCKOPT	Used by the application to request information about a named socket.

Figure 11.13 API calls used to access socket and host information.

Informational

There is another group, as shown in Figure 11.13, that can be used to obtain information about the socket interface and the network in general.

Data Manipulation

In developing a socket-based program, it is convenient to be able to transform and manipulate data fields. There are four API calls used to convert between host and network byte order, for short and long integers. These include:

- HTONL
- HTONS
- NTOHL
- NTOHS

The name in each case is self-explanatory. For example, HTONL converts a long integer from host to network byte order.

11.5 Programming Example

The exact use of the socket interface varies depending on the application, and can be quite complicated. However, it is possible to illustrate its basic operation with a simple example based on the byte stream (TCP connection) model.

Server Setup

The first step in socket setup is to issue the SOCK_INIT call. As mentioned above, this is particular to OS/2. It first checks the local environment, and then initializes the socket-related control blocks.

The SOCKET call is the official start of the program with respect to the interface. As shown above, the TCP/IP internet addressing family is declared along with the type of interaction desired. When using TCP, this is stream-oriented exchange.

A server will almost always issue BIND, which links the socket to a specific port and IP address combination. This determines which incoming connection requests will be honored, based on how they arrive at the server's host. An option also exists to effectively specify "any" for the IP address, allowing the server program to receive requests from any of the host's IP connections. Of course, this will only be relevant in a multi-homed (i.e., multiple IP address) host.

The next interface call used is LISTEN, which specifies the length of the queue to hold incoming connection requests. After this, the operating system can begin queuing the pending connections.

Finally, ACCEPT allows one client request at a time to be processed. For each new connection, a unique socket descriptor is generated, which corresponds to the connection and underlying TCB control block. The original socket descriptor is still available, and is used in subsequent

ACCEPT commands. To summarize, the single socket (originally declared) fields incoming client requests. Each of these is assigned a new
socket descriptor handle used by the application when sending and
receiving the data.

Connection Establishment by the Client

As with the server, the client will also use the SOCK_INIT and SOCKET
calls first. This provides a unique socket descriptor to be used with the
socket.

The BIND call can be used by the client to associate the socket
descriptor with a specific port and IP address. However, this is optional.

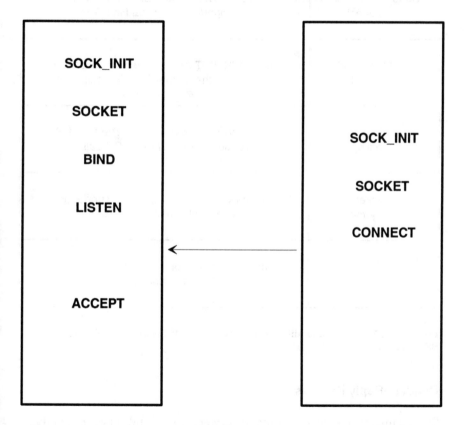

Figure 11.14 Simple example of connection establishment using the OS/2 socket
API.

The CONNECT function uses an underlying active TCP open to generate a connection request, which flows to a named server (port/IP). After the TCP 3-way handshake (discussed in Chapter 3), the connection is open and ready for business. Figure 11.14 presents a simple example of the socket-based connection establishment.

Difference	Description
Unsupported File I/O Requests	READ, WRITE, and CLOSE are not supported for normal file I/O.
Socket Initialization Required	The SOCK_INIT API call must be made first, before the normal SOCKET call.
Error Handling	To write an error to the device log, PSOCK_ERRNO is used instead of PERROR call.
Socket Management	There are two versions of SELECT supported, the version of which must be declared.
I/O Device Control	The OS/2 version of IOCTL differs from the BSD standard.

Figure 11.15 List of major differences between the OS/2 socket interface and the BSD standard.

Request-Reply Process

The format of the data exchanged between client and server depends on the application. Regardless, SEND and RECV can be used at either end in order to exchange the stream-oriented data.

11.6 Differences with BSD Sockets

For the most part, the socket interface provided with OS/2 is identical to the BSD standard. In this way, it serves as a model (for the new user) of how a socket API operates and what it contains.

However, there are several areas where the OS/2 implementation varies from the standard, as shown in Figure 11.15.

The differences result from the separation of OS/2 file I/O from the socket I/O. In UNIX, they are more closely linked. For example, in UNIX the SELECT call can be used to wait on file (disk) devices and sockets in the same call. With OS/2, this is not possible. Also, the file I/O calls in UNIX (i.e., READ, WRITE, CLOSE) are not supported in the OS/2 socket interface.

12

Network Support and Performance

In supporting the TCP/IP network, several commands can be used to gather information or affect operational change. These simple commands complement the more complete network management environment available through SNMP.

In addition, a framework exists for measuring network performance through established MIB groups. These objects can be accessed through a managing station such as NetView/6000.

12.1 Management and Control Primitives

There are several commands that are frequently used in administering a TCP/IP system, and the internetwork in general. They enable a basic capability to display and update certain operational parameters. And although SNMP provides the stronger foundation for network management, there is some overlap as many of these commands are still very useful and necessary. Figure 12.1 provides a list of the most prevalent of the text-mode operator commands. An important characteristic of their use, versus SNMP, is that a management station is not required.

Network Status and Connectivity Information

The first and probably most widely used of the commands shown is NETSTAT. It provides the status of the IP connections and lower-level physical network devices.

Command	Description
NETSTAT	A versatile command invoked to report on a variety of operational information, such as the contents of the IP routing table.
IFCONFIG	Used to initialize an IP interface, and to display its current status (e.g., active).
ARP	The Address Resolution Protocol table can be displayed or updated with ARP.
PING	A command used to determine if the IP capability of a remote host is active through the use of an ICMP message.
ROUTE	This command, with limited support by the IBM products, can be used to create and display entries in the routing table.
NSLOOKUP	The Domain Name System server can be manually queried using this interface.
FINGER	Used to look up information regarding a user or group of users on a remote machine using a service process.
RPCINFO	The pormapper process is a central repository for RPC servers, and can be examined with thsi command.

Figure 12.1 Commands used for network administration and basic management.

The command is general in nature, and must be issued with a parameter to qualify its operation for a specific instance. Though modeled after UNIX, its exact implementation, as with many other aspects of the TCP/IP protocols, can vary from platform to platform. However, the most commonly supported information that can be displayed includes:

- Local IP addresses.
- Local routing tables.
- Connected clients and servers with port numbers.
- Characteristics of an IP interface.
- ARP table being used.
- Status of UDP.
- Status of IP.
- Status of ICMP.

Other types of information can also be extracted, depending on the platform, such as the local buffer pool usage.

The interface configuration (IFCONFIG) command is used to display the characteristics of the local network interfaces in use. It can be used across the IBM product line, except for MVS and VM (where NETSTAT is used). In addition to displaying interface information, IFCONFIG can also be used to control the following:

- Token Ring broadcast characteristics.
- Use of and access to ARP.
- Driver-dependent debugging.
- Use and current state of a specific interface.
- Routing metrics.
- Maximum Transmission Unit (MTU) size.
- Subnet mask values.
- Status of ICMP.

The ARP command is used to access the Address Resolution Protocol (ARP) tables. For example, the mapping between IP and hardware addresses can be displayed and updated.

PING, short for Packet Internet Groper, provides a quick way to determine if a host is active. Actually, it tests the IP function on the remote host. In response to the command, the ICMP component within the local Internet layer generates a message to the target host. Like a submarine sonar ping, the message is returned indicating success. A text message is displayed, following the input, informing the user that the host is alive. Some implementations can include other information, such as packet round-trip time.

```
nic% ping ics.uci.edu
ics.uci.edu is alive
```

Figure 12.2 An example of the PING command.

Figure 12.2 contains an example of the PING command. In this example, the name for the remote host is used, therefore requiring a DNS lookup. PING also supports the use of the actual IP address, a format which is desirable when debugging problems.

Additional Commands

In addition to the network commands described above, several other commands can be used to access software-oriented data. As shown in the figure, these include:

- NSLOOKUP
- FINGER
- RPCINFO

Most of the time, access to the name server occurs "under the covers," where an application calls the name resolver function on behalf of the user. The NSLOOKUP command enables this DNS data, stored at the name server, to be accessed through the operator interface.

The FINGER command, part of a larger protocol specification, can be used to "put the finger on" a particular user or group of users. It must rely on a server at the target host using port 79. The information gathered and displayed by the command execution includes user details on the remote system, such as real name and date/time last logged on. For security reasons, the finger service is not universally implemented.

12.2 Remote Command Execution

While TELNET can be used to logon to a remote host, many times the connection and associated overhead are not required. Perhaps the user only needs to schedule a command at the remote host. In this case, there are two methods that can be used:

- Remote Execution Command Protocol (REXEC).
- Remote Shell Protocol (RSH).

A server is required to support the protocols at the target host, each of which is accessed through a separate TCP port.

Generally speaking, REXEC provides a more secure environment, where a user ID and password are used. The daemon REXECD is normally supplied.

RSH is usually limited to the UNIX environment, and does not require the security ID. In this case, the daemon RSHD provides the server function. However, many times the two are supported by the same background process.

Remote Execution Command Protocol

The Remote Execution Command (REXEC) protocol allows a command to be scheduled on a remote host. As with many TCP/IP applications, the functions are divided into a client and server. The target host server daemon accepts and executes each routine.

REXEC accepts commands from its clients, and can support the Remote Shell Protocol (RSH). Figure 12.3 includes a simple example. The first parameter is the name of the host, while the remaining text is part of the command string.

The steps used in processing the command include:

- User issues REXEC command locally.
- A TCP connection is established with the remote REXEC server.
- The user is prompted for a user ID.
- The user is then prompted for the corresponding password.
- The command is scheduled at the remote system, with output returned to the user or written to a disk file at the server.

Some implementations, including VM, MVS, and OS/2, allow the userid and password to be included on the command line.

The operation of RSH is similar, but in most implementations does not require a user ID and password validation. If this information is used, as in the case of the 6611 NP, it is sent as a part of the original command line.

```
rexec host1 comm1
```

Figure 12.3   An illustration of the REXEC command.

12.3 Debugging IP Routing Problems

Transporting data through the network is of course, the whole purpose of an architecture such as TCP/IP. When the datagram routing process is disrupted or disabled, the analyst or operator must determine its cause and correct the problem. This section illustrates the elements of problem determination in an IP internetwork. It builds upon the previous commands in order to present a framework to be used when approaching IP routing problems.

The first and most obvious symptom is, obviously, when an application on one host machine apparently cannot reach another (remote) machine. The primary vehicle used to test, as well as to verify the correction of, such a problem is the PING operator command. As mentioned above, PING creates an ICMP message that is transmitted to the specified destination. Note that, as mentioned above, PING will accept a DNS name or IP address. When a name is used, this adds a further layer of complexity because the name server must be involved. Therefore, the direct IP address should be used when debugging networking problems.

To summarize, PING is useful for testing and verifying:

- Physical network path
- IP routing activity
- Basic IP function at the target host

In the case where the host is not reachable, the operator must then attempt to locate the exact problem. There are several areas and aspects of the network to examine. This includes determining if the:

- Operating system is active.
- TCP/IP software is operational.
- Routing table contains the correct entries.
- Daemon supporting the dynamic routing protocol is active (e.g., ROUTED).

■ Network interface is active and usable.
■ Path through the intermediate internetwork is available.

It is fairly straightforward to determine if the local operating environment is functional. The next step is to examine the local environment.

Path out of the Local Host

There are several elements of the local host to examine. First, is the local TCP/IP (in whatever form) operational? Does the routing table have an entry for the destination (or at least a default entry)? Is the RouteD daemon used with RIP active?

In starting the process, the first step is to ping the local host. As a next step, the local network interface and routing tables should be examined. This can be done using the NETSTAT and IFCONFIG commands.

Pinging Your Way Around

To verify your path out of the local host, try to ping a device on the local network (e.g., LAN), so as not to pass through a router. If this does not work, then again the routing table is a likely source of the problem. Also, the ARP function supporting the mapping of IP address to link level address should be examined.

Finally, it is possible to gradually extend the reach through the internetwork with PING. Of course, this requires a knowledge of the network's topology. Try a device in the next network over. The process here is designed to move through the internetwork until a blockage is reached. Finally, if the ping is successful to a device in the target (i.e., remote) network, but unsuccessful for the desired host, then the problem must be with the remote machine. In this case, an onsite inspection (or some other type of access, such as dial in), is needed. The same sorts of elements can be examined in the remote machine as were inspected with the local platform, such as the operating system, TCP/IP software, routing table, ARP, and local network interface(s).

12.4 Performance Measurement Concepts

Network performance has always been an important topic for network analysts. What has changed, however, is the nature of the data available as well as the methods used in collecting it.

In the past, SNA performance data has been gathered from a diverse set of sources and tools. For example, each access method (e.g., VTAM) has its own performance characteristics, such as buffer pool utilization. Response time data can be collected using the Response Time Monitor (RTM) facility in the control units, or through a software approximation method (i.e., forced definite response). The NCP generates its own data through the NPALU, in cooperation with the NetView Performance Monitor (NPM) product. Of course, events and alerts are also directed to NetView, through VTAM over the SSCP-to-PU session or the more recent Management Services (MS) transport. And LAN monitors, such as Sniffer, can capture and analyze frames.

While these techniques are still important, and do have analogous functions within the TCP/IP world, a new paradigm also exists for measuring performance within TCP/IP networks. This is accomplished within the SNMP framework. MIB data is collected and stored at remote agents. Some of this information is directly applicable to performance and capacity measurement, and can be extracted by and reported at the management stations.

MIB Data Types

Part of the SNMP Version 1 architecture includes the specifications for the types of data fields that can be used within the MIB objects. These are detailed within RFC 1155, entitled "Structure of Management Information (SMI)."

SMI includes both universal data types, such as integers and character strings, as well as application data types. A list of these application data types is presented in Figure 12.4.

Of the types listed, two are particularly important with respect to the measurement of performance:

- Counter
- Gauge

Each of these generally functions as described, however, can be implemented and used in a slightly different manner depending on the MIB and resource(s) involved.

Data Type	Description
NetworkAddress	Used to select an addressing format; only IpAddress is currently supported.
IpAddress	This 32-bit field holds the Internet Family (IP) address.
Counter	A 32-bit unsigned integer value incremented from 0 to 4G, and then wrapped to 0.
Gauge	A 32-bit value that may increase or decrease, but remains "latched" (held) when reeaching its maximum.
TimeTicks	An unsigned integer which records time in 0.01-second increments.
Opaque	Used to pass data that is arbitrarily defined, and held within a string.

Figure 12.4 Application data types defined for use within the MIB-II definitions.

Types of Measurements

In using the counter and gauge data types, it is possible to gather and arrange the data such that several types of measurements can be made:

- Traffic
- Quality
- Capacity

Traffic is basically a measurement of the raw volume of data, such as the IP datagrams, transported. Where it is possible to establish an upper boundary, a corresponding utilization expressed as a percentage can also be calculated. Quality, as with some of the NCP-generated statistics for example, is a measurement of the volume of traffic transmitted compared to the errors encountered. Capacity contraints are reflected in the data packets that are either delayed or discarded due to an overload situation. This can often occur on the internetwork router nodes in a heavily used network.

Finally, it is also possible to establish other categories of measurement, in specific cases, that are not universally supported.

12.5 MIB Performance Data

All discussion of an SNMP MIB currently begins with the MIB-II standard, which establishes the framework for the support of many of the other optional MIB groups. Chapter 8 presented the IBM 6611 Network Processor, including most of the relevant extensions.

The first part of this section points to the sources of performance related data, as drawn from the established MIB standards. The next few subsections give specific examples of how this data, as drawn from two different areas, can be used in measuring performance. The final part explores considerations for basic collection and processing of this MIB data from the distributed agents.

MIB-II Standard

Almost all of the branches of the MIB-II definitions contain information that can be applied to performance. To summarize, these include:

- Interfaces group.
- IP group.
- ICMP group.
- UDP group.
- TCP group.
- EGP group.
- SNMP group.

This information can be enhanced through the standards, as defined in RFC extensions.

Additional RFC Specifications

Of the RFCs listed in Chapter 8, and supported by the 6611 NP, the following are important with respect to performance. Note that many are fairly recent, and have superseded the former RFCs, making them obsolete. The RFCs include:

- RFC 1398 - Ethernet group.
- RFC 1231 - Token Ring group.
- RFC 1406 - DS1/E1 group.
- RFC 1512 - Fiber Distributed Data Interface (FDDI), not included with the 6611.
- RFC 1229 - Interface Extensions group.
- RFC 1315 - Frame Relay group.
- RFCs 1471 through 1474 - Point-to-Point Protocol (PPP) group.
- RFC 1493 - Transparent Bridging group.
- RFC 1525 - Source Route Bridging group.

As explained above, each of these MIB groups hold object data fields that can be used to measure performance. Their availability and reliability depends on the agent implementation. Two examples from the MIB-II standard are presented below.

Transmission Control Protocol MIB Data

The Transport layer, particularly TCP, is normally used extensively on a host. Therefore, it can be beneficial to determine its usage and performance, as so many of the applications make use of its services.

The TCP data is under branch number 6 of MIB-II definitions. Within this section of the MIB there are many types of data available. As listed in the previous section, this information can be organized into three categories: traffic, quality, and capacity. Figure 12.5 presents all of the MIB variables involved.

The TCP traffic can be determined by adding the first two fields: tcpInSegs and tcpOutSegs. A measurement of transmission quality can be determined by dividing tcpInErrs by tcpInSegs (multiplied by 100) to determine a percentage. Capacity (or lack thereof), as measured by the percentage of retransmitted segments, can be calculated by dividing tcpRetransSegs by tcpOutSegs.

TCP Data	Description
tcpInSegs	This variable counts the number of inbound TCP segments.
tcpOutSegs	This variable counts the number of outbound TCP segments.
tcpInErrs	The number of datagrams that arrive (inbound) with errors are counted.
tcpRetransSegs	The number of segment transmissions that must be performed.

Figure 12.5 Variables within the TCP subtree which can be used to determine performance.

Internet Protocol MIB Data

The Internet Protocol is a required function, found in each of the internetwork hosts and routers. Therefore, its operation and performance is critical to the operation of the network as a whole. There are several variables that can be used in order to gain a perspective on IP performance, which is particular important for the backbone routers.

Figure 12.6 lists the fields related to the flow of IP traffic. One ratio to calculate is the number of forwarded datagrams (ipForwDatagrams) divided by the total received at the node (ipInReceives). This provides an indication of the amount of routing the node is performing. Another measurement that can be useful is the total number of datagrams handled by the node, both incoming and outgoing. The total incoming is readily available as indicated. However, the number of outgoing is not. This can be determined by adding the number sent by higher-level programs (ipOutRequests) and the number forwarded (ipForwDatagrams). Therefore, the total traffic can be determined as:

total = ipInReceives + ipForwDatagram + ipOutRequests

A measurement of quality can be made using certain values, as shown in Figure 12.7.

Also, constraints on capacity can be calculated based on the total number of datagrams discarded:

total discarded = ipInDiscards + ipOutDiscards

This number, divided by the total traffic volume shown above, provides an indication of capacity problems.

Error Indicators	Description
ipInHdrError	Describes the number of datagrams with IP header errors.
ipInAddrErrors	Number of datagrams with an invalid IP address.
ipInUnknownProtos	Datagrams with an invalid (unknown) protocol field in the header.
ipOutNoRoutes	Number of datagrams for which a route could not be found.

Figure 12.6 Four IP variables used to determine raw traffic volume.

Error Indicators	Description
ipInHdrError	Describes the number of datagrams with IP header errors.
ipInAddrErrors	Number of datagrams with an invalid IP address.
ipInUnknownProtos	Datagrams with an invalid (unknown) protocol field in the header.
ipOutNoRoutes	Number of datagrams for which a route could not be found.

Figure 12.7 IP variables counting errors, and therefore used to measure transmission quality.

The IP group also includes other fields related to the operation of the fragmentation protocols (e.g., number of fragments created, number of failures, etc.).

Techniques for Collecting and Processing the Data

Utilizing this MIB data within the SNMP manager-agent framework requires polling. That is, a central program must send an SNMP get request to each of the agents to extract each MIB variable. Of course, this requires overhead, both for the network and the two platforms involved (i.e., cycles). Also, there can be several ways to collect the data. The rsh command can be used, as in the case of the 6611-based agent. However, it is most productive and highly advisable to use a management station such as NetView/6000 as a base for data collection. After accessing the data, it must then be processed and displayed in some way.

To summarize, several issues must be addressed in establishing the data collection and processing procedures:

- Which devices will be polled?
- What MIB groups are needed?
- Which variables, from the selected groups, should be used?
- How often should each variable be read?

Each network device is used for a different purpose, and can also have different MIB data available. These factors, of course, influence the collection decisions. For example, hosts often perform little internetwork routing, but rather support the local applications. Routers, on the other hand, usually do not have much (if any) application activity, but rather route IP datagrams over various network interfaces. These as well as other factors influence the decisions over what devices and MIB groups to monitor. It is also important to understand the variables that apply in each case, so that an accurate and useful picture of performance can be ascertained.

Finally, after data is collected it must be processed and displayed. Each sample can be passed through a filter, which might be used to generate "alerts" when thresholds reach a certain level. The data can be logged for later use, and also displayed in real time.

13

NetView/6000

In the past when the subject of IBM network management was brought up, data processing professionals immediately thought of NetView (or maybe the original component products such as NCCF). This is due to the fact that for years the mainframe dominated the corporate landscape. IBM led the development of network management tools to support its commercial users. NetView became popular because, among other reasons, it manages SNA networks very well. SNA and the central mainframe, perfect together.

And recently IBM has worked to enhance NetView, with features such as the Management Services transport and Resource Object Data Manager (RODM), in order to position the product as the Manager of Managers (MoM). While its use in this role does have several advantages, there are also reasons why customers might look elsewhere for direct TCP/IP management:

■ NetView is a collection of previous products which, separately then collectively, were originally designed for SNA management; incorporation of TCP/IP management has been slow and operation can be cumbersome.
■ The product is somewhat removed from the LAN arena, where a significant amount of TCP/IP processing is done.
■ Mainframe computing has traditionally had a high cost associated with it.

As an alternative, IBM had offered a product by the name of AIX Network Management/6000. It ran on the RS/6000 platform, and was part of a collection of connectivity programs originally announced in February of 1990. The product provided generic alert reporting to the SNA host, as well as a basic SNMP capability.

Then in January, 1992, IBM announced NetView/6000 Version 1. This product was nearly a direct port of the OpenView product to AIX on the RS/6000 platform, as licensed from Hewlett-Packard (HP). In its first release, NetView/6000 focused on network management for SNMP agents and other IP-address devices. It immediately supported the new IBM 6611 router (i.e., as an agent).

NetView/6000 Version 2.1 quickly followed, with the announcement in September of 1992. It includes several new features, generally concentrating on providing support for a wider variety of network management protocols in the "open" enterprise. An entry level version of the product, which had several limitations such as the restriction of managing a maximum of 32 nodes, was announced in February, 1993.

In September, 1993 the older Network Management/6000 product was withdrawn from marketing, effective in December of the same year. Users were directed to migrate to the NetView/6000 Entry product.

NetView/6000, especially the latest Version 2.1, has generated a significant interest among network management professionals. IBM has enhanced the product to create its own environment in an attempt to differentiate it from OpenView. In fact, large parts of the product have been redesigned and rewritten by IBM. In the future, it is obviously in IBM's interest to own the product and terminate its relationship with HP, given the strategic and competitive nature of the market.

Further evidence of the product's acceptance can be seen with the license granted to Digital Equipment Corporation (DEC), which now supports it as PolyCenter NetView. And on March 29, 1994 IBM announced a port of NetView/6000 V2.1 to the Sun Solaris operating system.

So while NetView/390 can still be effective as the MoM, it will rely on the remote support of products such as NetView/6000.

13.1 Execution Environment

NetView/6000 can be positioned in basically two ways in providing network management:

- As the primary focal point for the management and control of a heterogeneous, multivendor network.
- As a remote data collection and command execution platform on behalf of the mainframe NetView product.

In either case, one of the product's strengths is the fact that it is in among the devices that it manages. It must have a direct connection to the TCP/IP network. This is frequently accomplished using one of the popular LAN protocols, such as Ethernet. Also, it was developed from the ground up, and tailored to the demands of the internetwork.

Product Uses

Each new release includes more functional capabilities. This has enhanced the product and its ability to take on a wider role in the enterprise.

With version 2.1, NetView/6000 has several features. These generally fall into the following categories:

- Manage the TCP/IP network through an association with the distributed SNMP agents.
- Monitor and display IP-addressable devices.
- Expanded network management capability, including non-SNMP protocols such as OSI.
- Dynamic discovery capabilities, including IP devices.
- Variety of MIBs, with support tools.
- In conjunction with MIB applications, can monitor network performance and generate reports.
- Adhere to the Motif GUI standard from the Open Software Foundation (OSF), linked to the X Window System.
- Provides an "open" platform for the development and integration of new network management application (e.g., documented APIs, support for mulitple standards, etc.).

In order to better appreciate these features, it is first necessary to discuss the framework within which the product operates.

Network Management Framework

Whereas NetView/6000 initially focused on SNMP management, Version 2.1 has expanded the framework within which it operates.

The SNMP protocol was first introduced in Chapter 4. Both OSI and SNMP have several common features, and generally operate in the same fashion.

A manager-to-agent connection is established, where the managing system (i.e., NetView/6000) relies on one or more agents. Network resources are represented as objects, and are defined within the MIB structure. The protocol exchanges between manager and agent are based on a common understanding of the MIB structure being used.

The OSI specifications are more complete and fully functional than those of SNMP. However, this has come at the cost of complexity, delays, and resource intensive implementations. Some of this has been allevi- ated by selectively providing support for the OSI protocols in the NetView/6000 product. OSI standards supported include:

■ Common Management Information Protocol (CMIP).
■ Common Management Information Services (CMIS).

Simply put, CMIS defines a set of services that are exposed to the higher-level systems management applications. Figure 13.1 contains a list of the CMIS services. CMIP is closely associated with CMIS, and defines the format for the OSI protocol data units transmitted through the network. In the case of NetView/6000, these protocols utilize the TCP/IP architecture as a transport, with the resulting combination depicted as CMIS/CMIP over TCP/IP (CMOT).

Also, interfaces created by X/Open are included:

■ X/Open Management Protocol (XMP).
■ X/Open OSI-Abstract-Data Manipulation (XOM).

Both are implemented as APIs available to the application devel- oper, as described later in the chapter. XMP is especially important because of its ability to allow consistent access to network management data. This is true regardless of the protocol, such as SNMP or OSI.

AIX Processing

NetView/6000 is designed to run on the RS/6000 workstation with AIX, a derivative of the UNIX operating system. The product has therefore been tailored to AIX, and adopts several characteristics of a UNIX-based application.

A large part of the processing is done using "daemons," another term for a background process. Daemons are usually designed to lay dormant, waiting for input. When a request arrives, they are activated and perform the work. These requests might be, for example, timer-driven. In addition, the user can launch foreground applications. These appli- cations interact through the user interface, as well as with the back- ground processes through interprocess communications (IPC).

CMISE Operational Service	Description
M-GET	Requests information.
M-SET	Updates object in target system.
M-ACTION	Requests that a specific action be carried out.
M-CREATE	Creates an object instance.
M-DELETE	Deletes an object instance.
M-CANCEL-GET	Cancels a previous request.

Figure 13.1 Operational services available through the defined CMIS element.

The X Window System is used to manage a Motif compliant GUI. A UNIX command-line shell is also available, through which commands can be entered.

Component	Description
SNMPRUN	Foundation for the management platform including GUI, IP discovery, trap management, and the MIB browser.
SNMPDEV	Provides both the OpenView (OVW) and NetView/6000 development environments as well as the on-line documentation.
NNMGR	A collection of MIB tools and applications as well as the event configurator.
DMRUN	Basis for communication, with support for XMP APIs, event management, and the Object Registration Services (ORS) database.
DMDEV	Includes code and overall environment for the development and integration of applications using the event management services.
IBMVA	Collection of development support options and code for integration into the larger IBM environment, such as mainframe NetView.

Figure 13.2 Major internal components of the NetView/6000 product, loaded one at a time during installation.

Internal Components

NetView/6000 can be broken down into six primary components, which are listed in Figure 13.2. These internal functions are implemented through background and foreground processes, as well as APIs and documentation.

MIB Support

A MIB is really a definition of resources within a hierarchical structure. It is virtual in the sense that MIBs are architectural frameworks, which then must be implemented in hardware and software. It usually resides in one or more files or databases.

There are a variety of MIBs available. The first way to organize them is based on the network management protocol being used. SNMP can be used with a number of MIBs, each of which collects like definitions into groups.

The NetView/6000 product supports a variety of MIB capabilities, as shown in Figure 13.3.

MIB Category	Description
MIB-II Standard	The MIB-II standard has been widely implemented and replaces the earlier MIB-I specification (which is still supported).
RFC Standards	In addition to MIB-II, there is a collection of MIB groups, each providing visibility and management of a resource, application, or protocol.
Enterprise-Specific	Each vendor can create MIB extensions specifically designed to describe and manage unique products.
Generic/Open MIB	NetView/6000 includes the ability to define and store a wide range of management data, regardless of its nature or the protocol being used.

Figure 13.3   Categories of MIBs supported by NetView/6000.

Because products and protocols are created so rapidly, the official standards often cannot keep pace. Also, each vendor frequently has special requirements for the management of its products. Therefore, while the MIB-II definition standard is widely supported, it is often augmented through the use of additional MIB definitions, or groups.

13.2 Installation and Customization

The product is shipped on a tape, and can be unloaded using the System Management Interface Tool (SMIT). The AIX SMIT utility provides a menu-driven technique for installing AIX software.

Installation Overview

Version 2.1 of the product will run on an RS/6000 POWERstation or POWERserver workstation with the proper hardware configuration and capacity. In addition, there are several software requirements, some of which are native to the system. These include:

- AIX V3.2 or above (with PTF U411928)
- AIXWindows Environment/6000
- X Windows System Version 11 Release 4
- X11 fonts
- OSF/Motif Version 1.1 or above
- SNMP agent
- TCP/IP
- InfoExplorer (optional)

During installation, the system is checked for all of the required software. Also, migration from the previous release is supported.

After the files are copied from tape to disk, a basic configuration is performed. This allows the system to then be immediately started.

Areas for Further Customization

There are several ways that the operation and use of the product can be enhanced through additional customization. These can be grouped into several large areas, including:

- General daemon management and default processing.
- Event management.
- Topology and map management.
- User interface enhancement.
- SNMP configuration.

Some of these topics are discussed further below.

Display Element	Description
Symbol	The graphical representation of an object, as displayed on a submap, with various characteristics such as type, position, and status.
Map	A collection of objects grouped together and described by a set of attributes (i.e., map name).
Submap	A map consists of one or more submaps, each of which uses symbols to represent objects.
Graphical Map	Using container objects and background maps, customized displays can be created which allow for a more intuitive and productive access to data.

Figure 13.4   Elements of NetView/6000 graphical interface used to display network management data.

13.3 User Interface

As mentioned above, the GUI used by NetView/6000 is based on the X Window System using the Motif style of presentation. This section begins with a few basics about the interface, followed by specific aspects of the product.

Windowing Basics

Products using an X / Motif interface, as well as other GUIs in general, have several common elements. These include:

- Menus
- Buttons
- Dialog boxes

Command	Description
OVSTART	Used to start all or a subset of the daemons defined in the file ovsuf, through an interaction with the process management daemon, ovspmd.
OVSTOP	Similar to ovstart, except used to stop all or selected daemon backgound processes.
OVSTATUS	Provides a status display of the daemons, and includes several different parameter options.

Figure 13.5   Commands used to control the operation of the NetView/6000 processes.

There are several types of menus (e.g., pull-down, pop-up) and buttons can be used to make selection. Menus are especially useful during navigation.

Dialog boxes are displayed, and allow an application to solicit additional information from the user.

Accessing Network Management Data

Internally, data representation with the NetView/6000 product is based on the concept of an object. Each object represents an entity (i.e., device) which has usually been dynamically discovered. Objects are stored in the NetView/6000 object database.

Figure 13.4 contains a list of the basic elements of the interface used in allowing access to the network management data.

A map, in NetView/6000 terms, is an internally maintained collections of objects. Symbols are used to represent each of the NetView/6000 objects on the displayable submaps. Under the covers, each application can access and display the object data within this framework of maps, submaps, and graphical maps.

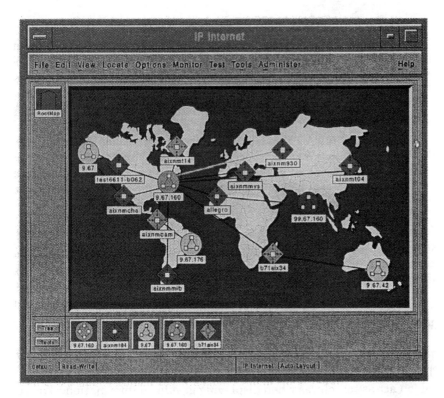

Figure 13.6   Internet map displayed with Version 2.1 of the NetView/6000 product.

Navigation at Startup

The "nv6000" shell script (i.e., procedure) is used to start the product, including the GUI display. The command is entered from an aixterm window. It includes several options, such as which maps are opened. In addition, three commands can be used to control the operation of the product, as displayed in Figure 13.5. These commands are really part of the broader category of process control, relating to the background daemons.

After the product has been started, four windows are displayed:

- Submap window
- Control Desk window
- Tools window
- Navigation tree window

The Control Desk window contains a list of active applications, and is initially attached to the submap window. The Tools window provides a way to access tools and applications. For example, it contains icons, which when selected, start applications to perform specific tasks. These are used, for example, to analyze internet traffic or SNMP errors, graph collected data, view the event history log, or send mail. In fact, additional Control Desk windows can be created from the Tools windows.

Figure 13.6 contains a display of the NetView/6000 Internet map, one of the display windows available with the product.

13.4 Data Organization

In order to support its operation, including the collection and display of network data, NetView/6000 uses several types of data files. Some of these are available as normal AIX files, while others are structured as databases.

Variety of Databases

Figure 13.7 includes a list of the primary databases that are included. The Map database holds maps, including symbol types and locations, which act as templates when displaying graphical information. The IP Topology and the Generic (or Open) Topology databases both contain information about the actual network resources. This information, as it is updated, is reflected in the displays.

The Object Registration Service (ORS) database allows non-SNMP agents to be registered and described. The NetView/6000 Object database is global in nature, containing fields that are fundamental to the operation of the product and its data collection activities by the distributed agents.

Open Topology MIB

This database is important because it can be used to integrate the data gathered from different network management protocols. In this way, both SNMP and non-SNMP nodes can be easily accessed by the user. This feature, called the Generic Topology Manager (GTM), is implemented as the gtmd daemon, in close association with the noniptopod daemon.

Database	Description
Map	The description of each map is stored in a separate database file, and contains information about map (e.g., symbols).
Object	Global object information, generic in nature, is saved and accessed by the various product components.
IP Topology	The IP discovery and display feature uses data stored in this file; this can be duplicated in the Generic Topology DB.
Object Registration Service	Agents that use protocols other than SNMP are identified, through type and location, and stored in the ORS database.
Generic Topology	This database forms the foundation for the representation of a variety of network topology information in a generic manner.

Figure 13.7   Databases used by the NetView/6000 product.

The database consists of tables. The tables are collected into groups; Figure 13.8 contains the four primary groups. For each there is a primary table, as well as one or more secondary tables. The groups act as generic building blocks used to describe the network content and organization. They are designed to be general enough so as to accommodate a variety of configurations.

The database also includes a model for how states of the resources are described and maintained. It follows the ISO document 10164-2 (State Management).

Group	Description
Vertex	Represents a vertex, or the highest reference point in the network.
Simple Connection	Describes a simple connection, or link, between two resources.
Arc	Depicts an arc, or curve, and contents.
Graph	Represents a graph relationship through multiple underlying tables.

Figure 13.8 Table groups defined within the Open Topology Database.

13.5 Background Daemon Processes

The concept of a background daemon is native to the UNIX programming environment. Each daemon, or background process, is designed to perform some function. It usually waits, in an idle state, until input arrives. This incoming request can come from the network, the user, or another daemon.

There are four categories of daemon processes supplied with the NetView/6000 product, as described below.

Process Management

Because of the large number of processes which make up the product, a daemon is needed just to manage and coordinate the activities of the other processes. This is not unusual. One might compare this to the job scheduling/management systems which run on operating systems such as MVS.

Daemon	Description
NETMON	Polls SNMP agents in order to dynamically discover network topology.
OVTOPMD	Maintains and updates the topology DB based on the activity of other daemons.
OVWDB	Controls and maintains the NetView/6000 object database through regular messages.
NONIPTOPOD	Manages generic topology information by accepting certain SNMP traps in association with non-IP proprietary daemons.
GTMD	Receives traps from non-IP applications and agents using the generic topology MIB.

Figure 13.9 Topology discovery and database operation daemons.

The daemon "ovspmd" implements the process management function. It establishes a communication link with the command "ovstart" (when issued) to receive requests and send status replies. Each of the daemons started by ovspmd is created as a child process, and runs under its control. In this sense, the process management daemon acts as the parent, or anchor, for all of the other background daemons. Therefore, ovspmd must always be active.

Each of the NetView/6000 daemons is described with a Local Registration File (LRF) stored in the directory "/usr/OV/lrf". An LRF is one of four types of registration files used to define an application; these are described in more detail later in the chapter.

The command "ovaddobj" can be used to read the LRFs to generate a startup file "/usr/OV/conf/ovsuf". The startup file, which contains an entry for each of the daemons, is used to control the start characteristics of each process. It is read by ovspmd.

In addition to processes supplied with the product, new daemons and agents can be created and installed with the product. There is an API provided to allow a process to be integrated with the Process Manager, also discussed below.

Topology Discovery and Database Operation

Another important function of NetView/6000 is to dynamically discover network topology information. Closely associated with this operation is the ability to access the corresponding database files.

Figure 13.9 contains a list of the background processes used to implement these two functions.

The processes listed perform functions which fall into three broad categories, including those that:

- Poll SNMP agents.
- Manage the generic topology data.
- Provide access to the NetView/6000 databases.

These programs, through a cooperation with the Event and Trap daemons, are able to dynamically determine the content and characteristics of the network resources.

Event and Trap Processing

In addition to discovering the network characteristics, NetView/6000 also accepts events generated by OSI managed objects, SNMP agents (i.e., traps), and internal processes. Figure 13.10 lists the daemons involved.

The daemon "pmd" accepts all incoming data, and acts as an internal router. It acts based on the content of each message, as well as information provided by the Object Registration Service (ORS) daemon ("orsd"), to direct each packet.

SNMP traps are sent to "trapd", which can forwards the message to applications that might be sensitive to the data (namely, ipmap). A copy of each trap is also sent to "netmon" (topology discovery), "noniptopod" (generic topology), and "tralertd" (conversion to an SNA alert).

Daemon	Description
PMD	Receives all incoming events or SNMP traps and provides internal routing.
ORSD	Maintains the ORS database, and accepts queries from the "pmd" daemon as to the nature and location of non-SNMP agents.
OVESMD	Implements the Event Management Services (EMS), acting as a sieve to process and filter incoming events.
OVELMD	The event log, which accepts and stores SNMP traps, CMIS events, and other data.
TRAPD	Accepts all SNMP traps from agents and other internal components; forwards the traps for additional processing as needed.
TRAPGEND	A NetView/6000 subagent that converts AIX errors to SNMP traps.
SNMPCOLLECT	Solicits, processes, and stores MIB values based on user defined parameters.

Figure 13.10   Event and trap processing daemons.

Events are sent to the daemon "ovesmd", which implements the Event Management Services (EMS) portion of the product. It can act as an event sieve, and deals with filter definitions. Events can be directed to daemons and foreground applications that have been configured to receive them. These applications, some of which are described below, can include:

- NETMON daemon.
- OVTOPMD daemon.
- TRALERTD daemon.
- IPMAP foreground application.
- NVEVENTS foreground application.

There is a similarity between event and trap processing, in that both types of messages are forwarded to other daemons in order to update topology information. Events sent to the "ovelmd" daemon will be logged.

Daemon	Description
TRALERTD	Provides integration of TCP/IP with SNA by converting traps to SNA alerts.
SPAPPLD	Implements a command interface to the host through the SNA-defined RUNCMDs

Figure 13.11   Host connection daemons.

Host Connection

There are two daemons that fall into this category, as listed in Figure 13.11. One is used to convert traps into alerts, and the other acts as a command interface to the host. In both cases, the AIX Service Point product is required.

13.6 Foreground Applications

The foreground applications, unlike the background daemons, can only be active after the user interface has been started. Most of the applications, which fall into five main categories, can be selected from the main menu.

Foreground Process	Description
IPMAP	Started to create topology maps based on IP topology of the network.
XXMAP	A counterpart to IPMAP which is designed to draw the topology of non-IP devices.

Figure 13.12   Map display foreground processes.

Principal GUI

The foundation for the display of graphical information is provided through the "ovw" application. It provides for map and menu management. It manages the user interface, based on the X Window System (Motif style).

The "nv6000" shell script first starts ovw, which then activates the following applications:

- IPMAP
- XXMAP
- NVEVENT

At this point, the user can begin to use the product.

Map Display

Figure 13.12 lists the two map display applications. The "ipmap" application is used to display IP topology information, as contained in the IP Map which represents the entire network. It does this by displaying submaps, each representing different aspects of the whole.

When first started, the application must go through a synchronization phase. The daemon ovtopmd can provide any changes in the IP Map structure since the application was last started. The Map is rewritten to the Map database. During steady state processing, it automatically receives status updates which are reflected in any of the open windows.

Foreground Process	Activation through Menu Item
XNMTRAP	Options..Event Configuration..SNMP
XNMSNMPCONF	Options..SNMP Configuration
XNMLOADMIB	Options..Load/Unload MIBs: SNMP
XNMBROWSER	Monitor..MIB Values..Browse MIB: SNMP
XNMCOLLECT	Options..Data Collection and Thresholds: SNMP
XNMBUILDER	Options..Application Builder: SNMP
XNMGRAPH	Monitor..MIB Values.. Graph Collected Data: SNMP (Main Menu)
XNMFAULT	Tools..Locate Failing Resources (Main Menu)
XNMRUNREPORT	Monitor..Reports: Site Provided

Figure 13.13 Menu operations foreground processes, showing the menu selection enabling the activation of each.

The "xxmap" application displays non-IP topology information. This information is accessed through the Generic Topology Manager, daemon "gtmd".

Event Display

As mentioned above, the Event Management Service (EMS) receives, processes, and stores event information. Part of this involves filter processing, as described below.

The "nvevents" application is used to display the events. After reading the event log at startup, nvevents receives updates from the EMS daemon, ovesmd. There are two presentation formats used:

- Event cards
- List

This application can show currently pending events, and is therefore a central part of the operator's approach to managing the network.

Menu Operations

The largest class of foreground applications, in terms of number, are those dealing with menu operations. They take their name from the fact that each application is activated from a menu item. Figure 13.13 includes a list of these applications, and the corresponding menu item with which they are associated.

The function of most of the applications is obvious from its name. For example, "xnmtrap" allows traps and trap processing to be configured. The application "xnmsnmpconf" is used to configure SNMP processing, including the polling intervals. The graph application, "xnmgraph," enables the creation of graphs based on the real-time or historical data collected from managed objects. The application "xnmfault" can be used to fastpath to failing resources.

There is a special set of applications allowing MIBs to be managed, including:

- XNMBUILDER - MIB Application Builder, used to create custom screens to display and manage network resources based on the MIB data.
- XNMBROWSER - MIB Browser, used to get and set values for both standard and enterprise-specific MIBs.

■ XNMCOLLECT - MIB Data Collector, used to quickly create functions to perform background data collection from network objects at regular intervals.

Taken as a whole, these applications provide the backbone of the product's functionality by allowing for the manual and automatic collection, update, and display of network data, through the MIB formats.

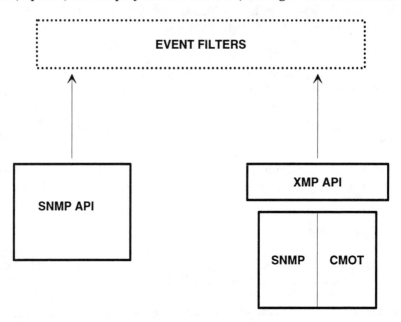

Figure 13.14 The NetView/6000 Event Management Service accepting unsolicited SNMP and OSI messages for processing.

Dialog Box Management

The "xnmappmon" application manages dialog boxes, each of which was dynamically created as the result of a user request. It can issue one of several commands under the covers, on behalf of the user. Because of this, it is considered to encapsulate the applications for management by and display for the user.

13.7 Event Management

As defined above, an event is an unsolicited notification of some occurrence sent to NetView/6000, and processed by the EMS feature.

Each event is passed through a filtering process which is used to determine its processing characteristics. Therefore, the systems administration has control over what conditions and network resources are passively monitored. The word "passively" is used because the product, through the MIB Data Collector application described above, can also "actively" monitor the network through a polling processing.

Event filtering is applied to data received through both the SNMP and XMP (SNMP and OSI) interfaces. Figure 13.14 presents an illustration.

Event Types and Characteristics

There are two major categories of events, as shown in Figure 13.15. The Map category results from an update operation, performed by a user or application, to the current map. Network events, on the other hand, are messages that flow in from the network utilizing either SNMP or OSI (i.e., over, or CMOT).

Event Type	Description
Map Event	Messages generated as the result of an application or user initiating a change to the characteristics of the current map.
Network Event	Notifications sent by an agent to the NetView/6000 platform for an SNMP or OSI managed object.

Figure 13.15 Categories of events recognized and processed by NetView/6000.

In addition, certain AIX system errors can be converted to events by the "trapgend" daemon, as mentioned above.

Each event is assigned a generic event number from 0 to 6, as well as a specific number. The first six generic event numbers have a specific number of 0. The last generic event (6) is reserved for enterprise-specific events, with the exact nature conveyed in the specific event number.

Event Filtering

It is important, especially with a large network, to limit the events that are handled by the product. This can be accomplished using event filters. Multiple event filters can be activate at the same time.

There are two manners in which filters can be created:

- Filter editor (operator interface)
- Filtering API (program interface)

The filter editor is accessed under the "Tools" menu bar selection. It is used to describe the characteristics of the filter, including the resource that it applies to. Each filter can be activated by using the "Filter Control" selection under the "Operations" menu bar option.

A program can also be used to create and register an event filter. There are two classes of API calls available, as part of the larger set of API calls that can be used by a NetView/6000 program:

- Filter creation
- Filter registration

Filter creation for an application performs a function that is analogous to that of the filter editor. Six API routines are available to build the filter definition.

After a filter has been created by the program (or through the filter editor), it can then be registered for use by the system. This works differently, depending if the SNMP or OSI (i.e., XMP) protocol is used. The XMP filter must first be converted into an XOM data structure before it is registered.

13.8 Application Development

NetView/6000 provides an open (i.e., well documented) and functionally rich environment for the creation of network management applications. It offers varying degrees of integration with the available services, topology information, and display capabilities.

General Characteristics

The first aspect of NetView/6000-based applications is to recognize that the operating system being used is UNIX (i.e., AIX). While this is obvious, the environment does carry with it certain characteristics, terminology, technology, and limitations that determine the nature of the applications.

Application	Description
Drop-in	An application with minimal integration with the established application framework, and started from a menu selection item.
Tool	A utility of some type which has been tightly integrated with NetView/6000, with an awareness of the objects.
Map	Can read and update the content of maps, namely the objects stored in the object database and represented by symbols.

Figure 13.16 Types of applications that can be created for use with NetView/6000.

A few of the application characteristics in this environment include:

■ Multiple processes (including daemons).
■ Single thread per process dispatching.
■ UNIX style directory structure and naming (filesystem).
■ C language use.
■ X Windows / Motif as the basis for the graphical interface.
■ Event-driven processing.
■ Multiple groups of system API functions available.

As with any application, some time should be spent at the beginning in determining its purpose, features, and design. There are several types of applications that can be created.

Categories of Applications

Figure 13.16 contains a list of the three main categories that NetView/ 6000 applications generally fall into.

The drop-in application has the lowest level of integration with the formal operating environment. It does not use any of the NetView/6000 APIs, but relies on the underlying AIX services as required. The application is made available to the user through a menu item.

A tool application is more tightly coupled with the application framework, and relies on many of the provided services. It has access to and awareness of the map contents. For example, it can be activated to operate on a selected object (i.e., symbol).

The map applications are created to access and update the objects through the maps. Submaps can be displayed through the graphical interface, allowing an interaction with the user.

Programming Interfaces

IBM provides a set of API functions that can be used by the developer. Figure 13.17 includes a list.

The XMP API provides a higher-level abstraction with which network resources can be accessed using multiple network manage protocols. In particular, SNMP and CMIS/CMIP support is provided. Both use the underlying TCP/IP transport; in the case of OSI this is termed CMIS/CMIP over TCP/IP (CMOT). In addition, an interface to an SNMP agent is provided through the native API.

The next two API groupings are particular to NetView/6000. The network logging and tracing facility can be used to track the activity of applications. This can be especially useful during development and debugging. The process manager interface allows an integration into the core control structure. For example, this allows for the graceful starting and stopping of applications, as well as the recording of process activity to the global log.

The event filtering API was first mentioned above. It can be used in controlling the processing of map and network events, and their subsequent display.

End User Interface Style Considerations

Each user interface has its own particular look and feel. This is dictated by the underlying technology, as well as by a desire to maintain a certain level of consistency in similar applications. Many times, a "style guide" is published, which helps the designer in making decisions regarding screen design and data placement (as is the case with NetView/6000).

API Family	Description
XMP	The X/Open Management Protocol (XMP) is a protocol-neutral API for accessing either SNMP or CMIS/CMIP over TCP/IP (CMOT).
SNMP	Access to the standard SNMP MIB variables and traps is provided for management applications.
OVuTL	A facility which allows for tracing and data logging is provided through these API calls.
OVsPMD	Applications can be integrated with the process manager daemon, ovspmd, in order to facility the orderly startup and shutdown of processes.
End User Interface	Over 200 API calls are available to control screen display and interaction with the user.
Event Filtering	A set of routines can be used to both create and register event filters for SNMP and XMP data.

Figure 13.17 Categories of API routines that can be used during application development.

There are three primary influences on the NetView/6000 user interface. These in turn affect how applications should be designed. An important part of design within this environment, due to the intuitive nature of the graphical display, is to maintain consistency (with the other applications). The major influences are:

- Use of X and the Motif style.
- Nature of the data being displayed (i.e., network resources).
- Design decisions made by the vendor (HP, and recently IBM) in how applications interoperate with the display primitives.

The End User Interface API can be divided into seven groups, as shown in Figure 13.18. Each supports a specific aspect of display and user interaction.

The structure allows, for example, submap stacking, navigation, and application management through the Control Desk. The designer is also encouraged to include other features which improve application usability, such as fast paths and graphical representation (e.g., using color).

Of course, the best advice is to use the product and explore the various features and components. Then build any new applications to be consistent with the standards already set.

Registration Files

Special configuration data sets, called registration files, hold information relating to the operation and use of NetView/6000 applications. Figure 13.19 contains a list of the registration files.

The Local Registration File (LRF) was already mentioned earlier in the chapter. Each LRF defines the processing characteristics of a background daemon. It is converted and stored in the startup file by the command ovaddobj, which is then available to ovstart.

The application file must be defined for each of the NetView/6000 applications. All of these files are read at product startup, as the result of the nv6000 command. The contents exactly describe the application's characteristics and determine its integration into the NetView/6000 product. Some of the definitions include the menu bar framework, the nature of the dialog boxes used, and how the commands can be invoked.

13.9 Trouble Ticket/6000

The Trouble Ticket/6000 (TT/6000) application runs on the RS/6000 and complements NetView/6000. It was announced in February of 1993, and supports both Versions 1 and 2.

EU API Grouping	Description
Application Integration	Establishes the link between an application and the NetView/6000 environment.
Object DB Access	Objects and their fields can be created, updated, and read by the application.
Symbols	Used to create symbols and control their display characteristics.
Map and Submap	Provides the ability to work with the map and submap structures.
User Verification	During interaction with a user, these routines can be used to verify requests.
Dynamic Registration	The NetView/6000 structure can be dynamically updated through the API functions in this grouping.
Callback	Used to establish response routines scheduled by NetView/6000 to communicate specific application events.

Figure 13.18 The End User Interface API organized into functional groups.

TT/6000 is roughly equivalent to the Information/Management product on MVS, which can be connected to NetView through the NetView Bridge Adapter.

The Trouble Ticket product must first be installed using the AIX SMIT facility. During the process, an entry is made in the Tools menu through which the application is accessed. Referring to the previous section, TT/6000 is therefore a tool application, with an awareness of the map structure and object content. It can therefore be activated within the context of one of the displayed symbols (representing a network device).

Registration File	Description
Application	This file must be used for each application, and describes its characteristics and menu integration.
Field	Used to define object fields, assigning attributes such as boolean, integer, or character string.
Symbol Type	Used to define new symbols for display at the user terminal based on classes and subclasses.
Local	The LRF must be included for each daemon, and then converted to startup file format for use.

Figure 13.19   Registration files used with the product.

An important foundation for the operation of the product is its integration into the NetView/6000 dynamic discovery process. This network information is used to populate the inventory database.

And of course its primary function is to support the management of problems. An incident report represents a potential problem and can be converted into a trouble ticket. Trouble tickets can be manually created by the user, or automatically generated through the information available in an event. The reference data included with the product enhances the usability of the product by adding contact information and escalating codes to the incidents and tickets.

The application supports automatic notification, and can of course be used to track problems and their resolution. In addition to the active problems, the log can be scanned for historical information.

14

Distributed Systems Management

The previous chapter presented the NetView/6000 product, which is ideal for managing TCP/IP networks. It can act as the management focal point, or interoperate with NetView/390 in order to keep control at the mainframe.

In addition, there are several other products which augment both of these management platforms. This chapter presents the primary supplements, as well as some of the concepts important with distributed systems management.

14.1 System Monitor

The System Monitor/6000 product was first announced by IBM in September, 1992. It is a separately priced and packaged product which interoperates with NetView/6000, extending its reach and enhancing its capability and performance. Specifically, the System Monitor acts as a remote monitor for each of the platforms it is installed on. It can also be configured as a type of sieve, filtering events based on performance thresholds, thus enabling local analysis and automation.

Since its original introduction, support for several other environments has been announced. The products in this family now include:

- System Monitor for Sun Solaris
- System Monitor for UNIX NCR
- System Monitor for HP-UX
- System Monitor/6000

The characteristics and basic operation of the System Monitor/6000 are illustrated below.

Functional Overview

As with other AIX-based products, the System Monitor is installed and administered using SMIT. Once installed, it can be positioned to perform two key functions:

- Provide system management data for the local system (i.e., where it is running).
- Offload NetView/6000 polling and remote management operations.

In order to understand how these functions are accomplished, first consider the three main components as illustrated in Figure 14.1.

The SMEUI application provides the end user with access to the product, and is integrated into the NetView/6000 environment as a tools application. It is used during customization of the tables, where configuration files can be created and saved. The user interface also provides access to the (enterprise-specific) MIB variables at each of the target systems.

Component	Description
SMEUI Application	This front-end application providing access to the product for the end user.
SYSMOND Daemon	A background process which implements the SMUX (subagent) protocol.
MIB	An enterprise-specific MIB, as well as extensions possible through various tables.

Figure 14.1 Operational components of the System Monitor/6000 product.

The SYSMOND daemon is controlled using the "sm6000" shell script, and runs as a background process. At startup, it reads the previously created configuration files which determine its operation. SYSMOND relies on the local SNMPD daemon for its link back to the central manager via SNMP. SNMPD communicates with the local System Monitor daemon using the SNMP Multiplexing (SMUX) protocol; this effectively positions SYSMOND as a "subagent" on the same node. The information provided by the System Monitor is presented to the managing station in the form of a MIB.

Data Available with MIB

As with all manager-to-agent interactions, the SNMP protocols are utilized to access the remote management data. The MIB provided with the System Monitor can be divided into two parts:

- Enterprise-specific extension.
- Customizable system management tables.

The enterprise-specific MIB is a group of variables created by IBM for the System Monitor. Referring to Chapter 4, this MIB has been placed within the ISO registration tree and is accessed through the object ID:

1.3.6.1.4.1.2.6.12

This enterprise-specific extension follows a fixed definition, that cannot be updated. It contains a wide variety of variables, most of which can be organized into several categories, as shown in Figure 14.2. Each of the MIB variables describes an aspect of the local system.

The MIB also includes extended data, represented as a series of tables, that is customized by the user through the SMEUI front end.

Customization Options

One of the first decisions that needs to be made is exactly how the System Monitor will be used. For example, it can be installed on one or more systems to monitor the local machine. Or, the product can be positioned to monitor sections of the network, so as to offload processing normally done by NetView/6000.

MIB Variable Category	Description
Local Configuration	Characteristics of the local environment, including machine name, devices, as well as the operating system configuration.
General OS Performance	Aspects affecting the overall performance such as status of the subsystems, paging devices, as well as CPU and device usage.
Process/User Information	The number and list of active processes and users.
Network Traffic	A measurement of the volume of network traffic (e.g., IP datagrams).
Adapters	Information regarding the status of the Token Ring, Ethernet, and X.25 adapters.

Figure 14.2 Categories of variables defined with the System Monitor enterprise-specific MIB.

For example, the System Monitor can:

■ Accept and filter incoming traps, forwarding only those requiring the management station's attention.
■ Poll downstream agents at regular intervals.
■ Analyze data, such as through a defined threshold.
■ Automatically generate commands in response to specific events.

Each instance of the System Monitor can be responsible for a group of machines in the network, reporting back to NetView/6000. Optionally, a three-level hierarchy is possible, where the "front-line" monitors report back to one or more System Monitors, which in turn connect to a central NetView/6000 platform.

Extending the System Monitor in this manner involves the use of several tables. There is no need to actually write agent code. The types of tables used with the System Monitor are shown in Figure 14.3.

Table	Description
Administration	This table contains information that can be used in managing the other tables.
Alias	Each entry in this table represents a group of nodes, providing a convenient method to organize and name parts of the network.
Analysis	The analysis table forms the foundation for how data is gathered and analyzed.
Command	Provides the means to customize the response to an incoming SNMP set or get request, by executing a command.
Filter	The traps received can be filtered according to several different criteria.
Threshold	Threshold values can be set for MIB variables which result in a trap being generated or command executed.
Trap/Destination	This table is customized by the user to determine where SYSMOND will send received or generated traps.

Figure 14.3 Types of tables that are used to enhance the capabilities of the System Monitor.

The Administration and Alias tables provide a foundation for managing the tables and the local node's view of the network (i.e., in terms of machine groups).

The Command table can be used to customize the System Monitor's response to incoming SNMP get and set requests. In each case, a command (e.g., UNIX shell) can be executed with the response returned in a MIB variable.

The Analysis table forms the foundation of the remote processing performed by the System Monitor. Each entry in the table describes an operation to be performed by the SYSMOND daemon, at regular intervals. An arithmetic expression is specified which includes the target MIB variables, as well as the IP address, host, or alias names of the remote host(s) (although local MIB variables can also be used). After collection and processing, the result can then be passed to the Threshold table for comparison.

The Filter table allows the traps, either received from the managed nodes or generated by SYSMOND, to be filtered. The Trap Destination table provides a technique to customize how the traps are forwarded.

14.2 NetView/6000 Management Applications

In addition to the System Monitor, described in the previous section, several other applications are available which enhance the usefulness of NetView/6000 and its network management capability.

Hub Management Program/6000

The IBM 8250 Multiprotocol Intelligent Hub family of products was first announced in September, 1992. Since then, the products have been updated on several occasions, each time adding improved capabilities and support for new features. For example, the 8260 was recently announced, and will be positioned to provide support for future ATM networks.

The design of the 8250 is based on a chassis frame with feature modules, each implementing a different protocol (e.g., Token-Ring, Ethernet, FDDI). It handles the transmission of LAN traffic, as well as bridging and LAN management. And of course, the hub itself must be managed. This can be done through a local ASCII terminal connected to the RS-232 port. Also, certain of the feature modules support a TELNET logon capability (e.g., Ethernet and FDDI). Finally, an SNMP agent which supports an enterprise-specific MIB is also included with the 8250.

While the 8250 agent can in theory be managed by any SNMP-compliant manager, it has a special synergy with NetView/6000. The basic support tools (e.g., MIB browser) can be used to access the 8250. In order to improve the display and data processing, however, it is recommended that users rely on the Intelligent Hub Management Program/6000 (IHMP/6000).

IHMP/6000 is an application integrated into the NetView/6000 environment. Version 1.3 was recently announced; some of the features of IHMP/6000 include:

- Tailored to the 8250 family.
- Provide network statistics.
- Autodiscovery.
- Support for the 8260.
- New Port Database, providing improved port management.

In addition to the NetView/6000 product, IBM now also offers a DOS-based version (as well as lower-level entry versions).

Router and Bridge Manager/6000

The IBM 6611 Network Processor plays an important role in anchoring the TCP/IP internetwork in an IBM environment. It was described, especially with respect to TCP/IP, in Chapter 8. The IBM AIX Router and Bridge Manager/6000 (RBM/6000) product was announced in March of 1994, and is tailored to the 6611. Like HMP/6000, RBM/6000 runs as a NetView/6000 application. It provides control and management for many of the features of the 6611. One or multiple NPs can be monitored through the support SNMP MIB variables. In particular, RBM/6000 provides a composite interface to the MIB data and other management features of the 6611 NP. The major features and support include:

- Integrated GUI display of one or more 6611 NPs.
- APPN.
- DLSw.
- System Manager (fast-path) command execution.
- Token Ring Source Route Bridging.
- Ethernet Transparent Bridging.
- Customizable polling rates.

In many ways, RBM/6000 is comparable to the HMP/6000, in the sense that both manage IBM networking devices.

RMONster/6000

It has taken a while, but IBM has finally created a monster - actually an RMONster. And it is not just one, but two products:

- RMONster/6000
- RMONster/2 Agent

Both products operate within the Remote Network Monitoring (RMON) RFC standard. RMONster/6000 requires NetView/6000, and acts as a central point for data collection, analysis and reporting. RMONster/2, as well as any other RMON-compliant agents, connect to the manager in order to provide remote LAN management. Specifically, the agents can monitor Token Ring and Ethernet LAN segments, including performance and media statistics.

In order to appreciate the use and operation of these products, it is first necessary to have a basic understanding of the RMON framework. The features and functions of RMON are implemented primarily as a MIB, in RFC 1271. In addition, extensions for the Token Ring environment are included with RFC 1513. Both of these standards are support by the IBM products. The standard was designed to address deficiencies of SNMP and the MIB-II. This includes, for example, the fact that each node being monitored must have an agent with corresponding MIB. Of course, this can create a significant processing overhead, especially with respect to manager-to-agent network traffic.

RMON was designed to limit the number of agents required, positioning a smaller number of remote agents that perform the management and monitoring functions. In addition, several other benefits, resulting from the design goals of RMON, can be summarized as follows:

- Continuous remote monitoring - the agents should have the ability to continually monitor the local environment, even if the manager temporarily suspends polling activities.
- Enhanced data collection - the RMON agent can include additional functionality, particularly with respect to the active collection of performance and error statistics, as well as problem detection.
- Local analysis - the agents can optionally include data processing functions, such as threshold comparisons.

As mentioned above, these objectives are met through the use of the RMON MIB. There are nine primary branches in which the data is arranged, as shown in Figure 14.4. The agents gather data locally, and make it available to the manager (in this case RMONster/6000).

MIB Subtree	Description
Statistics	This group defines the basic utilization and errors statistics for each subnetwork.
History	Samples are periodically recorded, based on the statistics data.
Alarm	A set of thresholds can be defined for the data collected, controlled by the manager.
Host	Dynamically discovers hosts on the LAN and maintains traffic counters for them.
HostTopN	A listing of the top "N" hosts, based on the measurement of a performance value.
Matrix	Used to hold traffic and error information between a pair of hosts on the network.
Filter	Filters can be used to monitor and optionally capture matching packets.
Packet Capture	Data that passes the filtering criteria can be organized for retrieval by the manager.
Event	Events can be defined based on MIB contents, and can result in an SNMP trap.

Figure 14.4 Main branches of the RMON MIB group.

14.3 LAN Network Manager

The LAN Network Manager has been positioned to monitor and manage the LAN environment. Therefore, it is an important aspect of the overall distributed management strategy. At the same time, IBM has begun to provide a closer integration with the other management products, such as NetView and NetView/6000.

Management of the Physical Media

LAN Network Manager (LNM), previously the LAN Manager, is actually a collection of several separate products. A list is provided in Figure 14.5.

The products focus on the management of the physical LAN media. For example, it supports:

- Token Ring segments.
- Token Ring adapter cards.
- Broadband PC Networks segments.
- Baseband PC Networks segments.

In addition, the product uses international standards (CMIP) in other areas, such in supporting the communication with LSM on the distributed PCs (i.e., CMIP over LLC, or CMOL).

Augmenting Network Management

LNM is therefore an important, and complementary, aspect of the enterprise network management. Some of the data collected by LNM can be directly accessed by LAN NetView. For example, LSM "speaks" CMIP which enables LNV to acquire that data in certain cases. Also, the service point capability, which enables integration with the host-based NetView, is described below.

14.4 LAN NetView

LAN NetView is a collection of products, based on international standards for network management, which is initially focused on providing systems management in the LAN arena.

Related Products	Description
LAN Network Manager (LNM)	The comprehensive solution, used to manage bridged LAN segments.
LAN Network Manager Entry	A more limited product, with no user interface, which can be controlled by the NetView host.
LAN Station Manager (LSM)	A type of agent that can be run on the DOS or OS/2 hosts, representing an implementation of the HLM (OSI) standard.

Figure 14.5 LAN Network Manager product set.

Family of Products

A family of products is provided, as shown in Figure 14.6, which establishes a framework for application development. It includes a rich set of features, such as a GUI tool (i.e., View), topology discovery and management, open APIs (e.g., XMP), and event management.

In addition, several supporting applications have been created by IBM to augment the product's usefulness. These include:

- LAN NetView Start
- LAN NetView Monitor
- LAN NetView Fix
- LAN NetView Tie

LAN NetView Tie can be configured to transform the OSI alarms into SNA alerts, which are then forwarded (through CM/2) to host NetView.

LAN NetView Management Utilities for OS/2, based on the earlier LMU/2 product, is designed to improve the management and administration of servers (e.g., LAN Server). It includes a basic SNMP capability when used within the LAN NetView framework.

LAN NetView Product	Description
Manager	Supports OSI concept of a managing system, providing central management from an OS/2 workstation using the Workplace Shell.
Enabler	Provides a subset of the Manager's features, such as a basic agent function, which enables the management of local or remote OS/2 machines.
Agents for DOS	Allows for the management of IBM and Microsoft DOS machines.
Agents Extended	An extension to the agent capability for OS/2 subsystems such as the OS/2 LAN Server product.

Figure 14.6   Members of the LAN NetView family of products.

Also, vendors continue to develop new LNV applications. One example is the NetWare Services Manager (NSM) V1.5 for OS/2. NSM is used to manage PCs running Novell's NetWare.

Focus on International Standards

The design and operation of LAN NetView is based on several international standards, including:

- Abstract Syntax Notation One (ASN.1)
- Basic Encoding Rules (BER)
- Common Management Information Services (CMIS)
- Common Management Information Protocol (CMIP)
- Guideline for the Definition of Managed Objects (GDMO), as well as other standards in the ISO 10165 series

- Simple Network Management Protocol (SNMP)
- X/Open Management Protocol (XMP)
- Systems Application Architecture (SAA)
- SystemView

In fact, the supplied agents shown in Figure 14.6 are CMIP-based.

SNMP Support

There is no direct SNMP API, although the more general XMP can be used. However, the emphasis is clearly on the OSI standards. To summarize, LNV can transmit network management data over three types of connections:

- CMIP over LLC (CMOL).
- CMIP over TCP/IP (CMOT).
- SNMP over TCP/IP.

Agent functionality can be integrated into the product framework. Basic SNMP get and set commands can be issued, however, its capabilities as a fully functional SNMP manager are limited.

The MIB-II, 6611 NP, and RMON MIBs are supported. However, it can be difficult to add new SNMP enterprise-specific MIB groups because of the internal format used, as LNV stores data according to the ISO GDMO formats.

14.5 Integration with Host Management

For many years, the IBM strategy with respect to network management had been solely host-centered. Even as new products found their way into the enterprise lineup, they would be subservient to NetView, falling under the SNA umbrella.

This has changed somewhat in recent years, particularly as new products have been introduced and enhanced. While SNA-based management from the NetView host can still be used, the NetView/6000 product provides a functionally rich alternative.

While SNMP managers had been around for quite awhile (e.g., SunNet Manager), NetView/6000 provides an option for the loyal IBM customers looking for consistency and improved integration among their products.

There are several things to consider when implementing the NetView/6000 product in conjunction with NetView at the host. The most important of these decisions include:

- Where is the center for network management?
- What protocol will be used by the manager?

For example, will NetView/390 or NetView/6000 be at the center? Also, will SNA or TCP/IP be used? When mixing the two worlds, where will the boundary be? This section presents the major configurations possible when integrating NetView and NetView/6000.

SNA Agents for NetView

The first, and earliest, configuration is based on retaining SNA network management at the MVS host using NetView. In this case, all information is accessed through distributed "SNA agents," primarily in the form of Service Points. The products that can report to NetView include:

- NetView/6000
- NetView/PC
- LAN Network Manager
- LAN Management Utilities/2
- Native Communications Manager/2 application.

The early configurations using each were based on the restrictive SSCP-to-PU session, which is now giving way to LU type 6.2 connectivity (i.e., NetView V2.2 and above). While all of these can be important with respect to NetView's distributed collection and management capability, the most useful in supporting an "outboard" TCP/IP internetwork is NetView/6000.

As part of the normal NetView/6000 internal processing, SNMP traps can optionally be converted into SNA alerts. The supporting software that must also be installed includes:

- AIX NetView Service Point (SP)
- SNA Services/6000

The "trapertd" daemon accepts the filtered traps, and creates the alerts using the SP API. The SNA Services/6000 product provides connectivity to the host through the SNA network.

In addition to forwarding SNA alerts, the NetView/6000 workstation can also accept commands (using the RUNCMD mechanism) from NetView, and return the replies.

NetView/390 as the SNMP Manager

Another configuration involves using SNMP rather than SNA protocols. In this case, NetView at the host can be implemented to act as the manager for the distributed SNMP agents. Figure 14.7 provides an illustration of the internal configuration at the MVS host.

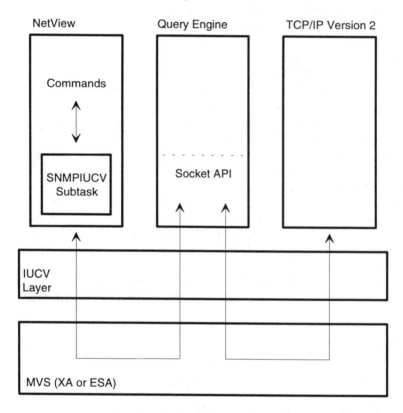

Figure 14.7 Structure used by NetView in accessing TCP/IP devices.

Here a separate subtask within NetView handles the communicate with the front-end Query Engine address space, which retrives the MIB variables. From there, the socket API is used in connecting to the network. It is important to realize that this configuration only enables a foundation upon which the management applications can be built. Also, it appears that, probably because of this fact, that this interface is not widely utilized by the NetView customers.

Host Management using NetView/6000

Where NetView/390 was previously shown as the manager, another set of configurations involves positioning NetView/6000 at the center instead. This can be done using two primary techniques:

- Support for SNMP-based management, as the foundation of NetView/6000 operation.
- SNA Manager/6000 product.

The first and foremost method is to implement NetView/6000 as the SNMP manager. There is an array of distributed agents that can be managed by NetView/6000, including the MVS host. That is, TCP/IP for MVS V2.2 includes an agent capability with MIB. When properly configured, NetView/6000 can access the MIB-II values, as well as certain enterprise-specific variables (e.g., 3172 support).

The SNA Manager/6000 offering enables direct access to certain SNA subarea information. The product was announced in September, 1993. It does not operate within the standard SNMP framework, however. Also, the product's capabilities are rather limited, focusing primarily on graphical display and basic command execution. NetView at the host must be available to interact with SNA Manager/6000 at the workstation.

While SNA and TCP/IP are battling it out in the corporate world, IBM seems to be helping TCP/IP along with its newly created APPN MIB.

APPN MIB

The foundation of the "new SNA" is based primarily on

- Advanced Peer-to-Peer networking (APPN).
- Advanced Program-to-Program Communication (APPC).

APPN enables a more dynamic connectivity and routing structure. It no longer relies on the central mainframe. In fact, APPN is actually very similar to TCP/IP in several ways. However, IBM has been very slow to bring APPN-compliant products to market. This process has accelerated recently, such as with its inclusion in VTAM and management by NetView (e.g., APPNTAM application). One interesting development is the recent release of an SNMP MIB definition for APPN. While the discussion of this MIB is not strictly related to the host management, it is of course very important to SNA in general. Currently, the APPN MIB is implemented within the 6611 NP, and will most likely appear elsewhere in the IBM product line.

MIB Subtree	Description
Node	Provides global information about the APPN end or network node.
Topology	Represents network topology, including network nodes and transmission groups.
Local Topology	Information about the node and its view of the network, including a list of attached end nodes (for network nodes).
Directory	Information used by the network nodes in managing its directory services.
Class of Service	The quality of network routes and the priority of traffic is maintained in a series of APPN tables.

Figure 14.8 Main sub-tree groups of the IBM MIB designed to support APPN.

The MIB falls under the enterprise-specific ISO registration tree branch, under the IBM 6611 product. Again referring to Chapter 4 where SNMP was introduced, the navigation path is:

1 . 3 . 6 . 1 . 4 . 1 . 2 . 6 . 2 . 13

Figure 14.8 illustrates the five major branches. In the future, it can be expected that the MIB will be enhanced, or perhaps augmented with support for related protocols (e.g., APPC). The interested reader should refer to the informational RFC number 1593, which was published by IBM in March of 1994.

14.6 Desktop Management Interface

The general techniques and technologies needed to manage the various types of traditional hosts, routers, bridges, control units, and front-end switches have been around for years now. Although continuing to expand, this framework become fairly stable. Over the same period, roughly the past 10 years, there has been an explosive growth in the number and variety of desktop computing resources. These PCs and workstations have now become a critical aspect of the corporation's computing strategy.

The Desktop Management Interface (DMI) is the most prominent example of a standard which has been created to address the management of these distributed computing resources. The Desktop Management Task Force (DMTF), which created the DMI architecture, was formed in May of 1992. The five founding corporations were:

- Microsoft
- Intel
- Novell
- SunConnect
- SynOptics

Since its founding, several other chapter members have been added to the group steering the standard's development (e.g., IBM).

The goal of the DMTF, and its DMI architecture, is to provide a consistent framework for the management of these desktop machines in an open, protocol neutral manner. Although not yet a part of the mainstream, the work of the DMTF will undoubtedly continue to grow in importance.

Inspiration and Mission

The founding members of the DMTF recognized the pervasive nature of LAN-based (desktop) computing resources. Each PC or workstation consists of a collection of hardware and software components. The goal of the DMTF is to define a set of common specifications for how the desktop PCs are to be accessed, regardless of the computer, management protocol, or transport.

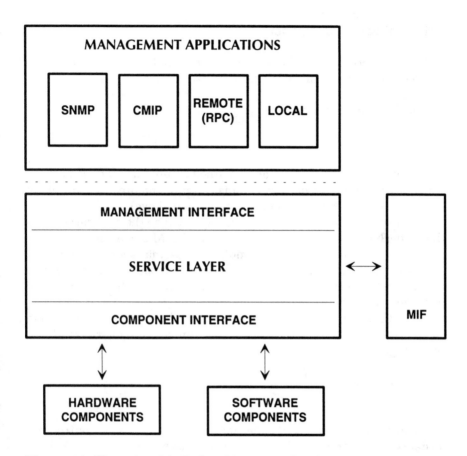

Figure 14.9 Illustration of the Desktop Management Interface (DMI) architecture.

While one or more of the interested corporations could create their own MIB definitions, there are several problems with this type of approach. Perhaps the biggest disadvantage is its inflexibility. Not only is SNMP tied to TCP/IP, but the MIB definition itself, once created, can be difficult to update or modify. Also, SNMP, while an option, is not universally accepted nor the best protocol to use in all cases.

In order to define a framework for desktop management that is flexible and extensible, it must be platform as well as protocol independent. DMI introduces a new protocol layer, implemented at each machine, which requires a minimal amount of system resources. It can then be used as the basis for other access protocols or applications, including SNMP, CMIP, or RPC.

DMI Architectural Components

Figure 14.9 provides an illustration of the DMTF architecture. It is divided into three primary layers:

■ Management applications.
■ Service layer.
■ Components.

A management application is defined as any program or protocol which accesses the service layer. This can implemented in a variety of forms, such as an SNMP agent (as mentioned above).

The services layer acts as an interface between the applications and the underlying components. As shown, the Management Interface provides access to this layer. It handles events, manages message flow, and generally enables a real-time access to the resources. For example, an application can request information regarding the various local hardware components installed.

The Component Interface provides the ability to access and manage each of the individual components. These components generally fall into two categories:

■ Hardware
■ Software

Hardware resources include, for example, adapters, controllers, modems, and system-level boards. The software components include both operating systems and applications.

An important aspect of the architecture is the Management Information Format (MIF) file. The MIF acts like a simple SNMP MIB, or datbase. It uses its own descriptive language, which is read and initialized by the service layer at initialization.

DMI obviously has the potential to grow to become an important aspect of enterprise-wide systems management. With respect to TCP/IP, DMTF has a direct relationship to SNMP. That is, an agent can be used in accessing the component data from a central managing system.

RFC Documents

This appendix provides a list of the most important RFC documents. It is not possible to describe all of the RFCs that have been created, with the corresponding protocols in use. Rather, the goal is to note the most fundamental for the operation of an average TCP/IP network, as well as those relevant to the IBM products and strategies.

In each case, the RFC number, as well as an informal title or description, is provided. Where a plus sign ("+") follows the RFC number, additional RFCs are associated, and listed to the right. Also, where necessary the current state/status has been included.

If any important RFCs have been inadvertently omitted or transcribed in error, please contact the author through the Internet. The final authority, of course, rests with the current RFC list and status of each document. These archives are constantly changing, where each day brings new and revised protocols within a growing body.

The RFCs can be accessed on-line through the Internet at several sites. For example, use the FTP command to access the server at:

DS.INTERNIC.COM

The directory "rfc" holds the files, each of the form RFCnnnn.TXT (where "nnnn" is the RFC number). You can also request to have one or more of the RFCs and/or the index printed for a nominal fee. For example, contact InterNIC at:

1-800-444-4345

The list below is divided into several categories, hopefully making it more readable.

Application Layer

821+	Simple Mail Transfer Protocol
	(RFC 822, 987, 1026, 1138, 1327, 1495)
959	File Transfer Protocol
854	TELNET
1576+	TN327E (enhanced version)
	(RFCs 1646, 1647)
1094	Network File System
1034+	Domain Name System
	(RFCs 1035, 1101, 1348)
1521+	Multipurpose Internet Mail Extensions
	(RFC 1590)
1411+	Kerbersos V4
	(RFC 1510 defines V5)
1460	Post Office Protocol V3 (POP3)
1123	Host Requirements RFC

Transport Layer

793	Transmission Control Protocol
768	User Datagram Protocol
1122	Host Requirements RFC

Internet Layer

791	Internet Protocol
792	Internet Control Message Protocol
826	Address Resolution Protocol
903	Reverse Address Resolution Protocol
951+	Bootstrap Protocol
	(RFCs 1532, 1533, 1534)
1112	Internet Group Management Protocol

Network Transport and Dynamic Routing Protocols

827+	Exterior Gateway Protocol
	(RFCs 904, 911, 1092)
1058+	Routing Information Protocol
	(RFC 1388)
1538+	Open Shortest Path First
	(RFCs 1245, 1246, 1370, 1403, 1584, 1586, 1587)

1267+	Border Gateway Protocol
	(RFCs 1268, 1397, 1403)
1434	Data Link Switching (DLSw)
1001+	NetBIOS over TCP/IP
	(RFC 1002)
1006	OSI formats over TCP/IP

Application Development and Programming

1014	External Data Representation (XDR)
1057	RPC Version 2 (Sun)
1592	SNMP Distributed Programming Interface

Network Management

1157+	Simple Network Management Protocol V1
	(RFCs 1155, 1213)
1352	SNMP Security
1271+	Remote Network Monitoring (MIB)
	(RFC 1513)
1441+	SNMP Version 2 (SNMPv2)
	(RFCs 1441 through 1452, and 1503)
1288	Finger protocol